The African Predicament

STANISLAV ANDRESKI

The African Predicament

A STUDY IN THE PATHOLOGY OF MODERNISATION

NEW YORK
ATHERTON PRESS

Copyright © 1968 by S. L. Andreski

Address all inquiries to:

Atherton Press, Inc.
70 Fifth Avenue
New York 10011

Library of Congress Catalog Card Number 68–57023

Manufactured in the United States of America

'Students of social science must fear popular approval; evil is with them when all men speak well of them.'

Alfred Marshall

CONTENTS

ACKNOWLEDGMENTS

I wish to thank my African friends, assistants and informants for helping me to understand their problems. I prefer, however, not to mention any of them by name in order not to implicate them in responsibility for controversial views. I should also like to thank Mrs Audrey Savin and Mrs Audrey Yates for their work on the typescript.

As my wife has collaborated in collecting the information on which the reflections presented here are based, and has discussed almost every issue dealt with on the pages which follow, she has a very large share in whatever merit resides in the present work.

I should also like to use this opportunity to thank Mrs Jean Floud and Professors Max Beloff, Sir Isaiah Berlin, Peter W. Campbell, E. E. Evans-Pritchard, Ernest Gellner, A. H. Halsey, H. A. L. Hart, George Lehmann, Hugh Seton-Watson, Edward Shils and Dr Michael Young for their help in various matters not directly related to the present book but without which I might not have been able to write it.

I am obliged to Ernest Gellner, Peter J. Rollings and Alexander Lopasic for numerous helpful suggestions although this does not mean that they agree with all my views.

Thanks are due to the following for permission to use extracts from works in which they hold the copyright:

Le Congo en Question by Roger Verbeek and used by permission of Présence Africaine, Paris, 1965.

A West African City by Michael Banton and used by permission of Oxford University Press London and the International African Institute.

The Anatomy of Uhuru by Carey Jones and used by permission of Manchester University Press, Manchester.

False Start in Africa by Rene Dumont and used by permission of André Deutsch Limited, London.

L'Afrique peut-elle Partir by Albert Meister and used by permission of Éditions du Seuil, Paris.

Rise and Fall of Kwame Nkrumah by Bretton and used by permission of Pall Mall Press Limited, London.

Africa in Social Change by P. C. Lloyd and used by permission of Penguin Books Limited, Harmondsworth, Middlesex.

FOREWORD

The purpose of the present book is to analyse the obstacles facing the new African states on the road to prosperity, internal peace and elementary freedoms. The treatment is on the whole confined to tropical Africa, and even here the Portuguese colonies and Ethiopia are mostly left out, as Ethiopia in virtue of being an old kingdom, and the Portuguese territories in virtue of being dependencies, differ markedly from the post-colonial states. As the same is even truer of North and South Africa, the remarks about these areas are made only to highlight certain points of argument from a comparative perspective.

Naturally, even within the confines of the new states of tropical Africa, the circumstances vary greatly. Nonetheless, they do exhibit certain important similarities, and it is these common features—or analogous social mechanisms, if you like—which constitute the object of the present inquiry.

I must stress that I have not attempted to give a well-rounded picture of African societies and cultures, but have focussed on the network of vicious circles which are perpetuating misery and strife. I have left out the more attractive aspects of African cultures not because I am not acquainted with them or think that they are not worth writing about; but simply because I prefer to concentrate on a topic on which I may have something important to say that has not been said before. Furthermore, the treatment is deliberately slanted towards the problems which seem to me to have been either unnoticed or glossed over or under-estimated by other authors and towards phenomena which are spoken of privately often enough but seldom written about. I see no point in repeating all the basic information about African traditional societies, political history, economics or demography which has already been competently provided by numerous publications. My aim has been to map out the crucial factors (and the causal relations between them) which can explain the sorry plight of the new African states. For this reason the present book must be regarded as an interpretative essay which assumes some knowledge of the basic facts rather than a self-contained introduction, let alone a systematic survey of the constellations of circumstances and forces which can be found in Africa.

Though perfectly understandable alone, the present book is in many ways a companion volume to my *Parasitism and Subversion: the Case of Latin America* which also deals with the social mechanisms perpetuating misery and strife. In addition to their primary concern with explaining the actual situation in the respective areas, both studies are intended as contributions to a theory of progress indicating the conditions under which poverty, oppression and strife may be eliminated.

By putting the word 'pathology' into the title of the present book, I do not wish to suggest that I have succeeded in establishing objective and ethically neutral (or value-free) criteria for assessing the health or goodness of a social order. By pathology I mean a systematic study of social phenomena which must be judged as evil from the standpoint of humanitarian ethics because they cause suffering and degradation.

University of Reading
January 1968

INTRODUCTION

The vast flood of literature on modern Africa contains few works which do not shun the less pleasant aspects of modernisation.* Recoiling, from attitudes of racial contempt or imperial high-handedness, writers of pink race do not dare to mention (or even to think about) the less laudable deeds of brown men. Outside southern Africa there are very few blatant racialists, and even unrepentant addicts to racial animosity conceal their sentiments under hypocritical assurances of friendship and admiration for the sake of business: as they can no longer be simply ordered about, the Africans must now be cajoled. Moreover, as during the colonial era the Africans had no power and were often humiliated and exploited, they have acquired in the eyes of the liberals and humanitarians an aura of martydom, while the fact that they were neither oppressing nor humiliating the Europeans was taken to be proof of their moral superiority. The error which underlay this idealisation of the Africans is analogous to that involved in the cult of the proletariat: the lack of power to do much harm was

---

* This, incidentally, is the reason why the present book is based to a much larger extent on seeing, talking to people and travelling, and less on the literature than my previous works. Whereas the most pungent exposures of the evils of the Latin American social order have come from under the pen of the indigenous writers—produced either during the periods of respite from repression or in exile—the publications of the African writers on politics and sociology are characterised by an apologetic rather than a critical attitude, which is understandable in view of their lack of self-assurance engendered by the scorn in which their race has been held for so long, and by the humiliations to which they are themselves often exposed when they live outside Africa. Perhaps the educated class is also of too recent an origin and still insufficiently numerous even in the most modernised countries to produce thinkers capable of sufficient detachment, although censorship and repression alone suffice to stultify critical commenting on anything touching politics. Truly realistic pictures of the African social and political scene can be found only in the novels of certain African authors; some of whom are very good indeed, but whose names I prefer not to mention in this context lest this might get them into trouble.

taken as evidence of virtue. Moreover, as in the case of the cult of the peasant in some countries of Europe, numerous intellectuals, who were bored or disgusted with the urban way of life, admired the peoples seemingly unspoilt by commercialism and industrialism, and hoped that they would create a better civilisation if given a chance. Thus the dogma that an African can do no wrong has gained an acceptance among European intellectuals.

As far as practical effects are concerned, this indulgence affects only the privileged Africans, without taking cognizance of what they do to their less fortunate compatriots, especially to women. In this way European and American intellectuals take the credit for chivalry to the underdogs while being on the side of the potentates who (though very weak on the scale of international power politics) are nevertheless in a position to offer to their foreign friends lavish entertainment.

There is another important point which, incidentally, illustrates one of the insuperable limitations in the study of human affairs: namely, that many touchy governments—and almost all dictatorships—ban foreigners who reveal what they would like to conceal. In consequence, those who wish to specialise in studying such areas, and pay further visits, have to be discreet in public utterances. Therefore, only somebody who does not particularly care whether he will be admitted to the countries he is writing about—in this case only somebody who has no vested interest in maintaining his position as an Africanist—can afford to be perfectly frank.

The students of communist affairs, to mention a parallel example, are divided into those who have written truthfully without dodging and those who have visited the homelands of socialism regularly; up till now nobody has been able to do both. Only countries with a fairly liberal government can be repeatedly visited as well as criticised.

The inverted racialism of the European and American intellectuals does their African counterparts little good, as it undermines their powers of self-criticism. It amounts, moreover, to a covert insult because it tacitly assumes that the Africans must be judged by less demanding standards than other men.

Whatever might be their deeper feelings, the African politicians find this dogma very useful, and promptly accuse of racialism anybody who dares to criticise them or the systems which they have created. Quite often however, their accusations are not without foundations, as there are many people whose carping on the shortcomings of the African states is undoubtedly prompted by racial animosity. For this reason, therefore, I must emphasise that I do not attribute the undesirable aspects of modern Africa to innate propensities genetically linked to pigmentation. On the contrary, the main purpose of the present work is to explain the present predicament of the African states in terms of historical antecedents and general social mechanisms. In any case, if we want to discuss the question of who is to be blamed for creating the present predicament, we must attribute the major part of the guilt to those who had most power and who arrogated to themselves the role of teachers . . . that is to the imperial nations. I do not think, however, that the apportionment of collective guilt is a very important topic. What really matters is how to improve the lot of suffering humanity, and the study of evil actions committed in the past is worth pursuing only in so far as it helps us to avoid repetition. True, improved understanding is of no avail against evil intentions or callous indifference, but it offers a chance of preventing misfortunes being brought about by misguided good intentions.

As this book is mainly about the Africans it must contain more references to their deplorable deeds than to follies and crimes committed in other parts of the world; but this does not mean that I regard them as more addicted to evil doing than other races. Anybody who has any preconceptions on this point should recall that only twenty-three years ago millions of human beings were being starved, tortured and murdered in the heart of Europe. The Roman arenas, the burning of heretics and witches, the treating of executions as a form of public entertainment, preferably on Sundays, the chaining of slaves for life to the oars on the galleys, the trans-Atlantic slave trade, the impalements of refractory serfs, the frightful treatment of small children in early factories and mines, the concentration camps, the monstrous despotisms from Nero to Stalin—all these and innumerable other atrocities amply testify to the evil propensities of the Europeans. The record of other races, however, is no better. It was the Africans themselves who hunted the slaves and sold them to the European traders for trinkets and weapons—often believing that the latter ate them up. They also practised head-hunting, infanticide, human sacrifice, cannibalism and a host of other cruel customs.

Regardless of continent or race, all the large states of the past have been based on exploitation and oppression, and nearly all of them were despotic. Though equally plagued by warfare, only small tribes were relatively free from exploitation and internal oppression—although even here the female class often played the role of the proletariat. Large societies without much violence and oppression have arisen only very recently, and remain very fragile and in constant danger of slipping back into the normal condition of mankind. This we must never forget when discussing African affairs; particularly as it is impossible to talk about the phenomena which contradict our professed ethics without using words loaded with moral condemnation.

For the readers who are interested in theory and methodology (the others can skip it) I should like to add two points. The first is that the traditional social systems rested upon an elaborate and steady equilibration of rights, duties and loyalties, sanctified by usage and religion, whereas the urbanised, commercialised and bureaucratised conglomerates contain no such intricate self-regulating mechanism, and their functioning is determined by unstable constellations of power and shifting avenues towards gain within the framework of constantly changing interplay between the remainders of the traditional cultures—some rapidly decaying, others curiously and vigorously surviving—and the new intrusive and corrosive forces. The organic analogy beloved of the anthropologists no longer holds and the Hobbesian model of a war of all against all is closer to the fluid reality. It might be of interest to mention incidentally that Peter J. Rollings, who has taught in Ghana for several years, tells me that the social theorist who always aroused greatest interest among his students was Hobbes.

The fluidity of the situation and the inchoateness of the elements which compose it place great obstacles in the path of anyone who tries to describe the circumstances with any precision or attempt any predictions of specific nature. No wonder then—and this is the second point—that the over-schematic 'theory of modernisation' does not carry us very far, particularly as it is based on the crudest imaginable version of the concept of unilinear evolution.

The introduction of mathematical formulae into economic theory has produced among economists a tendency towards splendid isolation, based on the belief that their discipline dealt with autonomous and measurable variables. This belief, however, appeared plausible only because the sociological assumptions of economic theory were more or less modelled on the dominant characteristics of the societies in the midst of which this theory grew, and to which it was most commonly applied. The evolution towards diffuse pluralistic collectivism, involving growing inter-penetration of government, pressure groups and the organs of economic control, has considerably enlarged the discrepancy between the current reality and the tacit sociological assumptions of economic theory (including even such recent additions thereto as the Keynesian models); but the arbitrary nature of these assumptions has been fully revealed only when conclusions about the affairs of underdeveloped countries, drawn on the basis of conventional economic theory, have proved to be manifestly false. The perplexity engendered by the failures of their predictions has given rise to an extensive literature supplying modifications of economic theories designed to fit them for dealing with pre-industrial economic structures. So far, however, only ad hoc qualifications have been proposed, without attempting to treat the fundamental problem of institutional limits to the validity of various parts of economic theory, let alone to erect a system of generalised economics like those adumbrated without much success several decades ago by Othmar Spann and Werner Sombart.

It is not surprising therefore that the plans worked out by the economic experts sent out to advise the governments of these unfortunate countries cannot be carried out. Economic theory will remain a steel construction built on foundations of sand until our understanding of non-economic factors is brought to the same level of generality and sophistication as the study of the strictly economic matters, so that economic and sociological theory form a continuum. That we are still very far from this goal is not only the fault of the isolationist economists but also the consequence of the sterility of the contemporary sociological theory which (as I have tried to show in a previous book) is being turned into a meaningless jargon by the most influential of its present exponents.

Everybody who has often been snubbed will remain touchy and suspicious, and therefore it is not surprising that many Africans are easily offended. But let us leave to the diplomats and public relations men the task of soothing their susceptibilities. A sociologist merits a place in the sun only if he tells people the truth about the nature and the consequences of their collective behaviour regardless of whether they like it or not: for correct understanding is a prerequisite of improvement. True, even among the best educated nations we can find enough examples of obdurate obscurantism to shake our faith in the efficacy of knowledge; nonetheless, whereas it is quite possible that better understanding will do little good, it is practically certain that action based on errors and illusions will produce no improvement if not lead to disaster.

Dealing briefly with a vast subject one cannot avoid being schematic with the consequence that the statements are only approximately true. However, as absolute exactitude cannot be attained even in cartography, we have to accept the degree of approximation which is the most useful for the given purpose. From a longer distance we can see the trees worse but the contours of the wood better; and although a large scale map will contain many more details than a small scale one, the latter will nonetheless provide us with the information which we could not find in the former. As with the proportions on the maps based on Mercator's projection, the statements made in the pages which follow are more exactly true about certain areas of Africa than about others. I have put qualifying statements wherever the discrepancies between the areas are so glaring that straight assertion would be palpably untrue, but to hedge every sentence with a string of reservations would make the book indigestible. For this reason some compromise was necessary, and the reader can take as the general guiding line that, unless stated to the contrary, my descriptions apply most directly to the most highly urbanised parts of Africa which are to be found on the West Coast. This is not merely because I happen to know this area (especially Nigeria) best but also because the present study is focussed on the factors and consequences of modernisation, and this process has advanced furthest precisely on the West Coast. It seems more likely that in twenty years' time Dar es Salaam will be like Lagos today than the other way round, although important regional differences will persist or even arise. Some areas, especially those inhabited by Moslem nomads, will probably remain unchanged for a long time to come. Other parts of Africa may fall again under a colonial rule or have a communist system imposed upon them. Nonetheless, the present trend of change throughout most of Africa appears to be in the direction of the type of life found around the bigger urban centres of the West Coast.

If you put rabbits and chickens through a mincing machine the resulting meats will differ less than did the animals (even when dead) while their structure was still intact. Likewise, the traditional African societies exhibited a greater variety than do the social agglomerates undergoing the process known as modernisation; largely because the external forces which are grinding them are the same: foreign big business, the mass media, the contacts with foreign models, the pressures of big powers, the enticements of international organisations, air transport and imported goods.

Chapter 1 TOWARDS STARVATION

The great hopes placed in the new African states have been disappointed. Instead of democracy—which so many European and American intellectuals naïvely expected—we see dictatorship or strife; and despite the implantation of new industries poverty is spreading. Perhaps it is less painful to be poor in the tropics than in a cold climate, nonetheless, the sufferings are very real. It would be wrong to speak of stagnation in Africa because, except where disorder and strife prevail, new factories, roads and buildings continue to appear, and the aggregate wealth is increasing in most areas. The trouble is that the population grows much faster. Indeed the economic difficulties are made unmanageable above all by the tremendously fast growth of population. This extraordinary increase is due to the lowering of the death rate without a corresponding lowering of the birth rate, which imbalance condemns to misery most of the world's population, and in Africa is greater than elsewhere with the exception of Latin America; although its impact is slightly softened by the greater amount of unused resources in Africa as compared with Asia. The rate of growth of its population is higher than that of any other continent except Latin America. Moreover, the rate of growth itself is increasing. The trend of the death rates is still downwards and if they dropped to the American or western European level, the population of Africa would more than double itself every twenty years.

Colonial rule has left as its legacy a trend towards impoverishment which cannot easily be reversed. This trend has not been created by exploitation (which except in the Belgian Congo and the regions of European settlement like Rhodesia or Kenya has been slight or non-existent) but by what would generally be regarded as the good works of the colonial administration, such as the abolition of tribal warfare, human sacrifice and infanticide, and the introduction of modern medicine, which have disturbed the age-long demographic equilibrium.

There have been many cases of very high profits for European

companies in combination with a treatment of the native labour
which by any ethical standards must be classed as exploitation—
like the famous construction of the railway from Brazzaville to
Pointe Noire in the French Congo during which many thousands
of indented labourers died. Nonetheless, the railway is still there
and the colonialists have not taken it to France. Despite all the
talk about colonialist exploitation nobody has yet tried to make
a statistical cost-benefit estimate; and prima facie it is by no
means clear that more was 'taken out' than 'put into' the colonies.
It was in the Belgian Congo that the metropolitan firms, settlers
and officials were appropriating the largest slice of wealth, but to
judge by the condition of the country since their departure, their
services were worth it. Of course it can be legitimately argued
that they have deliberately made themselves indispensable, but the
fact remains that the colonial rulers did develop their domains and
their former wards think that economic development is a good thing.

The effects of the population explosion upon the standards
of living could be neutralised only by a truly miraculous economic
expansion which neither the colonial rulers nor their successors
have been able to engineer. To organise a fast growing economy
is not a simple task, and may be beyond the ingenuity of even the
ablest leaders when cultural, social and economic foundations are
lacking. In the prosperous countries of western Europe a decline
in fecundity occurred spontaneously and without any encouragement from the governments, as the result of the rise in the standard
of living and the spread of a rationalistic outlook. It must be
remembered, however, that this happened in Europe when the
wealth was growing more rapidly than the population, which is
not the case in Africa today. At the time when the birth rate
began to decline, the population of Europe was growing less than
1 per cent per year. In Africa it is now growing three times as fast.
True, the Europeans of the last century did not have at their
disposal the technical knowledge of today, but they had ample
outlets for emigration, and above all they could become providers
of manufactured goods for the rest of the world whence they drew
needed raw materials. Those who regard industrialisation as an
automatic cure for poverty forget that it is impossible for all the
countries of the world to become 'workshops of the world' at the
same time. Britain, Belgium and Western Germany are prosperous
today because they can import food and raw materials, but they

would fall into utter misery if every country in the world tried to do the same. There is, of course, room for a lot of industrialisation, including modernisation of agriculture, but the unassailable point is that some countries can industrialise to the point of having to rely on imports of raw materials only if others have a surplus of them. When the supply of food is insufficient the indices of growing total production only prove that the rich use more mechanical gadgets. And as far as food is concerned, the position of Africa is becoming steadily worse.

A spontaneous decline in the birth rate cannot take place in a country where the majority of the population have neither an incentive nor even the material possibilities of practising birth control, and are too superstitious and improvident to care. As on the other hand the standard of living cannot be raised so long as the population grows so fast, we have here a vicious circle out of which it is very difficult to break. It is usually said that the remedy is to accelerate the growth of wealth until it overtakes the increase of the population, but apart from other difficulties we encounter here another vicious circle: an excessive growth of the population is not only difficult to catch up with simply in virtue of its speed but it also acts as a brake on accumulation of capital.

Owing to the age composition of their populations, the African countries suffer from the following disadvantages in comparison with countries with lower birth rate: (1) relatively fewer persons in the population are of working age; (2) the resources which could be devoted to raising the standard of living have to be used for combating its tendency to fall.

As a more numerous generation replaces the preceding, the current level of consumption can be maintained only if the amount of productive equipment is at least proportionately increased. In other words, investments must be made merely to prevent a deterioration in the standard of living. On the basis of certain not unrealistic assumptions it has been calculated that, if a population grows by 1 per cent a year, about 4 per cent of the total national product must be allocated to investments—called demographic investments—which merely counteract the effect of the growth of the population. This means, of course, that, given the rate of saving, the faster the growth of the population, the fewer are the resources which can be used for effecting an improvement. Unfortunately, however, even the rate of saving is not exempt from the influence of demographic factors. In a poor society with a low ratio of workers to dependants saving is difficult and therefore capital available for investment scarce, which means that the necessity of making heavy demographic investments rules out (or at least slows down) economic progress.

So long as the birth rates remain so high, every economic improvement will be nullified by the growth of the population, and there is no way of diminishing, let alone eliminating, misery. And as there are no grounds for hoping that under these circumstances the birth rate will decline spontaneously, we must conclude that all reforms are doomed to futility without a vigorous policy of encouraging and facilitating the practice of birth control. Naturally, there are many obstacles to such a policy. There is the economic difficulty: in the poorer countries of the world the poor are so poor that they cannot afford to buy soap, let alone more expensive products of chemical industry. Here the only solution would be a free distribution. Even very poor governments could afford it if they devoted to this purpose a fraction of what they spend on useless armaments and ostentation; and if they were unwilling to do so, contraceptive equipment could be provided as a part of international aid at the cost of a small fraction of its present amount. The real obstacles stem from traditions and attitudes.

The desire for the numerical increase of one's group constitutes one of the usual ingredients of nationalism and other kinds of ethnocentrism. Its roots stretch right back to the primeval horde, when the outcomes of affrays depended chiefly on relative numerical strength. Though outdated in the era of nuclear weapons and automation, this attitude impedes an adoption of a rational approach to the demographic problems. Moreover, attention to the problem of overpopulation can be prompted only by foresight and the concern for the public good, which qualities are nowhere over-abundant. Eliminating a demographic imbalance cannot put money into the pockets of any pressure group, and an advocacy of such a programme cannot have such popular appeal as a promise of a redistribution of the existing wealth. The most formidable impediment to a rational population policy in Latin America is the alliance on this point of two most powerful pressure groups: the Catholic Church and the Communist Party.* In

* See on this point *Parasitism and Subversion: The Case of Latin America*. Weidenfeld & Nicolson, London, 1966.

Africa, in contrast, the resistance stems principally from the tribal traditions ordaining procreation; although the Catholic Church also plays a sinister role in this matter wherever it is strong.

Overpopulation does not just produce a static condition of mass poverty but leads to a destruction of irreplaceable natural resources through soil erosion, and in this way creates a self-aggravating vicious circle. This process is of tremendous portent for Africa (as it is in fact for most of the world) but as this book is about the social mechanisms which perpetuate misery and strife and not about ecology—and as there are excellent books about the plundering and squandering of irreplaceable resources—I shall not dwell upon this factor beyond stressing that it underlies and overshadows every aspect of the economic predicament of Africa.

A population policy can never be an alternative to institutional reforms because without such reforms it is doomed to failure. Japan was fortunate in having a high rate of literacy and an efficient administration without which such a profound change in popular attitudes could not have been effected. It is difficult to imagine that such a change could be achieved by an administrative machine ridden with graft, nepotism and shirking, and operating in the middle of illiterate, apathetic and fatalistic peasants.

The vicious circle of poverty and demographic imbalance is even more difficult to break than the foregoing purely quantitative considerations indicate, because economic distress fosters parasitic tendencies and institutions, and stimulates strife and disorder, which in their turn aggravate the economic difficulties. As far as violence is concerned, the numerical preponderance of the young is of crucial importance because nothing makes a situation so explosive as a large number of unemployed or impoverished young men.

It is not surprising that the economic retrogression is greatest where disorder is worst. In his remarkable book, *Le Congo en Question* (Sociétè d' Éditions Présence Africaine, Paris, 1965), pp. 124-9, Roger Verbeck thus describes the situation (the wording and the arrangement of the extracts are mine):

'The agricultural produce exported in 1962 represents 60 per cent of the '59 tonnage. The amount of cotton sold abroad has decreased 8 per cent while not a single grain of maize nor a litre of peanut oil has been exported; the amount of manioc exported has fallen by 5 per cent. Crops with a stable return (coffee, tea, cocoa, rubber) benefit solely the Europeans and the Public Sector, that is to say, town-dwellers. When taking account of the fact that these same people control industry and trade, this means that scarcely 1 per cent of the population is receiving 50 per cent of the national income, and tries to export the greater part of this.'

'In the Equatorial Bumba region alone, rice production has fallen from 18,000 to 8,000 tons; in other regions, it is rumoured that rice production will be abandoned altogether. And rice is one of the subsistence crops supplying local consumers. 50,000 tons per annum are needed at the moment from American aid; and 40,000 tons of wheat flour have had to be imported to compensate for the lack of manioc on the town and country markets. In addition, the United States of America have sent out 70,000 tons of maize.

'It is said that the Congo farmer is discouraged by the drop in the retail price of his produce and by the lack of goods he can buy; that tribal and interprovincial struggles have ruined whole regions and paralysed their economic activities; that a large number of plantations were abandoned after the events of the summer of 1960. But these facts are not sufficient to explain such a decline in agriculture. . . . During the colonial period, the Congo peasant carried out his work . . . under the orders of the agricultural supervisor and cultivated his ground by semi-military methods, receiving his daily food and his meagre pay in return. He was normally nothing but a farm labourer working for the profit of those who had taken all his land; the State, the colonialists, the missionaries. (The total area of confiscated land has been assessed at around 13,000,000 hectares, including, of course, all the best land, which was mostly already under cultivation when the Whites came). But even when his strip of land belonged to him . . . he could only sell his produce at the extremely low prices dictated by the business monopolies.

'The colonial agricultural economy relied on the police. The granting of independence shattered the authoritarian system, suppressed all co-ordination and plunged rural organisation into anarchy. . . . "It was not until the few years before Independence that the administration set up centres in a few

villages which were to act as the basis for community development which should have been a primary objective decades
earlier. It was, of course, too late. Firstly, because the first
experiments never passed the level of authoritarian paper-
work . . . and nothing was done to give the peasants an
education which corresponded to their needs and their sur-
roundings. Secondly, because Independence now leaves the
organisation of rural life to the most mediocre elements of the
Congo youth. For to register in a school for agricultural
instructors one must have failed at everything else and have lost
hope of pursuing studies worthy of the name, that is, those
which lead to higher administration. . ." '

'Independence was the work of the évolués . . . without the
participation of the peasants. To this day, no agrarian reform
has ever been hinted at. The businessmen, missionaries and
colonialists have retained their vast properties. . . Peasants go
on selling their produce, when they have any, to foreign
businessmen and company agents who practise the same
usurious methods as four years ago. Workers and agricultural
labourers are still working at a subsistence wage for overseers
more tyrannical than ever before while the traditional chiefs and
the new officials add venality to the harshness of former white
Colonial officials. The disciplined brutes of the Force Publique
have become the despotic and disorderly mercenaries of the
Congolese National Army.'

Chapter 2 EXPLOITATION, PARASITISM AND STRIFE

Brutal exploitation has been the normal fate of the poor throughout history and wherever it abated it was in consequence of the operation of at least one of two factors:

(1) an increase of wealth faster than the growth of the population, or
(2) a shift in the balance of power between the strata.

Unless accompanied by the first, the second factor can only produce a temporary respite, and in any case the two factors are causally connected as the scarcity of capital in relation to the population enhances the power of owners, employers and officials over those who have to live by the effort of their brawn or brain. It is not surprising therefore that in poverty-stricken Africa the poor are exploited, although their fate is on the whole slightly better than that of their counterparts in Asia and most of Latin America or even the poorest parts of Europe.

As there are few large estates in tropical Africa, landlordism is confined mainly to the towns where, however, it appropriates a very substantial share of the wealth. In the new towns or the new parts of old towns—that is to say everywhere where the settlement is not by clans—labourers have to pay about one-fourth or even one-third of their wages for a dingy cubicle without water or sanitation, or even for a corner in a room. The newly-rich owners of the rentable property (most of whom acquired it with the proceeds of graft) expect to get their investment amortised in five or even three years. In Freetown most of the property belongs to the old established 'creole' families; while in Accra (which has expanded so much recently) the biggest owners of property are still the heads of the so-called royal lineages, though much property has been bought by wealthy cocoa farmers and market women; and the same is probably true of Kumasi. A more legitimate manner of acquisition, however, does not make the landlords necessarily more lenient towards the tenants who are not their kinsmen.

On the other side of the picture, the absence or extreme weakness of the trade unions (coupled with the venality of their leaders) enables the employers to keep the wages very low and extend the working hours regardless of any limitations existing on paper.

It is common knowledge that the native employers are harsher than the expatriate firms; and the reasons for this difference are not difficult to find and have little to do with any genetically determined racial inclinations, as can be seen from the treatment meted out to their African labourers by the settlers of European origin. The first part of the explanation is that outside the areas of European settlement the people who come into contact with African labour are managers of big firms who can take a less shortsighted view of labour relations, particularly as they can obtain no immediate personal gain from beating the wages down. Secondly, being wealthier and more efficient, the foreign firms can afford to pay better; and in fact the employees of the big expatriate companies constitute a real 'labour aristocracy'. By bestowing substantial privileges in the midst of poverty some of these firms obtain remarkably efficient and reliable work, which shows that the influence of the environment can be overcome by suitable incentives. Here is an example: as everybody who has lived in Nigeria knows, frightfully reckless driving is the norm. The ramshackle mammy wagons, for instance, are really terrifying engines of extermination. Nonetheless, the Shell Oil Company has succeeded in making their drivers into paragons of propriety and courtesy by a simple method of paying them at least four times the usual wage and dismissing them after the first serious accident without going into whose fault it was. As these drivers transport very costly cargoes this is simply good business, but only a wealthy and efficient company could take such a long-sighted view, which is either incomprehensible or impracticable for an owner of a back-street sweat-shop.

The domestic servants of the expatriates constitute a category very much superior in status and income to the drudges working in African households. The cooks able to minister to foreign tastes often accumulate a small capital from profits obtained through doing the shopping for their employers who find it more advantageous to allow a rake-off to one cook rather than be charged extra by every single trader. Such people regard it as utterly below their dignity to work as domestic servants for their compatriots. A little story from personal experience illustrates the point: when I was leaving the place where I had resided for nearly two years I tried to find jobs for my servants. All of them would have been happy to work for an expatriate but they would go back to their villages rather than consider employment in a household of one of their wealthy compatriots. The explanation was—as the cook put it— 'they will not treat me like a man'. As the nursemaid was from a family which had a teacher and a medical assistant among their members, she would not dream of taking up a similar job in a household of an African who was not her relative, as it would involve (apart from exhausting drudgery for next to no pay) making herself available sexually.

Generalisations about such matters must of necessity be very approximate and there are innumerable local and individual variations. The Ghanaians are said to treat their servants on the whole better and pay them a little more than the Nigerians, which may be explicable by a higher general standard of living (the calculated income per head in Ghana being more than double that in Nigeria). Nonetheless, the servants prefer to work for Europeans—and even better for Americans.

It is not surprising that people who come mostly from countries where labour is scarcer, as well as protected by the unions and effective legislation, and therefore has to be treated with circumspection, persist for a time in their more lenient and less ungenerous habits. It was probably different with the Victorians, used to treating their servants harshly at home, and it is certainly different with the pink South Africans—although I must say that when I went from South Africa to Spain in 1952 I was surprised to find that the condition of domestic servants was better in South Africa (despite the difference of race) than in Spain. Anyway, the point of raising the issue of domestic servants (very insignificant in itself) is merely to show that, contrary to the prevailing myths, the degree of exploitation does not depend on the differences in pigmentation, and that it is not true that people prefer to be bossed by somebody of their own race regardless of the quality of the treatment they receive. Many Greek, Portuguese and

Yugoslav labourers say that they prefer to work in Germany and Switzerland rather than in their own countries, not only because of better pay but also because there they are treated with more justice and civility.

Economic progress requires peace and order. Planning, saving and investment become unprofitable if nothing is secure. Strife impoverishes and may ruin a country if it is sufficiently serious. On the other hand, it is equally clear that generalised poverty and especially sudden impoverishment, generates strife and disorder; so that a vicious circle maintains a country in a pitiful condition. However, the relation between economic conditions and ruinous strife is complicated by the influence of the factor of the strength of political structure: a gust of economic adversity may break a weak political structure whilst a strong structure may withstand it. The African states which have to cope with such tremendous economic difficulties are terribly weak in consequence of ethnic divisions, the lack of competent personnel and above all the canalisation of all the energies into the struggle for power and its fruits.

Once a society is pervaded by predacity, no one has other choice than to skin or be skinned. He may combine the two roles in varying measure but he cannot avoid them: he cannot follow Candide's example and till his garden, relying on hard work for his well-being, because he will not be left alone: the wielders of power will pounce upon him and seize the fruits and tools of his labour.

The impossibility of opting out aggravates the ferocity which depends on the importance of the stakes—that is to say, on the expectations of what can be lost through defeat or gained through victory.

The greater and more general the poverty, the more important are the stakes of political contests. In an opulent country a man who is thrown out of office can usually find decent employment elsewhere but in a poor country full of paupers a loss of office usually means ruin for anybody who has no private wealth; and even the people in the latter category are safe only in so far as the rights of property are respected. In consequence, the fight for office becomes a matter of life and death for all the minor figures who cannot place large funds in foreign banks, and assumes the form of a struggle for existence fought with every available means and without regard for law or convention.

Under such circumstances the politics tend to oscillate between despotism and anarchy because a constitutional parliamentary government cannot function without a readiness to compromise and to observe the rules of the game. This applies even to oligarchy, but as far as democracy is concerned, it can be stated as a general rule, to which no exception has yet been found, that it can function firstly only in a society which is fairly prosperous, and, secondly, only where privileges obtained through political influence are not indispensable for making a decent living.

Nobody who has lived in tropical lowlands will fail to appreciate the magnitude of the handicaps under which mankind is striving in those regions. Uncontrollable vegetation, insects and all kinds of disease make minimal affluence and comfort much more difficult to attain. The heat affects not only the strictly physical activities but to a perhaps greater extent the mental as well. Much of the administrative inefficiency, bad planning and carelessness which we see in all the tropical countries must be due to the impediments of the climate. Malaria, for instance, from which most of the Africans suffer although only few die, brings convulsions on many children, and convulsions are well known to inflict a permanent or at least a long-lasting damage to the brain. Dr Mundy-Castle, of the National Institute of Health and Medical Research in Accra, has found strong evidence of brain damage as a result of malaria. There is no truth, however, in the common misconception that the Africans do not work much. This is true only of those who have the means of living without working, whilst the majority of the poor work much harder than the workers in opulent countries. Owing to the lack of machines and even more rudimentary tools (such as wheelbarrows or carts) they have to walk very long distances and carry heavy objects. We must also remember that what is condemned as laziness by superficial observers is often exhaustion and apathy resulting from undernourishment (including pre-natal undernourishment). We have here a vicious circle: starvation and disease make it difficult to raise the productivity of the worker, and without a rise in productivity these scourges cannot be eliminated. Apart from lack of food (especially during the months before the harvest) undernourishment is aggravated by food taboos (affecting especially women) and other traditional idiosyncrasies such as eating too much porridge which causes permanent intestinal defects. Cassava, so much eaten in many parts of Africa, has poisonous roots which may cause blindness.

There are limitations to an explanation in terms of climate, but we cannot disregard this factor. Durkheim's dictum that we must explain social facts in terms of social facts was a badly needed corrective to the facile geographical and biological determinism, current in sociology at the end of the last century, but dogmatic adherence to this dictum amounts to sheer prejudice. We have now innumerable studies in physiological psychology which show which temperatures are most conducive to various types of work; and even without them it is common knowledge that tropical heat makes work less pleasant, or more unpleasant, than it would be in a more congenial temperature.

The direct influence of the tropical climate upon the habits of industry, however, is less important than its indirect influence, exercised through social parasitism: the initial slight disinclination to work due to the climate stimulates the growth of parasitic institutions which then greatly strengthen this disinclination. Owing to the greater effort necessary for the accomplishment of a given task in the tropics a parasitic mode of existence has greater attraction than in colder countries, where the enjoyment of idleness is spoilt by cold weather. And once parasitism becomes widespread, it casts upon work the stigma of servitude which acts as a deterrent from work.

It must not be imagined, however, that social parasitism cannot flourish in the colder climes. On the contrary, as I have tried to show in *Elements of Comparative Sociology*, it can be regarded as the natural tendency of all large societies; and a certain amount of it can be found in all human societies: everywhere there are people who succeed in obtaining a large share of wealth without contributing in any way towards its production. There are, however, differences of degree which are of decisive importance: in some societies it is a residual phenomenon whereas in others it pervades the whole social fabric. As Charles Comte has shown 140 years ago, parasitism constitutes the most powerful brake on economic progress by destroying the link between the effort and the reward.

Nowhere in Africa do we find well-established and large institutions of parasitic suction like those we can see in Latin America: outside the areas of white settlement which we are not

B

treating here there are few big land-owners; the armies are comparatively minute, the Churches not very rich and even the political parties and the bureaucratic machines remain small in comparison with other areas of the globe. The exploitation of man by man—and even more of woman by man—is done mostly on a small scale but it is ruthless, all-pervading, and grafted on the still living traditions of slavery which nowadays often revive under the name of apprenticeship and education. It is a common sight, for instance, to see emaciated little girls carrying fat infants almost as big as themselves—they have been handed over by their parents in exchange for a lump sum to be 'educated' by a more opulent family. The rents charged for miserable hovels enable the landlords to recover the capital laid out in a couple of years. As we shall see later in greater detail, the practice of extorting bribes is universal and in contrast to Latin America not mitigated by class solidarity.

The causal relationship between parasitism and poverty is not unilateral but circular, and it exemplifies the principle of the least effort: all men seek the wealth necessary for the satisfaction of their basic needs, and wherever wealth can be conserved there are men who amass it in order to gain more power and glory. If the easiest or quickest road to minimal prosperity as well as to riches leads through participation in activities which add to the collective wealth, then men will put their energies into socially useful occupations. If, owing to circumstances among which general poverty usually occupies a prominent place, productive activities are unrewarding, then men will concentrate on devising ways of wresting from the others such wealth as already exists. In other words, the energies which in an expanding economy will be applied to production, in a stagnant or contracting economy will be canalised into open or veiled predation. Readers with a taste for theoretical problems might be interested in the analogy which the social mechanism in question offers to the mental mechanism brought to light by Freud (with whose detailed interpretation thereof we need not agree): when the basic propensities of human nature find no outlet, the mental energy turns inward to consume itself in internal conflicts. . . . In the same way, when social energy finds no outlet in constructive activities, it is used up in conflicts.

Another mechanism of conversion operates between internal

and external conflicts. It can be succinctly described as follows: external and internal conflicts represent alternative manners of predation and they constitute alternative and mutually compensatory releases of population pressure, as they are alternative methods of organising emigration to hereafter. From the psychological point of view, this mechanism offers an analogue to the alternation between extra-punitive and intra-punitive individual behaviour: by displacing resentments and aggressiveness towards the outsider, an external conflict helps to smooth internal quarrels, whereas the latter may incapacitate a collectivity for aggression or even defence. Thus, social energies can be regarded as having three main outlets: construction, internal strife and external conflict. The relationship between them is such that a blockage in any of them produces an increased flow through the others, whereas a widening of one tends to drain off the flow through the other channels.

The relevance of all this to Africa is obvious: a combination of economic distress with international peace has exacerbated internal predation. The growth of the population has nullified the benefits of increased production, creating new needs and multiplying energies without providing for them outlets other than predation and strife.

Intertwined with parasitism, but also deriving their strength from other sources, various other factors impede economic progress. The most obvious of them is the smallness of the markets, due in some cases to the sparseness of the population and the difficulties of transport combined with obstacles to foreign trade, and aggravated everywhere by general poverty. In very small countries the first two factors suffice to arrest economic development: clearly, no large-scale industry could exist on supplying only the markets of Dahomey or Gabon. Such states must either form part of a larger economic community or remain on a primitive level. Outside the lilliputian states like Gambia or Gabon, however, where size really is a severely limiting factor, the chief cause of constriction of the market is the poverty of the population, which buys derisory amounts of goods and lives almost entirely under subsistence economy. Poverty cannot be eliminated so long as production is insufficient, but expansion of production is held back by the smallness of the market constricted by poverty and waste. We have here one more instance of a vicious circle.

Unless there are forces which constrict it, smallness of the market cannot in itself be an insuperable obstacle to the growth of industry: all markets have been small initially and industries have grown nevertheless. A new factory throws goods on the market, but at the same time it pays its employees, shareholders, suppliers, etc., and this money may find its way into the hands of people who want to buy goods. But because the process of expansion is circular it must be gradual and harmonious: in a commercial economic system an ultra-modern factory established within a primitive economy is doomed to bankruptcy. This does not mean that the rate of progress must always remain the same and equal in all sectors, but simply that there is a limit to the incongruity beyond which it becomes disastrous. A large part of the economic difficulties of Africa stems from the tendency to jump the stages; to concentrate on grandiose schemes and to neglect more prosaic but more immediately useful investments; to make plans for heavy industry while neglecting the manufacture of spades and hammers and wheelbarrows.

One of the greatest obstacles to economic progress in Africa is the scarcity of competent and solid businessmen. In West Africa there is over-abundance of petty traders (who are mostly women) but the medium scale trade is mostly in the hands of the Lebanese and the Indians. In East Africa the latter monopolise it completely. What is worse, the advent of independence has undermined the slender basis for development of a sound business class such as existed in the colonial days, by making a small businessman an easy prey for bureaucratic extortioners. As will be shown later, foreign big business has the power not only to withstand but even to profit from the parasitic proclivities of the wielders of political power, but a small native businessman is compelled to pay and to cheat so much that he cannot acquire the habits of a sound and socially useful business practice.

High margins of profit are normal among the traders of the pre-industrial world, precluded from working on high turnovers by the undeveloped state of transport, and the force of persistence of this tendency has been reinforced in Africa by the insecurity which stimulates the preference for a smaller gain here and now instead of a much larger one in the long run. An equally important factor which accounts up to a point for local variations is the relative poverty of the traders (that is, how imperative is their need to get money here and now): money-grabbing even at the cost of alienating a customer for ever, is much more evident and prevalent in the markets at Ibadan, as is outright cheating, than in Accra, where a market-woman will undoubtedly cut prices for regular customers, and will also endeavour to increase their number by offering a special price to a newcomer, and adding 'so that you come to me tomorrow'. As far as more prosperous businessmen are concerned, this bias is connected with a low valuation of work which makes a smaller profit on fewer operations appear more desirable than a larger profit requiring proportionally more work—an understandable standpoint in view of the instability of conditions.

The combination of high tariffs with administrative corruption and inefficiency encourages smuggling, the prevalence of which has serious influence on the conduct of business as it puts solid firms at a disadvantage. The firms which keep proper accounting and refuse to enter into illegal deals have to pay much more for many of the goods which they require.

The dangers of wars, confiscations and pogroms play a considerable role in forming the mentality of businessmen but equally important is the uncertainty caused by violent and unpredictable changes in policies of the governments, who often suddenly institute or abolish without premeditation laws, tariffs, taxes, exchange controls, import and export restrictions. Some of the laws and regulations are clearly absurd and impossible to follow, and most businessmen circumvent them—just as they circumvent those which are wise and just—and illegality always implies uncertainty. Moreover, the expansion of governmental control over economic affairs make the businessmen dependent in many ways on the good will of officials (whom they try to influence by arguments, intrigues, bribes and threats); and this means that shifts in personnel of the ministries have serious repercussions on business prospects, and that the profitability of a venture may depend on the outcome of a struggle for power between ethnies or factions. In addition, the expenses incurred in cultivating the good will of the officials have to be recovered, which makes a very high rate of profit a necessity.

As the countries of Africa are dependent on a wide assortment of imported goods, but pay for them by exporting one or two staple commodities, even relatively minor fluctuations in the prices of the latter engender violent general dislocations. Expectation of such happenings discourages long-term planning and sound business practices. The difficulty of forecasting the cost of bribes introduces a further element of insecurity. Private enterprise can become profitable in a socially useful direction only if it can expect to reap the rewards of building up a reputation for cheapness and good service. Under conditions of insecurity these rewards must seem very uncertain, and not worth pursuing at the cost of forgoing opportunities of making quick and unscrupulous gains. Part of the insecurity stems from the political turmoil due to economic difficulties for which the anti-social conduct of business is partly responsible . . . again a vicious circle.

It remains to be added that as wages are low, shops, offices and workshops abound in semi-idle personnel with the consequence that productivity is so low that the wages cannot be raised.

Chapter 3 URBAN JUNGLES

The process of urbanisation has been very fast during the last decades. Since 1921 the population of Dakar has increased from *c*. 32,440 to *c*. 366,000 in 1963, that of Freetown from *c*. 44,000 to *c*. 100,000 in 1960, of Accra from *c*. 38,000 in 1936 to *c*. 338,000 in 1960, that of Lagos from *c*. 99,000 in 1921 to 450,000 in 1962. Kumasi grew from *c*. 24,000 inhabitants in 1921 to *c*. 190,000 in 1960, and the population of Ibadan which is now given as *c*. 600,000 has more than trebled since 1921. Abidjan in the Ivory Coast increased from *c*. 17,000 in 1937 to *c*. 187,500 in 1960, and Cotonou in Dahomey from *c*. 8,000 in 1931 to *c*. 54,100 in 1960. Most of this increase was due to migration: no less than 58 per cent of the population of Lagos consisted in 1950 of people born elsewhere, while according to the Ghana Census (1960) only 25 per cent of the population of Takoradi, about 40 per cent of the population of Sekondi, some 37 per cent of the population of Kumasi, and some 47 per cent of the population of Accra are of local origin. 52 per cent of the population of Takoradi and 36 per cent in the case of Accra had lived in those towns for less than five years, while in Ghana, as a whole, more than two-thirds of the urban inhabitants have been in the towns concerned for less than five years. In Freetown the influx has been less intensive, but even so about a quarter of all adults of tribal origin and over one-third of their children are of Freetown birth. Less than a quarter of the inhabitants of Port Harcourt were born there.

The early studies of detribalisation have concentrated on the process of destruction of the tribal and clan structures. Later writers, on the other hand, have emphasised that—as Michael Banton puts it*—'the changes that people undergo in becoming urbanised involve both a negative and a positive phase, a movement of disorganisation and a contrary movement of reorganisation', and have stressed the wide incidence of associations concerned with mutual benefit or with furtherance of occupational aims, leaning

* *A West African City*, O.U.P., London.

over backwards to show that they do not look down on the Africans. Consequently, the descriptions of urban life which have been published are true as far as they go—that is to say, all the statements which they contain are true—but the total picture is very misleading because they do not show the all-pervading element of strife which is so characteristic of large African towns. The authors emphasise the undoubtedly existing attractive features and leave out what is not nice.

A spectacular increase in the possibilities of consumption— combined with general poverty—leads naturally to an effort to increase incomes by all available means: through pushing and unscrupulous trade, stealing, prostitution, corruption, indebtedness (usurers in Brazzaville charge interest rates of 25 to 30 per cent per month); or cut-throat politics.

As Albert Meister points out . . . (p. 138, *L'Afrique peut-elle Partir?*, Ed. du Seuil, 1966) 'in contrast to Europe of the last century where the migration to towns began after agricultural productivity had increased, in Africa (as in other under-developed parts of the world) the rural exodus takes place without any increase in the agricultural production'. Inevitably, this must lead either to an intensification of the struggle for survival among the townsmen, or an aggravation of the exploitation of the agriculturalists by them or (as most commonly happens) both.

The following brief sketch of the evils attending unproductive urbanisation does not apply, almost needless to say, to all the areas of tropical Africa in equal measure. The violence and chaos accompanying the scramble for scarce goods depend in the first place on how acute is the scarcity— that is, on the relationship of the population to wealth. So it is not surprising that strife, squabbles and robbery are more conspicuous in Nigeria and the Congo than in Ghana and Ivory Coast, where the estimated income per head is about double. True, our analysis does not fit Somalia, Niger and Chad, which are a great deal poorer than Nigeria and the Congo, but there the old tribal structures have suffered little dislocation and consequently the pressure of population on resources takes the form of tribal affrays rather than of urban gangsterism and crookery.

Another note of caution must be sounded before we proceed further: we must remember that human behaviour can be described only in comparative terms: so that the notion of disorder and violence implies that of order and peacefulness; and it is all a matter of degree which more often than not we cannot ascertain with any precision. So I would not like to venture an opinion on whether the scramble for goods is more intensive or widespread in Ibadan than in Mexico City or Dallas, although I am sure that it is much more tumultuous and brutal than in any place in north western Europe. Certainly in no African town is gangsterism so well organised or so predominant as it was in Chicago in the days of Al Capone or is today in Manila. What is characteristic of the urban existence in tropical Africa is not organised violence but a kind of diffuse, unregulated scramble stemming from the fluidity of the social structures and the absence of efficient organisation. However, that unregulated petty strife can be common even under a fairly effective totalitarian rule is shown by the example of the Polish towns after the war where the so-called 'densification'—that is, the policy of putting several families into what used to be one-family flats—has called forth an unprecedented flood of rows and fights, usually starting in a shared kitchen or about a shared lavatory, and not seldom ending with murder. Are these conflicts more or less harmful than their African counterparts? I do not know. All one can say is that the common denominators are friction and scarcity.

One important difference between migration to towns in Africa as compared with most other parts of the world stems from the survival of the communal land tenure. With the exception of old Russia where the village community persisted much longer, a European peasant who went to seek a livelihood in a town usually had no property to return to, whereas an African migrant retains his right to land held under communal tenure. Consequently, there is much more movement to and fro in Africa. Coupled with the persistence of clan solidarity and the readiness to form associations for mutual aid among migrants from the same village, the bonds with the ancestral home prevent an utter pulverisation and degradation of the new townsmen. But while preventing the extremes of despair and misery, these factors impede the crystallisation of urban order.

Whether living in chaotic circumstances, precariously perched on the urban-rural divide, makes the African townsman unhappier than the inmates of well organised affluent societies must remain an open question. For order and efficiency may be attained at the price of standardising the individuals, pinning them down to a groove, and making life tediously predictable and stereotyped. How many denizens of overdeveloped countries are driven into melancholia, crime or drug-addiction by the monotony of living as hemmed in, well-fitted cogs of a super-efficient bureaucratic machine? In the tropics, moreover, so long as people are not starving, they suffer no physical pain from the absence of material goods which are indispensable in the colder climates; while sunshine infuses into life an elusive, vibrant quality which enhances enjoyment of momentary pleasures and allays fears for the morrow.

Though undoubtedly a source of many fears and much consequent misery, witchcraft also alleviates the feelings of helplessness, and helps to sweeten the bitter pill of failure by enabling the unsuccessful to lay the blame on the sorcery of envious rivals. These comforting faculties of the magic art ensure its survival (if not intensification) in cities, where tensions stemming from strangeness, helplessness and aggravated rivalry create a craving for a solace which more than outweighs the impact of the modes of thought deriving from science and commercial rationality. According to P. C. Lloyd:

'The great disparity between the aspirations of most West Africans and their real chances of success leads to a high rate of failure. And the response to these failures tends to be extra-punitive; the individual does not blame his own short-comings but shifts the responsibility to external agents . . . Witchcraft . . . is feared not only by those who fail but perhaps even more so by the successful. . . . To the spread of Christianity is attributed a general increase in moral laxity. Traditional deities were believed to punish swiftly and sternly. But the Protestant is taught that salvation can be gained through faith alone; the Roman Catholic confesses, and is forgiven his sins. Consequently one fears that one's enemies will be more likely to employ witchcraft or sorcery against one. Traditional methods of detecting witches are falling into abeyance. . . . To allay these fears of increased insecurity against witchcraft and sorcery there has, in recent years, developed a profusion of new anti-witchcraft shrines and of religious sects. The former operate almost entirely within the context of traditional beliefs, while the latter, founded by men and women who have often been prominent church members, are syncretist in character. The growing popularity of both indicates the degree to which the mission-established churches have failed to respond to the needs of their congregations.'*

In all societies individuals and groups struggle for their shares of the good things of life. The acerbity, frequency and duration of the resulting conflicts depend on the scarcity of wealth, the stimulation of the appetites and the force of the codes regulating the competition. In modern Africa the population is growing faster than wealth, the appetite for material goods and glory is intense, and the tribal morals are loosing their grip without being replaced by anything else, thus leaving behind a moral vacuum.

An African who goes to town does not usually sever his connections with his tribe and clan: he seeks his clansmen who seldom refuse to help him, and whom he is ready to help in return. Everywhere in the world, however, the tribal codes of ethics confine the duties and obligations within the tribe, and regard strangers as creatures without any rights. Until the rise of Buddhism and Christianity the idea that all human beings have some rights could only be contemplated by a few isolated philosophers; and even now humanitarian ethics receive more lip service than effective adhesion. However, in the old states the group centred limitations of the moral horizons operate on the level of social classes or nations, which are entities of roughly the same order of magnitude as the industrial and administrative units of the modern world. Whereas in Europe or Asia the processes of widening the moral horizon beyond the confines of the tribes stretched over many centuries, in Africa, the supra-tribal economic and administrative structures have emerged so suddenly that the change in attitudes could not keep the pace. In consequence the inhabitants of the big cities find themselves without moral guidance in their dealings with most people with whom they come in contact—for their clansmen or even tribesmen constitute usually a small part of the population of any large town.

The contrast between genuinely felt moral obligation towards one's clansmen and the lack of compunction in dealing with

* *Africa in Social Change:* P. C. Lloyd, Penguin, 1967.

strangers is illustrated by the behaviour of the Hausa traders. Most of them work in groups of kinsmen one of whom will be the legal owner of the shop or firm. He may employ his relatives (usually junior) in the shop or send them as itinerant salesmen. He pays them no regular salary or commission but feeds, houses and clothes them, buys them wives, gives them some pocket money if they merit a reward, and tries to set up the more capable of them in business on their own account, providing the initial capital. The itinerant sellers are under the obligation to hand over to their paternal boss all the money they make, but it is said that in fact they do so. Admittedly, it is very difficult to be sure that this is not a myth but whenever I inquired about this point I got an answer like 'but they could not steal from their senior brother'. Yet everybody knows that the same men will resort to every possible trick to cheat their customers, and if they get an opportunity to steal something from them they will do that too. And they treat their porters (who are in fact their slaves) like beasts of burden.

In the cities of West Africa clansmen or men from the same village often form curious associations for the purpose of making gifts to each member in turn: every month (or whatever period they agree upon) all of them will give an agreed amount of money to one of them, then to the next and so in turn. They enter into no contracts and could not sue the first beneficiary if he backed out and ran away after receiving a substantial gift. Nonetheless, the first generation townsmen take it for granted that this could not happen. The same people, however, will deploy great ingenuity in devising ways of stealing from their employers or any other stranger, and may even live by theft or robbery. Education does little to make people honest towards non-kinsmen: few of the bank cashiers, for instance, can resist the temptation indefinitely, and most of them vanish or go to jail.

Most of the inhabitants of African cities are very poor, although they seldom have to starve. In many cities the unemployed outnumber the employed, and a large number of women (perhaps even the majority of the young) gain their livelihood through prostitution. Particularly in the new towns, the overwhelming majority of the inhabitants (in some cases perhaps over 90 per cent) are under 30, men outnumbering women by 3 or 4 or even as much as 6 to 1. The unemployed young men live on the charity of their relatives. A good part of them take to stealing or smuggling or some form of crookery as their main occupation, while most of the others will not refrain from getting something by such means if an opportunity comes their way. The crime rate is rising very fast, and many towns which only a few years ago were quite idyllic now contain strong bands of robbers, some of whom work in collusion with the police. Those who own anything devote much time and money to protecting their property—the Africans using their poor relatives for this purpose while the expatriates make elaborate arrangements to prevent their servants from robbing them, employing at least one night-watchman for each house and sometimes a day guard as well. The more important people have police guards at their gates. The thieves are continually improving their techniques and no prize seems to be too small for some of them. Once I had a window curtain snatched literally behind my back from the room in which I was sitting.

In contrast to the problem of rising criminality in the affluent countries of north western Europe and north America, no subtle psychological explanations are needed to account for the prevalence of crimes against property in African cities where so many people have no other means of making a living. Most of the unemployed would like to work, and a mere rumour that there might be a job vacant will attract a crowd of 'applicants' in a matter of hours. In Nigeria, many young men give 'applicant' as their occupation—which in fact it is, as the literate among them write several applications every day for years on end. The Ibos appear to be the most persistent, while the Yorubas tend to give up sooner. Under these circumstances it would be miraculous if many of them did not take to crime, particularly as they have come to town with high expectations and feel embittered. The situation is further aggravated, however, by the moral confusion generated by the process of migration and urbanisation.

The villagers or herdsmen normally still obey the old customs which define their respective rights and duties, and regulate conflicts. This does not mean that they never transgress the norms or live in perfect harmony, but it does mean that their behaviour is more orderly and the clash of egoisms somewhat subdued. The greater incidence of crime in towns as compared with the villages is, of course, nothing surprising and it has been a recurrent theme of social thought in many parts of the world. In Africa, however, the contrast between the orderly and dignified behaviour of the villagers and the wild scrapping about money, stealing, cheating and robbing which goes on in the towns is particularly striking. The intensity and frequency of these daily conflicts vary considerably from place to place—mainly in response to the size of the population, the extent of disorganisation and the gravity of overpopulation. Thus the struggle for existence or opulence seems somewhat milder in Accra or Kumasi than in Ibadan, Lagos or Kinshasa. Nonetheless, the broad features of the contrast between the urban and rural way of life are similar throughout Africa between the Sahara and the Zambesi.

The first is that the African peasants were in some ways in a better position than their counterparts in most parts of the world: with the exception of the relatively small enclaves of enslaved or thoroughly subjugated populations such as Zanzibar or Rwanda, they were never reduced to serfdom and have continued until now to live in fairly independent communities bound by kinship, on the land which they jointly own. There have also been slave hunting and trading emirates like Zazzau where a large part of the tillers of the soil consisted of captured slaves. On the whole, however, the indigenous kingdoms like the Ashanti or Dahomey destroyed neither the communal economy of the village nor the web of tribal and clan affiliations—in contrast to the slave plantations in the Americas or the European manorial serfdom. What is more, until the colonial conquests large parts of Africa were occupied by completely independent tribes recognising no overlords. Such relatively happy condition of free peasants without lords or tax-collectors, as could still be seen in most parts of Africa within living memory in an almost unadulterated form, disappeared in Europe 2,000 years ago, and in the Near East 6,000 years ago, with the rise of states and the exploiting classes. When a Brazilian or Peruvian peasant goes to town he is entering a human jungle, but what he leaves behind is hardly better—a place where he has been exploited and ill-treated by the landlord, and where order is maintained not by tribal custom but by the power stemming from slavery and employing economic and physical coercion—whereas an African migrant more often than not leaves behind a society which he regards as just even though stifling. What he enters is a highly normless (or anomic, in Durkheim's terminology) society which resembles much more a gold-digger's camp than a well-ordered city.

Of particular importance is the embryonic character and deficient vitality of the professional groupings, as it is the pressure of the opinion within them that in old-established urban civilisations enforces the norms of which the law takes no cognizance. There are, of course, professional associations in Africa but they are too recent to hold genuine loyalty, and the codes of behaviour which they proclaim have not yet been internalised by their members, although some development in this direction could be detected in the lawyers' and medical practitioners' associations in towns with a longer established educated layer like Accra and Lagos. In the latter case any progress that might have been made has been nullified by the outbreak of strife. To visualise the comparison take, for instance, accountancy in a country where it has a firmly rooted tradition. Many of the new entrants will be following in their fathers' footsteps, but even those who are not will expect to spend their lives in this stolid group which may be the only social unit, larger than the family but smaller than the nation, to which they will permanently belong. For this reason most of them will take fairly seriously to heart the very useful even though not very inspired ideals of this profession.

There are in Africa some quite big towns (like Kano, Djenne or Timbuctoo) with a long tradition of urban living. Their social structures stand in strong contrast to the melting pots full of detribalised migrants (which is what the fast growing new cities are). In the old towns (or at least in their old nuclei) the settlement is by tribes and clans, and the web of kinship continues to operate. Most of such towns, however, stagnate and they represent the old semi-feudal Africa which is disappearing. Those which have been growing fast have acquired new quarters (like Kano's now destroyed 'sabon gari') where the dynamic sector of the economy is located, and where social conditions are similar to those in the completely new cities. The older coastal towns like Dakar, Lagos and Freetown contain substantial numbers of fairly Europeanised and mostly educated and privileged townsmen of several generations' standing, but they are a small minority in comparison with the recent migrants. Even within power elites, people of such origins seem to constitute a minority—especially in the countries which have experienced violent upheavals.

In a typical developing African town, the majority of the inhabitants are first generation. The professionals know very

well that in Britain or France people of their occupation have
certain definite ideas on how they should behave, but they
themselves have not been drilled in these prosaic virtues during
their most impressionable years. What is even more important
is that their convivial intercourse and their deeper friendships are
circumscribed by the boundaries of the clan and tribe rather than
of the profession. The only really recognised duties are those
towards the clansmen who are the only people who really matter.
A lawyer or an official is less concerned about his professional
reputation (except in so far as it affects his earnings) than about
whether he is well thought of by his kinsmen. The result of these
circumstances is that norms and ideals which might regulate
work and the social relations arising from it have either failed to
crystallise or have not acquired sufficient motivating force to
ensure compliance. One indicator of this state of affairs is the
absence of business partnerships between non-kinsmen. This
applies even to lawyers who have been trained in Europe—and
therefore constitute one of the most westernised social categories.
Apart from mutual mistrust, their function as battering rams on
behalf of their clans would lead to a break up of the partnership
as soon as a clan brother of one of them would come into conflict
with the clan brother of the other. In Ghana *all* business partnerships are likely to founder on mutual suspicion; it is said that each
partner suspects the other of salting away some of the funds and
therefore starts to do it himself, so that in the end the business is
ruined. It also seems that Ghanaian firms seldom survive their
founder in each case; in Kumasi there are, for instance, only two
African firms which have continued for more than one generation.
In the Akan areas especially this may be partly a consequence of
matrilineal inheritance, as the heirs will not have formed any
involvement in the business; but it also appears to be the case
generally that relatives will vie jealously with one another over
the pickings from the estate and have no wish or interest at all
in getting together to preserve any part of it intact or to keep it
going. On the other hand, the continuance of an African firm one
of whose partners has died is not unknown—and such partnerships
could well be between non-kinsmen.

In the tribal societies the moral obligations did not extend
beyond the boundaries of the tribe: apart from quasi-diplomatic
occasions, the stranger had no rights and it was perfectly legitimate

to kill or enslave him. This must not be forgotten when we try to understand what appears to be a war of all against all which is going on in the African cities. In fact, it is not quite a war of all against all but rather a transplantation and transfiguration of the conflicts between tribes and clans brought about by a heaping up of tribal splinters in an urban environment where fraud, theft and politics have replaced the traditional tribal warfare. We have here a complete discord between the moral sentiments and the social structure: the urban societies where the only effective ethics are tribal. The resulting petty strife varies in intensity from place to place mainly in response to the differences in tensions stemming from the pressures of population upon wealth. Thus, for instance, the 'war of all against all' is far more evident in Nigeria than in Ghana, although there is plenty of mutual distrust in Ghana. It is perhaps a question of differences in overt behaviour rather than in underlying attitudes; it seems that strangers are received more hospitably, or at least treated with more tolerance in most parts of Ghana than in most parts of Nigeria. One thing which is very plain is that Nigerians are and have been for years much more readily received and assimilated in Ghanaian towns than Ghanaians are in Nigerian towns.

The embryonic and fluid state of the customs which are supposed to regulate urban activities (and conflicts arising therefrom) is primarily due to the novelty of the urban way of life, and up to a point may be regarded as a normal consequence of sudden urbanisation. In Europe this process has been much more gradual, and so to get a closer parallel we must look at the towns which have been created almost overnight in Siberia—shoddily built, without amenities and filled with masses of illiterate peasants herded at the point of a bayonet—where human relations were at least equally brutal, and even more painful because of the isolation and helplessness of the individuals due to the absence of clan solidarity. The manifestations of the conflicts, however, had to be different under the condition of all-pervading regimentation and terror.

In addition to the warring tribal splinters, the African towns contain a still small but rapidly growing number of truly detribalised individuals who have detached themselves from their clan and tribe without being absorbed by any other stable group, and have consequently become truly rootless and amoral. This human type is produced by all urban societies, and in Africa can be found

mainly in the big cities of the west coast. The variegated associations which have sprung up in all the towns undoubtedly do
help the migrants to find their feet in the strange environment but
they can do little to alleviate the effects of detribalisation which is
destroying the bonds on which they are based.

Disintegration of the family has been a regular feature of massive
migration to cities in all parts of the world with the exception of
Latin America where landlordism, slavery and serfdom have to
a very large extent destroyed the family bonds among the rural
proletariat before the migration to the cities even began. In
Africa the impact of transplantation is even greater than it was in
Europe at the time when the industrial cities began to grow
because the African migrants are not villagers accustomed to
systematic work but tribesmen who until very recently regarded
war and hunting as the only activities worthy of a man, and left
tilling of the soil to women. Many aspects of African modernisation
and industrialisation become understandable if we remember that
all the men have imbibed the tradition that work is the thing
for women only.

In most parts of Africa to get a wife a man must pay a substantial
sum to her father, but once he has done that he expects her to
support him rather than the other way round. This was a viable
arrangement in free tribal existence where constant warfare kept
the number of men well below those of women, and where land
was plentiful. The husband provided each of his wives with a
plot of land which he had cleared, built a hut for her and her
children, and then expected her to provide him with food. To
be exact, the provision of game and in some areas of yams were
men's responsibility, but on the whole it was the women who were
providing the food for the family. Such a distribution of tasks is
impracticable in the cities, and the consequence is a breakdown
of the family as an institution.

Although a townswoman has no land to till and therefore
cannot produce any food, her husband expects her to feed not
only herself and the children but him as well, and so provide him
with a return on his investment in the bride-price. His attitude to
the money he earns is analogous to that of his ancestors towards
war trophies: it is something not to be given to women. There are,
of course, local variations: the Ghanaian town artisan normally
provides his bride with a sum of money to engage in petty trading,

and out of the proceeds she is expected to feed herself and the children—but she is not expected to feed him from her own resources although she may well do so if she becomes prosperous. In any case he does not intend to support her. True, there are in most African cities thoroughly Christianised and intensely respectable people whose family relations bear more resemblance to the way of life in Victorian England than to the prevalent African pattern; but they are a small minority even among the educated classes. The ordinary townsman is a drone who gives little or nothing to his family, and spends an inordinate part of his earnings on his clothes, except when he is saving to get a wife. It is symptomatic that in the African cities the shops with men's wear figure much more prominently than those catering for women.

As clerks and shop assistants are mostly men, while the most lucrative kind of domestic service (namely, for the expatriates) has since the early colonial days also been reserved for men, the opportunities of employment for women are very restricted. Indeed whenever women try to enter any new occupation no matter how humble, the men attempt to drive them out . . . often by beating them up. Actually there are only two occupations which women can ply without harassment: market trading and prostitution, which are frequently combined. As trading requires a certain amount of knowledge of the town conditions and some capital, be it only a few shillings, prostitution often provides the only entry into trading for a girl who arrives from a village with nothing. Given the parasitic proclivities of the males, moreover, prostitution is very advantageous economically because in this way a woman is sure to get at least something for her services and for defraying the costs thereof in the shape of progeny. Furthermore, far from precluding marriage, prostitution often constitutes the only means (tolerated or even recommended by the husband) of feeding him and the children.

There are several additional factors which foster the spread of prostitution, the first of which is the traditionally mercenary attitude to marriage. Notwithstanding all the whitewashing by the anthropologists enamoured of the myth of 'le noble Sauvage', there can be little doubt that the custom of the bride-price involves a kind of sale: not of an absolute sale like that of a goat—for the wife retains in most tribes some rights, often very substantial—but a sale

nonetheless because the transaction is concluded by the father of
the bride mainly (though not always entirely) for the sake of
gain. Now, if the normal fate of a woman is to be sold—even if
the sale is hedged by various reservations and is under certain
circumstances revocable—then why should she not sell herself
for her own profit rather than that of her father, when in consequence of her move to a town he can no longer control her? On
the other side, the young men are often unable to accumulate the
bride-price which, for instance among the Ibos and the Kikuyus,
amounts to a few years' earnings of an unskilled labourer. In the
traditional rural society the wealth circulates within a small
circle as men pay the bride-price in cattle or other goods obtained
through the marriage of their sisters or what we would call cousins;
the wealth usually going to a common pool from which it is
allocated by the elders. In contrast, the dispersion and mobility
brought about by urbanisation have partly or completely removed
the migrants from such networks, and forced them to earn the
needed sums by individual exertions on the labour market, which
can be very difficult or even impossible for many. In addition to
the increased difficulty of paying for her, the returns on the
investment in a wife are meagre under the urban conditions, as
she is seldom able to feed her husband. Consequently, many
men prefer to obtain their sexual satisfaction for casual payment
rather than for a large lump sum. The girls, on the other hand,
often prefer to live by prostitution rather than be saddled
with the burdensome duty of supporting a husband for the sake of
procuring money for the father.

There is also a demographic reason for the prevalence of
prostitution in the African towns. Given the prices of food and
lodging in relation to wages, very few men are capable of maintaining a wife and children, whereas prostitution spreads the cost of
maintaining one woman over several men. Polyandry is normally
the consequence of extreme poverty; and from the point of view
of social accounting one could regard prostitution in African
towns as a kind of collective polyandry, as it were, which is
feasible because in the new or rapidly growing towns men greatly
outnumber women.

Before going further I must warn the reader that the foregoing
account suffers from a linguistic distortion. In English, 'prostitution' is the only word for the selling of sexual services to a

multitude of transient customers, but it distorts the African reality because it is loaded with condemnation and contempt, from which the African attitude to such transactions is free, except in so far as it has been influenced by the missionaries. The traditional African outlook does not brand sexual acts as sinister or filthy, but neither does it regard them as ecstatic or even very important; being free, in fact, both from the notions of pollution and from the ideas of romantic love. The taboos restricting sexual intercourse rest upon the fear of disastrous material consequences which their breach is believed to automatically bring about—not upon the feelings of guilt and shame. In accordance with this down-to-earth attitude, assuaging someone's sexual desires for payment carries no greater stigma than cutting his hair. Moreover, from the viewpoint of African custom (on the West Coast at least), the giving and receiving of money elevates rather than degrades a relationship, as it constitutes a proof of seriousness of the sentiments—which may be regarded as crudity or as a laudable absence of hypocrisy. An African woman will accept money from a suitor with equally few reservations as her European sister would flowers or ornaments; and a woman who demands cash is no more despised than a film star in Europe or America whose road to fame has led (as normally happens) through the beds of influential directors.

In addition to this unabashed materialism—so different in form rather than ethical content from the furtive and veiled Euro-American variety—an important determinant of the situation is the existence of different kinds of marriage with the corresponding variations in the status of the wife. In many parts of Africa being a wife may be a matter of degree rather than a 'yes' or 'no' question and the various functions which the Judeo-Christian tradition treats as indissolubly united may be parcelled out to different persons. Many relationships, which occur in Western civilisation but without the benefit of customary or legal regulation, are fully institutionalised in traditional African societies where we can find (to use our meagre vocabulary) half-wives, co-wives, temporary wives and other varieties. There is one kind, for example, which the father can reclaim from the husband after a few years. There are also women hired out (as the Europeans would say) not so much for the purpose of providing sexual satisfaction as (what seems more curious to a Westerner) for bearing children.

A childless wife or even an unmarried woman, may keep a permanent or temporary child-bearer and appropriate the latter's children; while a man without sons may not allow his daughter to marry but encourage her to produce offspring which he will claim as his own.

One can generalise more easily about the defects and failures of urban, industrial and political institutions because the obstacles to their successful implantation stem from the clash between the imported foreign patterns and the most general features of the tribal society; but the customs regulating sex and kinship vary not only from area to area but often from village to village, so that even a most cursory survey of these matters would require a separate volume. Compelled, therefore, to skip the issue, I shall only stress that although (especially in its more business-like forms to be found in the bigger cities) commercialised promiscuity undoubtedly contributes to the disintegration of the traditional bonds of kinship, neither the women involved nor their children suffer to any great extent from a social stigma or the subjective feelings of degradation, except in the most thoroughly Christianised enclaves.

Even in the biggest towns, where commercialised promiscuity assumes a more business-like and unequivocal character on the European pattern, the practitioners are called 'free women' and, because of their independence as well as affluence, their status is not necessarily lower and occasionally higher than that of wives who normally have to work and obey.

The spread of commercialised promiscuity was particularly easy in the areas inhabited by matrilineal tribes where a man's heirs are his sister's children, while the marital bond is traditionally of little importance and the husbands are often transient figures without much authority; although it would be untrue to say that matrilineal inheritance invariably goes with weakness of the father role. This is not, for instance, the case in the Akan areas, where the male is head of his household, which often contains several wives, and there is no doubt about his authority. In those societies promiscuity was common anyway and what urbanisation is corroding is not so much the institution of marriage as the bonds of matrilineal family and clan.

The disintegration of the conjugal as well as of the extended family cannot fail to stimulate crime and the generalised ruthless scramble for money. It affects even the first generation townsmen, many of whom roam around as irresponsible drones, but who would have been moving within a strictly enforced code had they stayed in the ancestral village. Even more prone to crime or semi-criminal behaviour are the second generation young townsmen who have been brought up in the slums without parental control, and who have been thrown into heartless urban environment at an early age to fend for themselves. They could hardly be expected to show many scruples in the struggle for existence. Almost needless to say, this type of human being is not confined to Africa and has been known in all parts of the world. In post-revolutionary Russia, for instance, large roving bands of syphilitic young delinquents infested the cities as well as the countryside, until Stalin had applied his favourite cure of extermination.

The picture sketched above does not reflect in equal measure the social reality in all African towns. In East Africa, for instance, where the process of urbanisation is much less advanced, its attendant evils are naturally less massive. In old-established towns like Ibadan in Nigeria a lot of settlement is by tribe and clan and in consequence a large section of the inhabitants are firmly embedded in a definite social structure while the floating population is less important. Since, however, most of the contacts in the course of making a living take place between non-kinsmen, this in no way attenuates the scramble for goods. In any case, even in the old and relatively static towns the human flotsam is numerous and exhibits most of the features sketched above. As might be expected, however, it is in the towns which have been growing most rapidly or have recently sprung up that we can find the closest approximation to the Hobbesian conditions of the war of all against all.

Many of the most painful aspects of African development stem from the fact that the dissolution of the old ethics and of the tribal and clan solidarity goes on faster than the emergence of new norms and ideals. Naturally, some ethnies resist the corrosive influence of modernisation better than others, but the educated elite are almost everywhere morally disorientated: torn between the traditional values which they have imbibed in childhood and the so-called civilising influences from abroad, many of them are completely unsure about what is right and what is wrong, and oscillate between incompatible patterns of behaviour.

The preceding grim account of city life raises the question of why do the villagers go to the towns already full of paupers? In the first place owing to the pressure of the population on land which, of course, varies in density from place to place. Given the state of agricultural skills and the meagreness of the output, there are too many people in the villages, and many of them are condemned to idleness and hunger. Secondly, as the rural society is gerontocratic, the young men and women have to work very hard and are obliged to surrender most of the fruit of their exertions to their elders; and so by going to town they can escape from this severe discipline. The most important inducement, however, seems to be that migration comprises an element of a gamble. A man who stays in the village knows that he may accede to certain privileges with age but he will certainly remain poor to the day he dies, whereas if he tries his luck in a city he may end up even poorer but at least he has a chance of getting something very much better. Objectively his chances of success may be very small but young men are usually given to optimism, which in the new African states has been stimulated by the sight of incredible careers made through the process of decolonisation.

Chapter 4 STILL-BORN NATIONALISMS

Everybody talks about the new nations in Africa although it is far from evident that such entities really exist in any but purely legalistic sense. When talking about these problems in English or French one is particularly likely to confuse the socio-psychological with legal aspects because of the poverty of terminology. The languages spoken east of the Rhine have different words for citizenship (in the sense of being a subject of a given government) and nationality in the sense of consciously adhering to a nation as an entity distinguished by customs, language and specific culture, and characterised by a widely shared desire for political independence. This linguistic discrimination reflects the far-reaching divergence between state frontiers and the areas occupied by the nations as defined above, which has been a characteristic feature of central and eastern Europe for many centuries; in contrast to Britain and France where this discrepancy was much less noticeable and gave rise to fewer conflicts. For this reason the French and English 'nation' refers both to the sum of the citizens (or subjects) of one state, and to the culturally defined aggregate exhibiting a will to political independence and a consciousness of belonging together.

If by a 'nation' we mean the sum of the subjects or citizens, then, of course, a number of new nations have been created in Africa. If, however, we look for some psychic reality behind the legal categories—for something that we could call national sentiment or national consciousness or patriotism, uniting the subjects of the state—then we shall find that there is only one nation-state south of the Sahara—the Somalis—and that even in the ancient kingdom of Ethiopa mental identification with the state is confined to the Amharic ruling race.

As the prospects of the new states depend in a very large measure on the nature of the bonds uniting their citizens, the question of national consciousness has great practical importance; but to discuss it realistically we must discard the shibboleths and the clichés with which it is surrounded. Another difficulty stems from emotive loadings of the words, and from the fact that they designate social relations; so that by altering their meanings we may be suspected of attempting to subvert the present situation. If we define 'nation' in such a way that it does not fit the sets such as 'the Kenyans' or 'the Zambians', we shall be deemed to have been guilty of attacking their right to a seat in U.N.O. and of insulting them, as forming a nation has come to be regarded as a badge of respectability. Notwithstanding these perils, we must put some order into the terminology because in its present confused state it hamstrings understanding; and some of the usages are patently absurd.

Take for instance the word 'tribalism', which is usually applied to the solidarity or separatist tendencies of any ethnic aggregate smaller than (or simply not co-extensive with) the population of the state, even if the aggregate in question is as numerous as the Yorubas. Why should 13 million Yorubas be called a tribe but the much less numerous Latvians a nation? Because the former are Africans and latter Europeans? We can be using the word 'nation' only in a purely legal sense if we apply it to the heterogeneous population of Uganda or Tanzania but not to the Yorubas or the Ashantis. Why should we call the opposition of the French Canadians to the English Canadian domination nationalism, and the analogous attitude of the Ibos to the Hausas tribalism? Are the protagonists of the official view of African affairs not indulging in crypto-racialism when they call the same thing nationalism (which sounds good) when it occurs in Europe or America, but 'tribalism' (which sounds bad) when it occurs in Africa?

If we take such criteria of nationhood as numbers, distinctiveness of culture, language, territory and political tradition, the Yorubas seem to satisfy them, even though their desire for political independence and unification with Yorubas beyond the borders is not very conspicuous. On the other hand, the word 'tribe' designates in ethnological literature very much smaller units enmeshed in one kinship network and organised for collective action. The Yorubas fall into hundreds of units which are usually called tribes, and therefore cannot be jointly described as a tribe. If we take the will to sovereignty and political unification as the decisive criteria, then the Yorubas appear as not quite a nation—

or at least not so much a nation as, say, the Germans—but they are certainly nearer to being a nation than a tribe.

The question arises: what should we call social aggregates of this kind? We could use 'people' but this word has so many meanings and is so vague that it should be avoided in any but the colloquial sense. The French call such entities 'les peuplades' which is slightly less ambiguous than 'les peuples', and recently the term 'une ethnie' has been introduced into sociological literature. As this term is very convenient, inoffensive and of Greek origin, it can be imported into English without any modifications, and we can speak of an ethny or ethnies, rather than of ethnic groups. The latter term is not very good because we add to the confusion if we call groups entities whose components are relatively isolated from each other; particularly as what they have in common are cultural traits rather than organs permitting collective action.

An ethny, then, is a social aggregate exhibiting a certain uniformity of culture but not organised for collective action, where the feeling of collective solidarity is rudimentary, and where there is no will for political unification and independence (or preservation thereof). A nation can be defined as an aggregate characterised by the following features: (1) a set of cultural traits (such as customs, beliefs or language) which distinguish it from other similar aggregates; (2) a widespread desire amongst its members for political unification and independence, that is to say for a government of its own, staffed by its own members; (3) size larger than any network of kinship could embrace, which feature distinguishes a nation from a tribe; (4) absence of analogous divisions inside it: which implies a readiness on the part of the members of any of the territorial components to accept individuals from any other component as their supreme rulers. The last criterion enables us to decide such questions as, for instance, whether the Scots, the Welsh and the English constitute nations or parts of the British nation: if it matters little to most members of each collectivity from which of them the prime minister and his cabinet colleagues come, then they constitute one nation; if there are strong feelings on this matter, then they do not. It would be unthinkable that a German or a Frenchman should become a prime minister of Britain or the other way around. As with everything else in human affairs, national unity is a matter of degree: an Englishman could become a commander of a Scottish regiment but hardly a Mayor of Edinburgh. When we saw that after Nigeria became independent the Ibos were being eliminated from posts in the Northern Region even if sometimes they had to be replaced by specially imported Europeans, then we could conclude that the Nigerians did not constitute one nation. One could compile all kinds of interesting indices of national unity and segregation by estimating resentment or indifference to interchange in positions of authority; bearing in mind, however, that this variable has a vertical (or class) as well as horizontal or territorial dimension.

Having sharpened our concepts we can know better what we are talking about but we cannot avoid the perplexities stemming from the state of flux and transition. In Europe, America and most of Asia it is fairly clear what is a nation and what is not, but in the Arab world, the Indian peninsula and Africa, the attributes of nationhood singled out above pertain to different aggregates with overlapping boundaries. Thus the Yorubas have a language and culture of their own, but they are living in two states: Nigeria and Dahomey; and it is questionable whether there is among them any strong desire for unity or independence. If we look at Nigeria as a whole, it would be untrue to say that there is no desire whatsoever to preserve the unity, but it is highly debatable how widespread and strong it is.* Indeed it is highly doubtful whether there would be any popular resistance to a complete re-drawing of the political map of Africa. There is no reason to imagine that a passionate yearning for re-unification would spring up in the Congo or even Ghana were they to be divided. No equivalent of irredentist nationalism which sprang up in Poland after the partitions could be expected to arise among the population were Nigeria to disappear from the map, its Northern Region joined to the Niger Republic and the Western Region to Dahomey.

Few people who have no first hand acquaintance with Africa realise how great are the contrasts between the ethnies comprised within the present state frontiers. The diversity of African languages is greater than anything that can be found in Europe even if we include Basque, Hungarian and Finnish—which at least are all syntactic, whereas in Nigeria syntactic Hausa as well as tonal

---

* This was written before the massacres of the Ibos in the North had destroyed the embryonic sentiment of unity. Just as the revision of the present text has been completed, Biafra has declared independence and a civil war has broken out.

Yoruba and Ibo are spoken, Indeed the difference between Hausa and Ibo is greater than between English and Russian or Hindi, as the latter three belong to the Indo-European family, whereas geographic propinquity of the speakers is the only thing which connects Hausa with Ibo or Yoruba.

The customs and the basic values of the Moslem Hausas are totally unlike those of the christianised or pagan inhabitants of the Niger delta such as the Ijaws. To mention one of the most profound contrasts: the former are patriarchal and keep their women in submission and seclusion, while the latter are more or less matrilineal with husbands and fathers as unimportant and transient figures. Indeed the contrasts between these two cultures seem more fundamental than between the American and the Russian. The old Hapsburg empire was homogeneous in comparison with the ethnic variety not only of the largest African states like Nigeria, the Congo and the Sudan, but even of the much smaller Sierra Leone or Cameroun. Apart from perceptible differences in bodily features, the Arabized Moslems are divided from the Christian and pagan inhabitants of southern Sudan by language, customs, religion and a deep hatred rooted in the long memory of wars and slave raids. Putting them together into one state was less justified than would be to make one state out of Germany and Poland.

It is significant that the African languages have no names of indigenous derivation to designate the existing states with the exception of Ethiopia and Somalia, so that the names had to be invented either by the colonial rulers or since the independence. This applies to Ghana too: there had existed a kingdom of that name but it lay to the north of the present republic, so there is no continuity of any kind. There is nothing wrong in inventing new names for new polities, but bearing in mind how recent these baptisms are helps us to appreciate how weak is the tradition on which these structures rest.

When Tshombe was trying to set up a separate state in Katanga an outcry was raised against his treason and the iniquity of tearing off from the Congo its richest province. But in reality the Congo is merely the area which the Belgian king, Leopold I, succeeded in seizing, and it represents neither an ethnic nor economic nor any other unity. Apart from the administrative frontier there is nothing which the ethnies composing its population have in common and which distinguishes them from the ethnies living beyond the borders. If the inhabitants of Katanga have no right to keep the wealth obtained from the subsoil of the area which they inhabit, why should the Iraquis not have the duty of sharing their income from oil with the Egyptians; or why should the Swedes have the right to exploit for their own benefit the iron ore found on their territory rather than share the proceeds with the Finns? Or why should the British have the right to prevent the Portuguese from coming here and enjoying the benefits of the Welfare State? Having been ruled by one conqueror creates no obligation to preserve the unity once the masters have gone; or if it does, then we should condemn all those who have contributed to the break-up of French Equatorial Africa or British India or the Hapsburg Monarchy or, for that matter, of the British or the Roman empires. It is true that Tshombe was a partner (or, as some would put it, a stooge) of Union Minière but he was no more docile towards it than President Tubman of Liberia is towards Firestone Rubber Corporation; and in any case most rulers of Africa are under the influence of either foreign big business (and French or American secret services) or of the communists, or both—sometimes trying to play off one against the other, though seldom with much success. Partly in virtue of being a son of a Lunda chief, also related through marriage to another powerful chiefly family, Tshombe had the backing of the largest ethnies in Katanga, and had there been a plebiscite the Leopoldville government would have found very little support. Katanga would have become a separate state which could perhaps have emulated Ivory Coast as one of the few relatively well ordered and prosperous countries in Africa. The real reason for Tshombe's unpopularity abroad was that he was tied to a weak partner—the Belgians—whereas Lumumba was backed by the Russians, and Kasavubu and Mobutu by the Americans; and there can be little doubt about who had ampler means of organising a world-wide wave of journalistic indignation.

With the exception of Somalia, none of the states in tropical Africa derives its existence from the patriotism or national consciousness of its citizens; and their integrity remains precarious. The bigger formations of former French Africa have split up soon after receiving independence, others (like Nigeria and the Congo) hover on the brink of disintegration, in others still the unity is maintained by the stronger part oppressing the weaker, as in the Sudan and Ethiopia.

The strongest force countcracting the fissiparous tendencies is the interest of the principal beneficiaries of the existing structures in preserving them. As the benefits of the top politicians and officials depend on the size of the body politic which sustains them, they hesitate to break it up unless the struggle for power turns into a civil war, particularly as every bureaucratic machine once set up acquires a certain force of persistence through sheer habit and inertia. However, a vested interest of the beneficiaries can preserve the system only in so far as they can impose their will upon the rest of the population.

Without the suppression of separatist tendencies by force all the existing African states would disintegrate (with the possible exception of Somalia). The prophets of the one-party state like Nkrumah and Nyerere are quite right in saying that competition between parties does not correspond to the needs of the African states because it is true that, in the absence of any widespread loyalty to the state, any open struggle for power is likely to transform itself into separatism and irredenta; and consequently, only an authoritarian government can prevent disintegration; although even this is far from certain in many cases.

The mono-parties of Africa either constitute a mechanism of domination by one ethny or are based on some kind of compromise about sharing the benefits of office between the leading personalities of the most powerful ethnies, while the weaker ethnies are usually deprived of all access to power and wealth, and consequently find themselves in a situation considerably worse than under the colonial rule.

Although nothing is quite so simple, we can say that the conflicts between the parties, which broke out as soon as independence was achieved, were an emanation of the struggles between the ethnies, as by and large the political sympathies were determined by ethnic division sometimes reinforced by religious differences. In the Sudan, where the gulf between the Christian or pagan and the Moslem accentuates ethnic animosities, the party struggles have led to the ousting of the Christians from all positions of power. Apart from its connection with a conflict between the old-established middle class and the 'new men' the victory of Nkrumah over Busia involved also a victory of the Nzimas over the

Ashantis, while the defeat of the Action Group in Nigeria has meant that the Yorubas would get a smaller share of the spoils than they might have done otherwise. The correspondence between party and ethnic membership, however, is far from perfect because in any ethny there are 'quislings' who will join a party dominated by another ethny for the sake of personal advantage.

In the case of Nkrumah, for instance, until quite recently his ethnic affinities were consistently ignored in Ghana politics, which may be due to the fact that his ethny, the Nzimas, are a small and quite remote group as far as most Ghanaians are concerned. There is very little evidence that ethnic considerations ever influenced either the composition of the C.P.P. or the choice of Ministers to more than a marginal extent: Nkrumah's chief lieutenants for a long time were Kojo Botsio, a Fante, and Komla Gbedemah, an Ewe, while his chief hatchet-man during the period of consolidation of his power after independence was Krobo Edusei, an Ashanti, and his chief disciple and adulator later was Tawia Adamafio, a Ga. There were other Ga's also prominent around Nkrumah. Northerners were somewhat lacking, and from the first felt generally left out of the scene—hence the Northern People's Party, which ostensibly came into existence to redress the balance. However, the general under-representation of Northerners at the centre was as much a function of the rarity of educated Northerners, and Nkrumah did go out of his way to appoint a few among the most eligible. The C.P.P. was not in any way a tribal party, although its opponents, other than the Ghana Congress Party, were regional tribal or religious groups (in the case of the Moslem Association Party). Nkrumah's own ethnic identity has always been a matter of doubt, anyway, it being widely believed that his Nzima ancestry is largely fictitious and that his actual father was a Kru seaman from Liberia. (This is something he would be interested in concealing on other grounds than that Krus are not Ghanaian, by the way: they are known in Accra and elsewhere as night-soil removers). Towards the end of his regime, however, more and more Nzimas started appearing in important Party and government positions, especially in posts connected with his personal security.

For a few years Nigeria seemed to constitute an exception to what was said above about the one party rule being a condition of preserving the integrity of the post-colonial states. The peculiarity in Nigeria, however, was not democracy (which was purely nominal) but that it was a federation of one-party states under the hegemony of the Northern Region; and its unity was based on a truce rather than on patriotism.

In some of the African states a full-blooded repression of separatist resistance movements is going on. Northern Kenya, for instance, no longer has any effective administration, and is the scene of fighting between the Somali tribes and the Kenyan troops. In the one-third of Ethiopia populated by the Somalis intermittent warfare has been the way of life for centuries and still remains so. The biggest bloodshed, however, is taking place in southern Sudan where the ground has been prepared by a long tradition of slave hunting which has been stopped only in this century by the British occupation. Actually a number of tribes and kings of southern Sudan had surrendered to the British in exchange for a promise of protection against the Moslem slave raiders from the north; and the abandonment of these people to the mercy of their age-long enemies (which has been called 'granting of Independence to Sudan') has amounted to an ignoble breach of trust.

In the Chad Republic the boot is on the other foot, and it is the better educated Christians who control the government and are keeping down the school-shunning Moslems whose resistance has now taken the form of guerilla warfare with the aid of weapons supplied through the Sudan. Substantial areas are under the control of the rebels.

It is strange that people who are outraged at the racial discrimination in Rhodesia and South Africa do not care about the mass slaughter in Sudan, although more people have been killed there during the last six months than in Rhodesia between the arrival of Cecil Rhodes and the year 1966. In Sudan the Moslems from the north are trying to exterminate all the educated infidels and convert forcibly to Islam the remaining Christians and pagans, while reducing their number at the same opportunity. Neither the British government, nor the friends of Africa in Europe and America, nor U.N.O. have voiced any objections to this policy. However, it is not my purpose here to examine the relative demerits of Rhodesian racial discrimination as compared with more brutal but less colour-idiosyncratic oppression perpetrated in most African states. The main point is that the unity of African states rests on coercion rather than consensus, though the relative

C

weight of these two elements varies from case to case, and from one province to another.

The Amhars, for instance, show a great deal of devotion to the unity of Ethiopia which they rule, but the other half of the Kingdom's population has to be prevented by force from breaking off. The Somali guerilla warfare has already been mentioned and it remains to be added that the Galla tribes too are kept down by terror. The nature of the rule is indicated by the fact that for distributing anything printed in Galla one may be sentenced to death. Local resistance movements have been put down in blood in other countries too—in the Tiv area of Nigeria, in the Bamileke area in the Cameroun, in Ghana, in the Congo—although with less bloodshed than in Sudan. In fact every African state has engaged in repression of this kind.

Relatively mild forms of coercion can maintain the integrity of most African states not because the factors of cohesion are strong but because the centrifugal forces are weak. The units which command real loyalty are the clans and the tribes a few thousands strong—not the large ethnic aggregates like the Ibos or the Fantis which are often mistakenly called tribes. The smaller entities, however, are too small to provide a basis for an independent state; and for this reason a separatism on this level cannot be alluring to educated men seeking or enjoying bureaucratic or commercial posts. A strong separatist movement has to be organised on an ethnic rather than tribal plane, and on this level it would in most cases have to be created. Thus there is no Nigerian nationalism but neither is there any Ibo or Hausa or Yoruba nationalism. The Ibo have a language and customs in common but they have never had a state of their own, and they did not realise that they had anything in common until their contacts with other ethnies became frequent and intensive in consequence of their forcible incorporation into a British colony. Hausaland, it is true, has been ruled for more than a century by one feudal hierarchy recognising the sovereignty of the sultan of Sokoto, but the population is divided into the Fulani aristocracy descending from the last wave of conquerors, the Hausas, and the non-Hausa Moslem, Christian and pagan subjects; and further subdivided into a multitude of tribes, clans and castes.* Political awareness and the sense of solidarity extending over the entire Northern Region

* See F. S. Nadel, *Black Byzantium:* O.U.P., London.

is confined to Fulani aristocracy. Before a Hausa nationalist movement could arise a great deal of ethnic amalgamation would have to take place, and the mental horizon of ordinary peasants would have to be radically widened. Probably the nearest approximation to nationhood—in the sense of belonging together, of ·a feeling of solidarity as against strangers and of loyalty to a collectivity larger than a tribe—can be found in a medium sized and fairly homogeneous ethny like the Ashantis, who had built a strong state before the British conquest and have fought many wars as a unit. Faced with this potentially very explosive force, the Nkrumah regime clung to semi-totalitarianism for the sake of self-preservation. The rise of the National Liberation Movement, however, while unquestionably it was based on Ashanti, and while it was led by one of the Asantehene's chief linguists, had a great deal to do with discontent about cocoa prices and the use of the Cocoa Marketing Board's funds for other purposes than those approved by cocoa farmers. The Somalis—who as pastoralists move around and maintain contacts over long distances—show relatively little cultural diversification and a great deal of awareness of their apartness as well as considerable solidarity, despite the extremely rudimentary economy, absence of big towns, general illiteracy and the persistence of tribal conflicts. They squabble and fight among themselves but readily combine against their neighbours, and are constantly attempting to free the Somalis under foreign rule. It is significant that the Somali Republic is the only state in Africa which came into existence through a fusion of territories hitherto ruled by different colonial powers; the usual process being a breaking up of a colonial domain into smaller states. To be exact, the Camerouns are the second example (as the British Camerouns have voluntarily joined the French) but the birth of the new republic has been accompanied by one of the biggest irredentist uprisings in Africa which could be overcome only with the aid of the French soldiers. So we cannot say that the integrity of this state rests upon a consensus. It is interesting that in Africa we find real nationalism only where it should not exist according to those who regard it as determined by the level of economic development, urbanisation and education.

The movements for independence in tropical Africa have been much weaker and less broadly based than most writers on African affairs make out, and it is even questionable whether they can be correctly described as nationalist. True, in Ghana and Nigeria the demands for independence had a considerable measure of mass support and gave rise to big party machines but the movements thus generated had nonetheless the nature of temporary alliances of the ethnies against their European rulers, and they lost all cohesion as soon as the latter departed. Up to a point, of course, this is true of all resistance, revolutionary or reformist movements —and it is all a matter of degree—but the relative weight of durable internal bonds in comparison with a mere tactical alliance does make a difference to the subsequent evolution.

Perhaps a feeling of nationhood would have arisen if the struggle for independence had been long and bitter—something like the 150 years of Polish national resistance or the much shorter but frightful Algerian war of independence or the present American-Vietnamese war.* As it happened, however, the colonial masters vanished either without any fight at all or after a few skirmishes, and in consequence the common effort was far too short and feeble to leave a durable imprint on the minds of the participants. Moreover, as the demands for independence were justified by an unassimilated democratic ideology incapable of stirring genuine emotions among people still rooted in clans, the real motivation behind the movement remained almost purely economic.

The Mau Mau revolt was the bloodiest and the most protracted uprising against the European rule which took place in tropical Africa but it was a Kikuyu affair from which the other ethnies kept away—it certainly was not a *Kenyan* national insurrection. It was not accidental that it was precisely the Kikuyus who rose up, as among all the Kenyan ethnies they had the largest proportion of educated or urbanised people as well as the largest number of landless labourers on the farms owned by the European settlers. The Kikuyus' land hunger was partly due to the salubrity of the Kenyan highlands which permitted especially fast multiplication.

Although nationalist movements often generate such fanatical devotion among large numbers of people that they are ready to

* The appalling American predicament in Vietnam illustrates the importance of sociological understanding and the danger of falling victim to one's own propaganda. The decision to intervene was obviously taken on the assumption that no nation can genuinely be converted to communism, and that nationalism and communism cannot converge. The situation in Latin America in this respect is examined in *Parasitism and Subversion*.

immolate themselves for the cause, the economic motivations play an important part; which is not surprising in view of the fact that secessions and conquests determine who will occupy a given territory or at least the top positions therein. It could hardly have been accidental, for instance, that when Poland was partitioned the striving for independence was much stronger in the Russian part where the Poles were excluded from the higher administrative jobs, than in the Austrian part where they were not, and where in addition they could play an active role on the general political scene. Among primitive tribes as well as among totalitarian states practising mass expulsions not only opulence but the very existence of entire populations may depend on who retains or seizes power over a given territory. In most historic states, however, conquests usually affected only the occupancy of higher administrative and military posts and ownership of large estates. Given the static nature of agrarian economies, the number of lucrative positions could be enlarged only through territorial expansion, and the demand for suitable positions for the multiplying scions of the higher classes inevitably generated imperialism. In the European conquest of Africa the desire for new administrative posts—in other words the expansionist tendencies of the civil and military bureaucracy—played an equally important role as the search for markets, sources of supply and fields for profitable investments—although the latter motives have received more attention in the literature.

It is worth noting that decolonisation has obversely confirmed the thesis formulated in 1900 by a disregarded forerunner of Keynes, J. A. Hobson, in his *Imperialism: an Economic Study* (later taken up in a debased form by Lenin) according to which a drive to conquer new fields for investment abroad stems from the declining profitability of investment at home due to over-saving and under-consumption, which in turn are caused by the very unequal distribution of income. It is significant that the imperialist nations became willing to give up colonies when a partial redistribution of income and a much more radical increase in the public spending have eliminated over-saving, under-consumption and unemployment, tilted the balance in the direction of inflationary trends, and, in combination with increasingly rapid technical progress, ensured a continuous expansion of opportunities for investment at home. Moreover, whereas until about 1930 the rate of profit on investments in the colonies was higher than on investments in the highly industrialised countries, afterwards (especially after the Second World War) it was the other way round. It is equally interesting from this point of view that the country which clings most tenaciously to its colonies—Portugal—has a stagnant economy.

To return to the economic motives behind the African independence movements: there was nothing surprising in the desire of educated Africans to displace the Europeans from the best posts which they had monopolised; and it was very easy for the African politicians to convince the urban proletariat and even the peasants that their poverty was due to the rapacity of the foreign masters who were carrying away all the wealth. The peculiarity of these movements—I must repeat—was not the presence of economic motivations but only the virtual non-existence of a truly ideological element. It could hardly be otherwise in view of the artificial and heterogeneous character of the entities which were the objects of the recently imported and unassimilated nationalist oratory.

Evidence from other parts of the world as well as from Africa suggests a generalisation that a collectivity can inspire genuine loyalty among its members only if it is sufficiently homogeneous and differentiated from other aggregates to generate a clear 'we-image'. A national consciousness can acquire neither clarity nor emotional loading when the nation is defined in such a way that its frontiers not only do not coincide with any cultural, religious, linguistic or racial dividing lines but even cut right across the natural affinities. Nor can the we-image become vivid and capable of stirring emotions when its object consists of juxtaposed ethnic cysts, or cysts which (though ethnically related) are divided by religious taboos, as in the case of Indian castes. Even rigid class barriers stultify national consciousness, and European history shows a relationship of mutual reinforcement between nationalism and egalitarian tendencies, both of which were stimulated by the advent of mass warfare, as shown in detail in *Military Organisation and Society.**

So long as the European masters were there, the African independence movements remained founded on a kind of class solidarity; but as soon as the foreign rulers departed, the chasm between the newly privileged and the less fortunate appeared and

* Routledge & Kegan Paul, London, 1968.

superimposed itself upon the older ethnic divisions—without, however, overriding them. The intersections of the horizontal and vertical dividing lines in a way help to preserve the integrity of the new states in so far as they prevent a crystallisation of clear-cut ethnic or class conflicts; but, in the absence of firm overall bonds which could reduce their intensity, they produce a collective paralysis.

It is one of the safest generalisations of sociology that a common struggle against outsiders generates solidarity within a group, and induces its members to make sacrifices for the common cause. Thus, for instance, the earliest manifestations of French and English nationalisms can be traced to the Hundred Years' War. German nationalism was awakened by the Napoleonic invasions and cemented by the victory over the French in 1871: and there are many other examples to the point. The image of national identity, moreover, acquires firmer contours in consequence of successive conflicts with different enemies. The African independence movements, however, had only one enemy—the European masters who have retreated without putting up a proper fight except in Algeria. And as the big powers do not allow the new states to fight one another, they have no chance of forging a national consciousness and solidarity through war.

Viewed from this angle the brandishing of the imperialist bogey by Nkrumah and others, as well as the outcry about Rhodesia, appears understandable and may have been designed to stimulate the growth of national feeling. This method, however, cannot be fully successful because the enemy is too distant, while the internal conflicts involve direct personal contact with the enemy. Prompted by unrealistic vanity, moreover, Nkrumah has spoiled his own work by harping about Pan Africanism—a chimera with which he was distracting the Ghanaians from attending to their own affairs.

There are no unmixed blessings in this imperfect world, and the peace forced upon the new states by the hegemonic powers is preventing them from acquiring a cohesion resting upon a foundation of collective sentiment, and from diverting aggressive pulsions towards outside, which would attenuate the internal conflicts between ethnies, tribes, clans and classes. Moreover, as the tribal ethics are crumbling, the factors which impede the emergence of a sense of duty towards the nation and the state, contribute towards a creation and perpetuation of a normless and pulverized society without a generally accepted code of behaviour, where everybody tries to snatch from everybody as much as he can without any restraints from deep rooted collective ideals: indeed, a state of affairs not very remote from 'war of all against all' adumbrated by Thomas Hobbes.

The readers interested in sociological theory might like to be referred again to the mechanism of conversion described earlier: a fight or even a sheer feeling of hostility towards outsiders drains off aggressive impulses from the internal arena and contributes towards its pacification. Given the quantum of aggressive impulses, a diminution of the flow through one outlet produces an increase in the flow through the other and the other way round. The quantum of aggressive impulses, however, is not constant and fluctuates in accordance with the amount of frustration, which becomes particularly explosive when people suffer from poverty and discontent-producing social dislocation; provided the poverty is not so severe as to debilitate them to the point of making them incapable of active protest, as has happened to the most downtrodden classes in India and Egypt. As poverty depends on the relationship between the population and the resources, the psychological mechanism outlined above is enmeshed with the demographic mechanism of alternation between internal and external fighting as regulators of population pressure. The purpose of mentioning these principles once again here is that they enable us to forecast a further aggravation of internal strife in African states.

Instead of drawing the population together, the employment of French or English as an official language cuts off the elite from the commonalty just as the use of French in eighteenth-century central and eastern Europe did. Having English or French as the official language prevents a crystallisation of a national consciousness because the graduates have no vested interest in anything that could be called national culture. It is probably because in fact they do not know where they belong that the African writers insist so much on their *Negritude*. Furthermore, not understanding the official language, the ordinary people can neither identify themselves with the state nor acquire even the most rudimentary information about public affairs. Another important consequence of the linguistic situation is that when one is compelled to use a language which one does not command perfectly one cannot say anything involved or subtle; and (what might have even more serious political consequences) one incurs the risk of cutting a comic figure in the eyes of those whose mother tongue it is. This often aggravates the inferiority complex, the feeling of insecurity and the need for individual or collective self-glorification which often prompt political or economic follies.

The picture presented on the preceding pages will appear incredible to those who have built their picture of Africa from what they have heard from African intellectuals and students, whose accounts are coloured by understandable desire to give a good impression of their countries. Being a nation or belonging to a nation has become a hallmark of respectability, the right to which has come to be regarded as reserved for the artificial creations of the colonial powers, and denied to ethnies such as the Ashantis or the Yorubas disdainfully labelled as tribes. For the sake of respectability, therefore, the Africans must insist that their political formations belong to the species of nation-states. As in so many other ways, a façade adopted for the sake of imitating wealthier and more powerful countries clashes with the contrasting reality behind.

Notwithstanding what I have just been saying about the weakness or even non-existence of nationalism in tropical Africa, it would be a mistake to conclude that, say, Ghana or Senegal are purely legal entities, and that their inhabitants have no feeling at all of belonging together. The reality is more complicated: it is true that the populations of the new African states do not constitute nations in the European sense, but on the other hand the political and administrative unity tends to mark the way of life with a specific imprint, and therefore to create a partial foundation for national consciousness. Labels have a certain suggestive power even if they are initially affixed in an accidental manner; and so some sentiment of belonging together has been created within the populations of the new African states, even though in most cases it is extremely weak even among the politically articulate citizens. As mentioned earlier, there are perceptible differences in this respect between the countries: for instance, the Ghanaians are nearer to being a nation than the Nigerians, and the Tanzanians (or rather Tanganykans) nearer than the Congolese. Apart from the influence of the factors such as ethnic homogeneity and the duration and scale of joint efforts, these differences depend on the numerousness of the educated elite who have a material stake in the preservation of the unitary political apparatus. It is not certain, however, that further development will lead to the emergence of nations as defined by the present frontiers; for it may happen that the spread of education in combination with growing dissatisfaction may lead to an emergence and crystallisation of nationalisms along dividing lines more congruent with the ethnic boundaries, and to an eventual re-drawing of the political map. This may, but need not, happen because political integration can exert enormous cultural influence and eventually induce ethnic amalgamation and homogeneity. In Europe the delimitations of national consciousness have largely but not wholly been traced by political frontiers determined by outcomes of battles, dynastic liaisons and other evanescent phenomena. So it is not impossible that notwithstanding their arbitrary origins, the present frontiers will circumscribe the future nations. Much will probably depend on whether a population comprised within the frontiers has a distinctive indigenous lingua franca (like Swahili in Tanzania) which could become their national language. Where (as in the Congo or Nigeria for instance) this is not the case, the chances of unitary nationalisms emerging are much less. The second decisive factor will be religious homogeneity: the gulf between the Christians and the Moslems is so profound, and manifests itself in so many crucial aspects of life, that it seems most unlikely that it could be encompassed within a single national consciousness, particularly when it coincides with the linguistic barriers and the economic differences between the life in the desert or the savannah and that in the tropical rain forest. There is therefore no reason to expect that there will ever be such a thing as a Nigerian or Sudanese nationalism as defined by the present frontiers.

The European nationalisms crystallised slowly over the centuries, and therefore it is not surprising that the new African states lack a foundation in national consciousness. The crucial difference between Europe (apart from the Balkans) and tropical Africa lies in the fact that in the former part of the world national sentiments have emerged before economic development became rapid, and before the governments have built intricate administrative machinery and assumed the task of regulating a complex economy. In Africa in contrast, attempts are being made to organise big bureaucratic machines capable of guiding or even initiating rapid industrialisation, but which receive no support from genuinely-felt collective ideals of service to the state. It is this psychological vacuum rather than the lack of skills that is primarily responsible for the disorder and graft which afflict the African states. The situation is further aggravated by the population growing faster than wealth, which naturally inflames the internal conflicts. And as internal strife impedes the emergence of the patriotism required for administrative efficiency, political order and therefore economic progress, the vicious circle is complete.

In Europe we have witnessed the evils of inflamed nationalism, whereas in Africa we see the deleterious consequences of its deficiency. The sentiments of national solidarity, the habits of co-operation in a large mass and the concern for efficiency have undoubtedly been stimulated, if not created, by the wars which the European nations have waged during several centuries. And it may not be due to solely material advantages that the nations renowned for efficient military organisation, like the Germans and the Japanese, have also been successful in catching up in the industrial race. It is difficult for an adherent of the humanitarian ethics to advise the African states to wage war on one another in order to forge national solidarity and to learn the habits of efficient co-operation on supra-tribal level. Nonetheless, we must recognise the sad truth that in this imperfect world every good thing has its disadvantages, and that in Africa as in Latin America the absence of the struggle for survival between the states eliminates one of the most decisive factors of cohesion and efficiency.

The war in Nigeria (or Biafra)* can nominally be classified as 'civil' but in reality amounts to a war of conquest—for never have the Ibos been ruled by either the Hausas or the Yorubas. True, they used to take orders from Lagos but it was from the British governor.

Assuming that the Federation was a good thing—which is by no means obvious in view of its heterogeneity—it is very difficult to apportion the blame for its break up. To be sure, the first military coup, which overthrew the post-independence government, was directed by Ibo officers; and although the initial leaders were jailed or at least pushed out, it was another Ibo—Brigadier

* The rest of this chapter has been added at the end of 1967.

Ironsi—who took over. It is also true that while killing Hausa and Yoruba politicians and officers, the conspirators have spared the lives of the Ibo luminaries of the civilian regime. However, before we put the blame on the Ibos for first drawing the sword, we should make sure that there is no substance in the claim that the revolt was in fact a pre-emptive strike aimed at forestalling a coup from above accompanied by a purge of southern officers, planned by the Hausa leader, Ahmadu Bello, and his puppet prime minister, Tafawa Balewa. Anyway, whatever might have been the real moves behind the stage, many people suspected Ahmadu Bello of harbouring such designs, particularly as he did not conceal his desire to establish a Fulani Hausa domination over the southern infidels.

During his brief reign Ironsi inevitably favoured his Ibo compatriots (though by no means excessively), and the planned replacement of the federal structure by a centralised administration would no doubt have led to an Ibo ascendancy, as they had the largest number of qualified men for the civil service and the officer corps.

When the northern soldiers rebelled, killed Ironsi and replaced him by Major General Gowan (a Christian from a small ethny in the North, who tried to act as an umpire and has never attained real power) the menace of Ibo domination has disappeared. However, to forestall such an eventuality for ever the northern politicians have instigated massacres which brought death to tens of thousands of Ibos living in the Northern cities, and led to a flight of hundreds of thousands to the Eastern Region. The refugees, who had been filling all kinds of skilled jobs in other regions, had to abandon all their property and have also left a vacuum which has greatly impoverished the Northern Region. As education-shy Moslems could provide no replacements many Yoruba job seekers have found an opportunity in the north, which partly explains their acquiescence in the Hausa domination of what remains of the Federation. Neither this advantage nor the bait of partaking of the spoils of office (including the Ministry of Finance for the Yoruba leader, Awolowo) can eliminate a widespread, though forcibly muted, desire for independence from the North, and the dislike of the Hausa soldiers among the Yorubas, which must be the reason why Lagos has the appearance of a city under foreign military occupation.

The former Eastern Region—now baptised as Biafra and claiming independence—has a larger and much better educated population than most African states, and by all standards of professed political ethics eminently qualifies for sovereignty. True, the Ibos account for only about two thirds of the inhabitants, and the minorities resent their domination and might prefer the old Federation. The ethnic differences, however, are not so great as to prevent an eventual amalgamation and fusion into a nation—which is impossible for Nigeria as a whole.

Biafra would no doubt have been allowed to secede if the oil wells did not lie within its boundaries. But coveting the revenue, the Moslem generals, with the blessing of the Lagos government, have launched their troops upon a cruel war of conquest which has already claimed more victims than the British Imperialism had throughout the entire period of its activity in Africa.

Fearing extermination, and helped by their superior education, and the newly risen true nationalism, the Ibos are resisting valiantly against the invading troops supplied with weapons by the British as well as the Russians. Their own arms come through the Portuguese colony of Saõ Tomé. If, as is quite possible, the Ibos succeed in repulsing the invaders the rest of Nigeria may well fall apart, exhausted financially and no longer united by the prospect of booty in the shape of revenue from oil. Administration and the economy have already seriously deteriorated, while corruption appears even more rampant than in the opulent days of the arch kleptocrat Okotie-Iboh.

The refusal of other African governments to recognise Biafra is contrary to their professed respect for 'nationalism', and stems from reluctance to create a dangerous precedent which might lead to unpredictable changes, which attitude resembles the Holy Alliance of the European monarchs in the early nineteenth century against irredentas and popular uprisings.

It throws curious light on the true motives of the most vociferous friends of Africa that they do not worry about massacres (even verging on genocide) so long as these are perpetrated by the Africans—as if the colour of the assailant made any difference to how much it hurts. It did not help the Poles that they were indistinguishable from the Germans by physical traits, and that many of the S.S. men had names of Polish origin.

Chapter 5 MORAL DISORIENTATION

Most teachers and parents find that children learn each other's vices quicker than virtues; and the same can be said about most cases of contact between civilisations. Anyway, we can see an unmistakable exemplification of this tendency in Africa of today. The Africans have, of course, learned many useful skills and have abandoned some of the practices which were unquestionably evil by humanitarian standards, but as far as really effective general standards of value are concerned, they have imbibed through their contacts with the Europeans only the burning desire for money and the things which it can buy. The higher ideals which have inspired those who made Western civilisation what it is (or should we say was?) appear even to the African intellectuals as words which are useful to invoke but which are devoid of any motivating force. To see things in the right proportions we must remember that the same is true of the immense majority of Europeans too: everywhere in the world the idealists are few and their usual fate is to be squashed by tyrants and their hirelings to the applause of the ignorant populace. Nonetheless without a sprinkling of idealists, and without the circumstances which give them some freedom and influence, no decent social order can survive let alone emerge. Now one of the most depressing (to a liberal humanitarian) features of the new African social order is the complete absence of idealism of even the most watered down quality: the worth of everything and everybody is measured by money . . . to an even greater extent than in post-war Germany. True, everywhere in the world an observer who can bear the sight of unpalatable reality will find that much of human behaviour (and not only in politics but even in 'cultural creativity') can be explained along the lines of 'who gets what, when and how' but there are usually also forces which cannot be accounted for in this way, such as intense nationalism or doctrinaire fanaticism or even a dose of altruism. It must be remembered, however, that a devotion to an evil ideal can be much worse than cynicism and indifference; and that much suffering could have been avoided if, for instance, the German youth had been less ready to sacrifice themselves for the Nazi principles and their beloved Fuehrer. Similarly, the Russian revolutionaries probably constituted the largest body of self-sacrificing individuals that the world has ever known, but the fruit of their victory was a regime equally unique in its monstrosity. To repeat however, some measure of adherence to good ideals constitutes an indispensable condition of a decent social order. In the new African states the political and cultural creeds receive absolutely nothing but lip service. This can be explained sociologically.

The first thing to remember is that ideals and creeds are collective products. Their devotees may be few but they must communicate and inspire one another. Nobody can develop a burning love of science if he has never heard that it might be a laudable pursuit. Patriotism cannot flourish without a well-established identity and delineation of its object, and without being shared by a large number of individuals. Dutifulness in public service can become or remain common only if the civil servants are esteemed within their social circles in accordance with how nearly they live up to this ideal. The norms and ideals are products of social evolution and require as their bearers crystallised groups which can exert the pressure of collective opinion upon their members. Such a crystallisation of group structures and of normative codes requires time. The minimum seems to be one generation because, although people may change their views while accumulating experience, their basic values are as a rule formed by the time of adolescence. For this reason many defects of the new African states can be understood if we bear in mind that the habits and values necessary for minimally efficient working of a large organisation were completely beyond the mental horizon of the great majority of present members of the African elites during their formative years. Moreover, being motley crowds suddenly and haphazardly assembled, the African elites could develop neither the coherent codes of behaviour nor the social mechanisms for effective indoctrination of the new entrants. Furthermore, their exposure to clashing scales of values has turned them into practical cynics and theoretical ideologues. In the ancestral village they were taught the tribal code of behaviour which was later derided by their teachers (most commonly missionaries) who preached something quite different. When they went to a university (or what was even more shattering, to London or Paris) they met leftists who told them that the missionaries were imperialist lackeys who told them a lot of lies. So their disorientation was complete and they have merely learned to invoke phrases and principles which strike no chord in their hearts.

The exposure to the imported mass media has radically accelerated the spread of moral disorientation but the phenomenon itself is well known in other cases of culture contact, and in Africa it had been noted many decades ago by Mary Kingsley who has observed that the worst villains were people whom the missionaries have failed to convert but who have lost their old beliefs in the process.

Generally speaking, perhaps more important than grand idealism is the more prosaic everyday identification with the institution one is working for, which may lead men on the verge of retiring to have a concern for its future. As every realistic observer of social life knows, this kind of concern is scarce enough in any country but among the members of the African elites it cannot be found at all; the explanation being that their attachment to the clan overrules all other loyalties, and that it goes against the grain of their entire upbringing to identify themselves with a collectivity not cemented by kinship. This is slightly less true about the Moslem populations where religious confraternities have played an important historical role, although even there an adhesion to a new sect or confraternity was commonly a matter of a collective decision by the clan or the tribe, so that the bonds of kinship and religion tend to overlap.

The imperviousness to the sentiments of solidarity transcending the bonds of kinship accounts for (among other things) the extra-ordinary spectacle of two or three hundred white mercenaries being able to chase around the Congolese 'revolutionary' forces more than a hundred times as numerous, as well as for the complete absence of any resistance to Smith's government in Rhodesia. When the issue at stake and the action falls within their traditional ways of thought and feeling—when it is a case of a tribal war about land, cattle or water sources—the Africans are naturally capable of great bravery, but (as all the writers of military manuals never tire of saying) a good *esprit de corps* constitutes an indispensable condition of military prowess, and this is what the armies of the new African states are incapable of developing.

This factor is crucial especially within the higher echelons which have to show initiative and collaborate in making decisions, whereas simple drill and personalised loyalty to their officers can carry common soldiers quite far—which was the reason why the colonial armies officered by the Europeans could put up a very good performance on the battlefield. To appreciate better the situation we must remember how proverbially difficult it is to maintain the unity of action of an army consisting of allied troops...let us think of N.A.T.O. and de Gaulle or Foch and Haig. Now imagine this kind of thing going on at every level of command and you will understand why the grand alliance of the African states tries to browbeat the British government into sending troops to Rhodesia but does not dare to move against the lilliputian army of Ian Smith.

I have mentioned the weakness of the African armies not because I have a special admiration for the military *esprit de corps* but to illustrate the principal source of weakness of all modern institutions in tropical Africa, which is the incompatibility between their functional requirements and the traditional patterns of social solidarity. On the whole the Africans have not yet evolved any moral bonds beyond the confines of the clan and the tribe, and for this reason usually act in urban settings as 'perfect economic men' whose attitudes are purely mercenary, because most of the people with whom they come into contact in shops, offices and streets are not their kinsmen but strangers in the primeval sense of this word.

Strange though it may seem, the mercenary approach to human relations has many roots in the traditional way of life—at least in West Africa. In many areas, for instance, courtship expresses itself in gifts of money. Anniversaries, weddings, celebrations of return or success and other festive occasions usually involve giving money to the feted persons on the part of the visitors. When visiting somebody one is also expected to make him a present of a sum of money which will be larger if the host has a higher status. A girl will regard gifts of money as a proof of the serious intentions on the part of her suitor. The West Africans do not feel that passing the cash on such occasions is in any way improper;

and we can describe this attitude in accordance with our preferences either as lack of refinement or freedom from hypocrisy. The custom of punishing children by withholding food probably also stimulates cupidity. The rewards, too, assume this form whose efficacy is assured by the usual scarcity of food. In any case, the most common pattern of allocating food stands in direct contradiction to anything which might be called chivalry: the strongest (that is to say, men) eat first, take the best bits, and leave what remains to women and children. Among children the bigger take the best bits and the small ones get whatever remains and in consequence suffer from hunger throughout their early years. This custom no doubt helps to keep the population down and ensures the elimination of the unfit, as only very tough individuals can survive such a trial, but it must leave a deep imprint on the attitude to material goods.

The sight of the European residents living at a standard which in relation to prevailing poverty was and remains fabulous, must have deeply influenced the scale of values because it was this aspect of civilisation which was most easily noticed, particularly as the local exponents of this civilisation did not exactly exemplify its higher ideals. The majority of the European residents in Africa went there for material gain and, especially at the beginning when life in Africa was dangerous and uncomfortable, they comprised a large proportion of ruthless money grabbers not even averse to robbery and murder. With the spread of regular colonial administration in Africa the scope for semi-criminal adventures diminished and the British and French colonial civil services were able to attract some higher-minded recruits many of whom developed a considerable sense of duty and genuine attachment to the people they were governing—surpassing by far in this respect their indigenous successors. Nevertheless most of the Europeans who went to Africa did so only because they could live there much better than at home. This was particularly the case with the commercial employees, who seldom developed any sentimental attachment to the country, but up to a point applied even to the missionaries.

The decolonisation has brought about a very marked deterioration in the moral quality of the European residents because a category within the ranks of which some dedication could be found—the civil servants—went home while the number of the commercial employees has increased and continues to rise as new industries are set up. The arrival of the personnel of the international agencies has brought no compensation as it contains a very large proportion of work-shirking intriguers and political secret agents. The only category of expatriates which contains a sizeable proportion of really dedicated people are the missionaries although among them too one finds a large number of mercenary-minded people. Some expatriate University and secondary school teachers could also be described as dedicated, often by contrast with their African colleagues.

Apart from the old customs, orthodox Christianity, whether of Catholic or the Protestant variety, remains the only moral code which finds genuine adherents. There are millions of devout Christians who find the religious tepidity of the European residents deeply upsetting and are shocked by the sight of the Europeans drinking and lounging scantily dressed around the swimming pools when they should be going to church. Nonetheless, it cannot be said that the Christian faith has made much impact on the tenor of human relations in Africa. As in other parts of the world, for the great majority the religion is a matter of the ritual and a few taboos—mostly without any ethical significance. The missionaries have succeeded in making people ashamed of nakedness (which, incidentally, was one of the reasons why in the early days they got financial support from the cotton manufacturers) but not of polygamy. And as for honesty and veracity towards non-kinsmen or dedication to work, the missionaries might not have been there at all.

Concerning the African's lack of inhibition about telling lies—which forms one of the favourite topics for denigration among the expatriates—it is important to realise that the tribal customs not only do not enjoin telling the truth to strangers, but even recommend dissimulation. In some tribes the children are deliberately trained to give untrue or evasive answers to any questions which a stranger might ask lest he be seeking information with hostile intent. We must not forget, moreover, how widespread is hypocrisy and deception in all countries of the world; and that (as Herbert Spencer has pointed out in his *Principles of Sociology*) mendacity and evasiveness characterise all human groups which live under fear.

The popular press, the trashy books, the shoddy films, records, and above all, television, are doing enough harm in the industrial societies but in the poorer countries they smash the very foundations of the social order by undermining the traditional values without putting into their place anything except anti-social hedonism and the worship of money. One can believe that life is worth living only for what money can buy, and still remain a fairly law-abiding and decent citizen if one has enough for comfort and entertainment; but what can a covetous hedonist feel and do who sees that he is condemned to poverty for the rest of his life? If he is daring and strong or clever enough he will try robbery or crookery. It is significant that the biggest centre of gangsterism in Africa is Liberia and in Asia the Philippines (while in Latin America it was Cuba)—the three countries which have had most contact with American mass media in their respective continents.

The repugnance which so many Asiatics feel for the American Way of Life appears perfectly understandable if we put ourselves into their shoes and realise how unbearable must be a hedonistic scale of value when one is condemned for life to poverty and backbreaking work. Apart from its present identification with the resistance against the invaders of a totally alien race, communism appeals to the Vietnamese largely because of its puritan streak— and it cannot be denied that puritan dedication to work must become widely accepted in any country which wants to lift itself out of misery.

In Africa the strength of clan solidarity and of the tribal and ethnic divisions makes a genuine conversion of the masses to communism impossible in the near future, and even the unsuccessful members of the educated class are not yet sufficiently de-tribalised to become fanatic doctrinaires; although owing to the prevalence of disorder and venality, a few agents can achieve a great deal by intrigue, cajolery and intimidation. In contrast to Asia the hedonist indoctrination through imported mass media has up till now stimulated only money-grabbing and the ruthless exploitation of the poor, but no powerful ideological currents.

In a number of African cities we can see television masts
towering above expanses of insalubrious shacks where there may
be no running water (or at best one tap for hundreds of inhabitants),
where people defecate and dump refuse into open ditches which
may not drain at all and which permanently exude all-pervading
nauseating smells. The decision to spend money on television
rather than on sanitation well illustrates the scale of priorities adopted by the rulers of Africa. True, they are not the only rulers to
be addicted to vanity. The Americans too prefer to spend money
on firing rockets into space rather than on slum clearance; while
the leaders of the British Labour Party would rather let the
education and the health service deteriorate than forgo the
opportunity of unveiling a supersonic airliner which will deprive
millions of innocent citizens of the remainders of tranquillity
for the sake of conveying a few thousand top people a couple of
hours earlier to New York, so that they may have a little more
time for fatuous speeches and grinning in front of television
cameras. It has also been said with some justification that the
poorer the country the more resplendent are the churches.
However, in addition to being a common proclivity among the
rulers of all nations, the squandering of scarce resources on
frivolities has special roots in the feeling of inferiority common
among the educated Africans.
Nobody worries about his shortcomings in terms of a scale
of values which he does not accept. He may feel angered or
aggrieved by the treatment he receives from the upholders of the
foreign values but not by the mere fact of being unable to excel
in what only they regard as laudable. A hunter and warrior will
smart under the restraints which are compelling him to abandon
his old way of life and become a labourer, but he will not feel a
genuine shame at not possessing the latter's skills or even being
unable to read and write. He will, however, fall prey to feelings

of inferiority as soon as he accepts the standards which he cannot
or at least does not yet attain. This applies not only to occupational
skills but also to such relatively trivial matters as manners and
the niceties of speech.

No European will be ashamed of not being able to eat rice
with sticks unless he has lived in China for so long that he has
become partly sinicised and has begun to aspire to be like the
Chinese. Another example to the point is the proficiency in
language: a tourist will not normally be ashamed of using a
distorted form of the local language, whereas a naturalised
resident of long standing will normally be embarrassed if he
makes a gross mistake. Putting it into more general terms we can
say that a transition from one culture to another cannot fail to
engender some inferiority feeling among those making it, especially
if the gap between the two cultures is large. This applies to trans-
culturation as well as to social mobility. When somebody brought
up in an African peasant household goes to study in London or
Paris, and then becomes a delegate to the U.N.O., the unsettling
effects incipient in all forms of social mobility are multiplied by the
disparity of cultures.

Though not always intentionally, the education dispensed by
the missionaries usually helped to instil into their pupils the
feeling of inferiority by teaching them to despise the custom and
beliefs with which they grew up, and to be ashamed of their fathers.
Even the second or third generation Christians are not immune
to this insidious influence because, even though they need not
despise their mothers and fathers for being pagan, they are made
to feel ashamed of most of their countrymen. As the missionaries
abhor nakedness which still remains associated with humble
status and poverty, their teaching has contributed to instil the
sentiment of the moral value of wealth and disdain for poverty . . .
which is not exactly what Jesus preached. In the past the African
pupils were openly taught that they belong to an uncivilised and
naturally inferior race by the missionaries who were simply
imparting what they regarded as an obvious truth. Nowadays, such
instruction is less common, or at least better disguised, but many
examples can still be found; and the patterns of thought and feeling
formed under such circumstances will persist for some time.

In contrast the Moslems are free from the touchiness and other
tensions stemming from feelings of inferiority, and despise the

infidels whose gadgets and knowledge are contemptible in comparison with the Faith which opens the gate to eternal bliss. Though many of its tenets constitute serious obstacles to modernisation, Islam does rule out the difficulties stemming from a complex of inferiority.

The feeling of inferiority—or the anxiety about imputations of inferiority—fosters an obsessive concern for collective and individual status symbols. On the individual plane, this manifests itself in the preoccupation with cars and other mechanical gadgets, punctilious attention to dress and a great concern about decorum. Unlike the Rhodesian estate owners (usually misleadingly called farmers) few Africans of equivalent status would roll their sleeves up or take a necktie off—let alone stoop to soiling their hands. On the collective plane, this tendency leads the rulers of Africa to give priority to obtrusive symbols of modernity—such as show-hospitals, airports, big industrial projects, television stations and assembly halls—and to disregard more important but less conspicuous matters like the fostering of small workshops. The economic planners will advocate importation of ruinously expensive tractors but not of introducing wheelbarrows and scythes which would bring much more palpable benefits.

It is not only in Africa, of course, that 'economic planning' often amounts merely to 'talking big', and making plans is regarded as a laudable activity regardless of whether the plans have any chance of being carried out or not. In the new African states, however, the gap between planning and the possibility or realisation seems to be particularly large, and reminds one of autistic thinking in children, some forms of which the child psychologists attribute to an insecurity complex. The following example from my personal experience illustrates how unrealistic a supposedly serious discussion can become.

In 1963 I was attending in Nigeria a conference on housing in which a number of high ranking politicians and civil servants took part, and we came to the topic of a design appropriate for mass re-housing. Seeing that the debate proceeded on a rather unrealistic plane I made what seemed to me an obvious suggestion that we should try to find out what would be the cheapest type of house compatible with the elementary demands of hygiene. I was told that this would not do because 'the Nigerians deserved the best'. When I asked where the money would be found, I was given the answer that it would be raised on the capital market in Europe and America. When after a quick calculation I had pointed out that the interest on the capital needed to re-house the Nigerian slum dwellers would exceed the total value of exports from Nigeria, another discussant replied: The United Nations will provide the funds. My retort that the United Nations had a big deficit already and had no funds for this purpose was simply ignored, and the discussion continued on the plane of fairy tales.

On the whole, I have found that whereas the African politicians and intellectuals would talk very realistically about the power game, they were unwilling to face reality on economic questions. Apart from the status anxiety and the very inexperience of the new rulers, the use of a foreign and imperfectly understood language may be conducive to play with words without much regard for what they mean. Perhaps even more important is the fact that so many members of the elites which took over from the colonial rulers ascended the ladder of success by passing examinations in subjects completely unrelated to what they were doing or could see, such as the British constitution or history lessons designed to make them into French patriots. The incapacity of so many African leaders to think realistically about general problems (as distinct from the day-to-day tactics) remains one of the major obstacles to an improvement in the condition of their countries. As on so many other points there seems to be a vicious circle here, because the tendency to fall into word magic when talking about economic problems may well be due to the hopelessness of the situation. The phenomenon of flight from reality into some kind of make-believe can often be observed in communities facing insurmountable difficulties; and it seems to square well with Malinowski's theory of magic; the main point of which is that even people living on the most rudimentary level of culture think rationally about processes which they can control, but fall into an autistic mode of thinking when dealing with completely unmanageable and unpredictable phenomena. Given their means, the Trobrianders (as described by Malinowski) are very logical about how to build a canoe, but adopt irrational attitudes towards the weather or disease.

In the discussions of the plight of the tropical countries, not enough weight is given to the handicaps ensuing from imitating the fashions of dress unsuitable to the climate. The jackets, collars and ties, long trousers and sleeves, closed-up shoes seldom cause discomfort in northern climes. In southern Europe their deleterious influence on the will and the ability to work is already perceptible but in Africa it is crippling. True, the modern European dress is relatively comfortable in comparison with the velvets worn in the eighteenth century by the slave-owners of Brazil or Cuba, whose irascibility and indolence do not appear surprising if we remember that they were suffering acute discomfort nearly all the time—covered with boils, heat rashes and sores, afflicted by indigestion and respiratory and heart troubles due to the lack of ventilation, excessive perspiration and unhealthy diet—so that every effort was extremely painful. Although modern dress is not quite so incapacitating in the tropics, it nevertheless constitutes a severe handicap. In the tropical lowlands one can move about reasonably fast only when scantily clad. This factor affects particularly the work of people in positions of authority who can avoid moving around if so inclined; for the drudges are forced to work hard (even if inefficiently) by the pressure of poverty. Since independence, shorts as well as open-necked and short-sleeved shirts have come to be regarded as relics of colonialism, while jackets, collars and ties and long trousers have become obligatory. In consequence an African manager hardly knows what is going on on the shop floor owing to his reluctance to leave his air-conditioned office.

Laudably, like the deposed Brazilian president Janio Quadros, the Nigerian leader at the time of writing, Major General Gowan, used to appear at the beginning of his rule in an open-neck shirt with short sleeves. The absolute minimum attire for managers and civil servants is trousers, short-sleeved shirt and tie, or a well-cut American-style jacket-shirt worn outside the trousers without a tie. In recent years a compromise suit, generally called the 'political suit' in Ghana because of its popularity among the former politicians, has come increasingly into vogue. In this, jacket and shirt are combined into a single light-weight garment, with open neck and no tie; as a smart 'prestige' form of attire it is made of expensive material and very well cut—the best being those made in Abidjan.

The needless imitation of European and American ways makes life in the tropics uncomfortable in many other ways too: thus for example, much money is spent on importation of tinned foodstuffs (the consumption of which has become a status symbol) although better things can be bought fresh and very much cheaper locally. Despite the hordes of unemployed ready to work for a pittance, uneconomic tractors or even washing machines are imported to be used as status symbols. Similarly with houses: although the colonial style houses can be quite comfortable even without air-conditioning, they have two faults; they are colonial and not European-European, and they smack of rusticity. The most common new models are much more urban European with the result that they are like ovens where nobody can work well or even be comfortable while doing nothing without air-conditioning. We must not forget, however, that aping the rich and powerful is a general human tendency in no way peculiar to Africa; for instance, after every war all the armies adopt some features of the uniform of the victors as if the victory had been determined by a badge; and in England people now like to use the ugly word 'know-how' simply because it comes from rich America, although it must have been invented there by some illiterate immigrant whose vocabulary included neither 'skill' nor 'knowledge'.

Contrary to naive general preconception, bringing people from different countries need not do them any good, and can even have unfortunate results. The African students who come to Europe or America learn not only the skills in which they are trained but also the habits of consumption which are ruinous for their countries. An African doctor who wants to live like his British or French (let alone American) colleague must become a tremendous sucker of wealth absorbing at least as much as a hundred labourers. Similarly the personnel of the various agencies of international or bi-lateral aid do probably more harm than good because they stimulate in their indigenous colleagues the desire for a standard of living out of all proportion to the wealth of the country. The European (let alone American) salary scales amount to fantastic luxury in relation to the average income but no expatriates will come if they are offered less; and even if they are paid by their own governments, their mere presence constitutes a source of difficulties as their African colleagues will feel humilitated and rancorous if they cannot mix and entertain on the same level. The only foreign helpers who are prepared to live on a level appropriate for Africa are the Chinese which accounts for such popularity as they enjoy despite their intolerant dogmatism and having nothing to give. Even without racial and cultural differences it is difficult for the poor to be entirely at ease in the company of the rich, and the influx of opulent expatriates prevents the establishment of sensible scales of remuneration and fosters consumption mentality in countries where modest living and hard work are needed. This influx may be necessary for various reasons but it has very serious drawbacks.

Chapter 7 KLEPTOCRACY OR CORRUPTION AS A SYSTEM OF GOVERNMENT

As the word 'corruption' implies a condemnation of the practices to which it refers, it indicates an outsider's view of African affairs because very few Africans have any deep feelings about the states to which they belong. The ideals of impersonal service are often voiced in deference to the higher prestige of the European countries, but they have not been (to use a psycho-analytical term) introjected. What is regarded as dishonesty in countries well indoctrinated with political ideals, may appear as morally in order in a society where the bonds of kinship are strong and the concept of nationhood remains something very recent and artificial. For these reasons it seems better to use the word 'venality' rather than 'corruption', as it does not imply a fall from a previously attained higher standard.

However, as the word 'corruption' is most commonly used, I shall not attempt to avoid it completely, and shall use it to designate the practice of using the power of office for making private gain in breach of laws and regulations nominally in force. Where, for instance, a traditional judge is allowed by custom to receive a payment from a petitioner we cannot regard it as corruption. On the other hand, an official who bases his claim to be obeyed on the body of laws and regulations which forbid him to solicit payments, nevertheless does so, can be said to practise corruption, regardless of the fact that he may not feel he is doing anything wrong. The additional difficulty here is, of course, that compunction, shame or remorse is a matter of degree, often subject to alteration and ambivalence.

Although corruption is common in all parts of Africa north of the Zambesi, there are considerable local variations in its importance. Where there is less wealth to circulate, where trade is less intensive and detribalisation less advanced, where there are fewer officials and politicians, and a larger part of the population lives in remote, self-sufficient villages, it is natural that there will be fewer occasions for bribery and embezzlement, and that the amount involved will be smaller. It is not, therefore, surprising that corruption is more pervasive, and on a larger scale, on the West Coast than in the less developed countries of East and Central Africa like Tanzania or Uganda.

Everybody who has lived in any of the African states knows that venality is a common practice there. The interesting question is not so much how widespread it is, but rather why it is so common. Nevertheless, some description of the phenomenon must be given because the conspiracy of silence on the part of the great majority of European intellectuals, due to inverted racialism, prevents the dissemination of knowledge about this phenomenon. However, in view of the danger of libel suits, the subject of legally illicit gains from public office is not one which can be amply illustrated by well-documented cases. In *Corruption in Developing Countries** Ronald Wraith has given some facts obtained from the trials which took place in Nigeria shortly before independence, but these are merely tiny splinters of a vast iceberg. Anyway, no such trials have been held since independence although the gains from office have vastly multiplied.

It lies in the nature of graft that we cannot have statistics which indicate its extent but there can be no doubt that in all African states the wealth acquired through illegal use of public office looms large. Everywhere people fear the police and their exactions, of which the most common form is imposition of fines for fictitious offences, the fines naturally going into the pockets of the police-men. The police are regarded by the ordinary people as extortioners or even uniformed bandits. The clerks who deal with innumerable small formalities expect individual payment, and if they do not receive it they attend to the matter with deliberate delay or invent a pretext for shelving it for ever. Especially in Liberia, it is quite impossible to get through any official business without the services of special contact men who know how and to whom to pass a bribe, part of which they keep for themselves.

Licences of various kinds and exemptions from import duties on articles which can be sold at great profit are frequently given to the favourites of the government or in exchange for bribes. Fabulous sums were obtained for granting concessions to foreign companies, and fortunes were made from sales of lands belonging

* Ronald Wraith and Edgar Simpkins, Allen & Unwin, 1963.

to the state. A relatively minor form of corruption is the mis-appropriation of movable objects.

The study of venality well illustrates the inescapable limitations of sociological inquiry: here we have an extremely important phenomenon which decisively affects politics, administration, business, education, relations between classes or even sexes, and a host of other crucial aspects of social life; yet it cannot be studied with the aid of interviews, questionnaires or statistics, and even the documentary evidence provided by trials vanishes when the phenomenon becomes all-pervading.

The use of public office for private enrichment is the normal and accepted practice in African states and the exceptions are few and inconclusive: a top politician who is not known to have acquired a vast fortune is singled out for praise as some kind of ascetic. To keep a sense of proportion, however, we must remember that the situation has been similar in most of the states recorded in history, and that the custom of refraining from using the power of public office for private gain constitutes one of the most recent and fragile conquests of civilisation, and that in no country in the world are bribery and embezzlement unknown. In Britain (which scores high in respect of probity) outright bribery is rare but its subtler forms are noticeable: when, for instance, a high ranking civil or military officer obtains a directorate in a firm with which he has been dealing on behalf of the government, expertise may not be the only ground. The members of elected bodies appear never to accept cash; nonetheless, the devotion of some of them to various financial interests or even foreign governments does not seem entirely selfless: after all, apart from such things as free trips and other perks, being on good terms with wealthy and influential people opens all kinds of doors to oneself as well as to one's friends and relatives. Scandinavia, Britain and Switzerland are the countries least afflicted by venality, which is much more common in the rest of the highly industrialised countries, such as France, Italy and the United States. The prevalence of bribery in southern Europe and Latin America is well known, but what merits notice is how common it is in eastern Europe: in communist Poland, for instance, the act of passing a bribe has been nicknamed 'a socialist handshake'. It is true, however, that under a communist system nobody can become a millionaire by accumulating the proceeds of graft which, in consequence, is practised commonly but only on a relatively small scale: whereas in Latin America and 'free Asia' it is big business in which fabulous fortunes have been amassed.

Enough has been said to show that there is no justification to regard venality as something peculiarly African; and the immunity thereto as typically European. The mere fact that attitudes vary from one period to another shows that they cannot be genetically determined, and therefore have nothing to do with race. Cupidity arises easily in human souls, and in order to understand the variations in the incidence of graft, we must look into the moral restraints which a given society imposes upon uses to which power may be put. Obviously, I cannot embark here upon a systematic inquiry into this problem, but I must dispel the common preconception that it is all a matter of opulence and industrialisation. There is more graft in the U.S.A. than in poorer Britain; more in Britain of today than thirty years ago; and in Germany it appears to have been increasing step-by-step since before the First World War.

The foregoing considerations must be borne in mind if we are to see things in the right proportions, but they do not alter the fact that venality pervades through and through the fabrics of African states. After only a few years in office the top politicians have amassed fortunes worth a hundred times the sum of salaries received. Many of them have simply transferred big sums from the treasury to their private accounts, but the practice of getting cuts on government contracts constitutes the chief fount of illegal gains. In Nigeria the customary cut is 10 per cent and for this reason the expression 'ten-percenter' is often used to designate anybody active in politics. Nonetheless, the small fry also take part in this business, though naturally on a scale corresponding to the power they wield. People like municipal councillors and district officers or provincial commissioners can make substantial gains on local contracts and awards of licences for market stalls. Scarcely a waste paper basket is bought for an office without somebody getting a tip from the seller, who then gets it back from the public funds by charging a higher price than he could get from a private buyer.

Collection of taxes, excise and custom duties offer ample opportunities for graft. With the aid of bribes people can have liabilities drastically reduced or may even avoid taxation altogether, whereas those who refuse to play will receive most stringent assessments—which in cases where the amount of income cannot be exactly proven, could become exorbitant and crushing. Thus cupidity and the desire to evade the legal liability, and on the other hand the fear of victimisation, enmesh everybody who runs a business (regardless of the size) in a network of bribery. Powerful politicians, however, do not have to pay for preferential treatment: their debts to the state are simply overlooked until they show a lack of party discipline or are dislodged by their opponents.

The forms of bribery and embezzlement are profusely variegate and many of them must appear incredible to people who have always lived in better ordered countries. I have known hospitals in West Africa where the patients had to pay nurses to bring them a chamber pot; where the doctors (who were receiving a salary from the state and were supposed to treat the sick free of charge) would look only at those patients who had given them money, and saw those first who had paid most, regardless whose condition was most urgent. Those in charge of the dispensary stole the medicaments and then sold them either to the patients on the premises or to the traders. The doctors did the same, taking the medicaments for use in their private consulting rooms. Patients unable to pay got injections of coloured water. Many who did pay were cheated and got exactly the same.

The picture painted above is unpleasant, but the reader should not imagine that all the people guilty of such deeds are monsters. The less well placed of the staff would find it very difficult to mend their ways because very often their salaries do not come— sometimes being delayed for months, sometimes vanishing altogether. Many owe substantial sums borrowed to pay for their training or as bribes for getting the appointment. Their tasks, moreover, are so utterly overwhelming that it makes little difference what they do. Even if they worked without sleep or rest, they could attend only to a small fraction of the crowds which are waiting and dying in the yards, corridors or staircases. The quantity of the medicaments is so small in relation to the number of the sick, that even if they were dispensed in accordance with the regulations, only a tiny fraction of the patients would get what they need. Such circumstances, as well as the bad example of the old hands, extinguish all dedication among the newcomers and breed callousness. Furthermore, as in many other walks of life, (and not only in Africa) a person whose probity and sense of duty shows his colleagues in a bad light will be slandered and pushed out.

As in so many other fields we have here a sad example of the senseless implantation of an institution unadapted to its environment. A free medical service which is quantitatively utterly inadequate must become a mockery which embitters the patients and corrupts the practitioners. What is the point in employing doctors and nurses when no money is left to pay the cleaners, and in consequence the hospitals become dangerous disseminators of disease? It would be much better to end this bitter joke and abolish the so-called free hospitals; at least people would not be teased with what they are not going to get, and would feel less wronged.

The hospitals run by the missionaries usually constitute islands of relative efficiency and honesty; and, viewed against the true background, the criticisms levelled against Albert Schweitzer on the ground of his paternalism can only be regarded as preposterous. The missionary clinics, however, function mostly in outlying areas where the tasks are a bit more manageable than in overcrowded and insalubrious towns; and in any case they are mere drops in the ocean.

It must be remarked, incidentally, that it is absurd to use the word 'paternalism' in a pejorative sense because the world would be a much better place if the rulers felt as benevolent towards their subjects as an average father feels towards his children. What we normally get in politics is a pretence of paternalism; and the common relationship is analogous to that of a shepherd who keeps on fleecing his sheep and eventually goads them into a slaughterhouse. Schweitzer's attitude was that of true paternalism: he was convinced that he knew best, he expected to be obeyed by his staff and the patients, and did not want to be treated by them as an equal; but all the time he was performing all kinds of unpleasant tasks, giving unstintingly, and taking nothing in return—which is a bit harder than inviting a few educated and opulent Africans to tea and talking about equality while doing nothing for the suffering multitudes. Whatever the members of the African ruling classes may say, a sick peasant will always prefer Schweitzer's paternalism to the rapacity of his masters or their pink partners.

D

The schools suffer from venality too. Nobody can find out how many scholarships and certificates are obtained through bribery but people often talk about such practices and assume that this can be done—as far as driving licences are concerned it is generally accepted that one must give a bribe unless one is an important person. Teachers' salaries are sometimes embezzled by the headmasters or higher officials. Moreover in the same way as people in other public services, many teachers had to pay for getting appointed, and continue to pay ransom for being kept on the payroll. In some places the children have to pay fees although according to law they should not. I am personally acquainted with the case of a headmaster of a government secondary boarding school who has paid for a sizeable house for himself out of funds received from the treasury and the pupils for running the school. The pupils have on several occasions staged riots in protest against insufficient food but to no avail.

Officials in charge of public works use lorries and other equipment, materials and man-hours belonging to the state or the municipality to build houses for themselves or hire them to other people. Customs officers have, of course, plenty of scope for peculation: in exchange for bribes they pass goods without levying the duty or at least reducing it substantially, whereas people who give them nothing may have to face interminable delays with the added danger that their goods will be damaged or stolen. There are, however, limits to the customs officials' freedom of action imposed by the demand for income on the part of the treasury; and, as far as I can judge this elusive phenomenon, the situation is much better in this respect in the former British and French colonies than in many countries of Latin America.

The police are among the worst offenders against the law: they levy illegal tolls on vehicles, especially the so-called mammy-wagons (heavy lorries with benches and roofs) which usually carry many more passengers than they are allowed and transgress a variety of minor regulations. They are allowed to proceed regardless of the infractions of the law if they pay the policemen's private toll. There are innumerable cases of the police turning a blind eye to the activities of contrabandists, thieves and robbers in exchange for ransom. Sometimes they actively help the criminals. They guard effectively only the houses of important people or of those who pay them, while ordinary citizens have to rely on self-defence. Unless he has committed his deed before the eyes of numerous witnesses, or his victim has influential avengers, even a murderer may be left unmolested if he can afford an appropriate bribe. What is really astounding is that if he can pay a big sum, the police may even help him to erase the traces of his crime by framing up somebody quite innocent but helpless, and getting him hanged. This, however, can be done only in fairly big towns containing uprooted individuals, or among semi-detribalised rural populations. Where kin solidarity retains its full vigour (as in Somaliland) such an action would call forth a tribal uprising.

Verification of bicycle and car registration, trading licences and opening hours, enforcement of traffic regulations and hosts of other functions provide the policemen with the opportunities for squeezing out bribes. As they hardly bother to conceal these operations, and as everybody knows about them, it is clear that the highest officers must be conniving and participating in the gains. My most vivid experience of this kind of thing was in Liberia in 1964 when we were arrested in front of the presidential palace on a trumped-up charge of trying to obtain forbidden information about this building; and we were not released until my companion (a Pan-Africanist American Negro who has emigrated to Ghana) paid up. Liberia, however, is the most extreme case in West Africa, and such a thing could not happen in such a place in Ghana, Nigeria, Ivory Coast or Senegal.

There are limits to the disregard for qualifications in making appointments: to be engaged as a pilot one must be able to fly, and nobody without some special knowledge will be able to construct a building which will stand. Moreover, certain functions (such as those of a doctor or lawyer) have been effectively mono-polised by the holders of appropriate diplomas, which restrict the number of candidates. Nevertheless, within these broad limitations and with very few exceptions, the allocation of posts in public services (including the most humble) is mostly determined by criteria which have nothing to do with fitness for the job. Apart from a flair for manipulation and intrigue which everywhere in the world always helps the main criteria of selection are kinship and the ability to offer either a bribe or some other service in return—often on the principle of 'if you appoint my kinsman,

I shall appoint yours'. Almost needless to say, the new states of Africa are not the only places where criteria unrelated to the fitness for the job affect appointments: in England for instance, in addition to family influence, there are 'the old boy networks', the members of which identify one another by their old school ties, apart from cliques of newer type. The contrast with Africa is a matter of degree and the limits within which connections are allowed to outweigh qualifications. As a rough and a very general guess (and excluding such bodies as the diplomatic service, the guards and the court) I would say that in Britain qualifications counted for 80 per cent and connections for 20 per cent; and in Nigeria it would be the other way round. In Spain it might be 50/50. In Britain, moreover, reciprocity practically never takes the form of outright bribes. Another important difference is that in industrial countries nepotism and the old boy network significantly affect only the top jobs and a fairly small number of minor sine-cures, whereas in Africa obtaining employment as an office cleaner or a postman depends on personal ties or quasi-feudal tribute. Apart from the persistence of extended kinship in Africa, one reason for this difference is that there is more scope for nepotism and squeeze in apportioning jobs when candidates have no alternative opportunities.

Unless he receives a substantial bribe from a non-kinsman, an average African official will give all the appointments which he controls to his kinsmen, except in cases of more complicated arrangements based on bargaining between clans in consequence of which an official may appoint a kinsman of a man who has appointed or will appoint his kinsman in return. The relative importance of bribery as compared with kin-nepotism depends on the extent to which a given set has become detribalised, as detribalisation involves weakening of kin-solidarity and thereby gives more scope to unfettered cupidity.

An interesting point here is that bribery and nepotism are often combined; a man in the position to decide whom to employ will give preference to his kinsmen, but they will still have to hand over to him a part of their pay. The resulting network of social relations will somewhat resemble the old custom of giving presents to the heads of clans, and will be less ruthlessly mercenary than when strangers are involved. It will present a fascinating and intricate hybrid of kin-solidarity, commercialisation, quasi-feudalism and disordered bureaucracy. Unfortunately, such networks are difficult to study because they involve illegal actions about which people do not like to speak to strangers.

Our understanding of African venality might be improved by a distinction between solidaristic and egoistic graft—somewhat analogous to Durkheim's distinction between altruistic and egoistic suicide (the former being prompted by obedience to the norms of the society, as with Japanese harakiri, and the latter due to social isolation and moral disorientation). To designate a prevalence of the latter two features in a society Durkheim coined the term anomie (i.e. normlessness).

We shall classify a given case of graft as solidaristic when we have reasons to believe that it was prompted primarily by the desire to help the kinsmen; and as egoistic when the motives appear to be purely selfish or at most concerned with the welfare of the nuclear family. Almost needless to say, these types are ideal and their relatively pure exemplifications can seldom be found, the majority of the cases presenting a mixture of both. Nevertheless the variations in the proportions of the two ingredients are clearly perceptible, and they make a great difference to the functioning of a given society.

With the partial exceptions of Liberia and Sierra Leone, where the elites descend largely from detribalised slaves resettled in Africa, the African administrations are staffed mainly by people who have been brought up under still vigorous systems of extended kinship, and whose exposure to the ideal of impersonal public service has been brief and backed neither by the tradition nor by genuine sentiments of nationalism. They feel deeply about obligations to their kinsmen but have no sense of duty towards the state—an artificial creation of the foreign masters imposed upon them by force only a few decades ago. A typical African official has been educated at the expense of a large number of his kinsmen who were patiently making collections to pay for his schooling in the expectation that he will look after them when he reaches a high position. If he put his duty to the state above this debt of gratitude, they would regard him as a despicable traitor, ostracise him and perhaps demand an immediate repayment in cash of what they have spent on him. Disowned by his kin he would find himself unable to rely on anybody's backing or loyalty in an environment where the struggle for existence is very bitter, where it is not customary to have close friends who are not relatives, and where his competitors enjoy the support of numerous kinsmen. Under these circumstances the regard for his own interest as well as deeply ingrained sentiments prompt a man to break or twist a law which prevents him from helping his kin, which he regards as his foremost duty.

An African who has reached the top is expected to provide jobs for hundreds of his clansmen, to give decent presents to a vast array of relatives as well as to the clan elders when he visits his village, to make contributions befitting his station to the association of people from his village who reside in the same town as he, to provide in his house food and lodging for kinsmen who come to the town seeking jobs and not finding them for months or even years: to help to pay for the education of the children of his poorer relatives, and last but not least to provide feasts and to defer the costs of sacrifices or funerals (including his own) apart from making donations to the church. As he cannot meet such extensive obligations out of his salary, he is compelled to squeeze bribes, embezzle public funds, take rake-offs and so on. He feels no remorse about doing this because everybody else who can, does the same, and nobody feels that it is something wrong. Solidaristic graft, then, inevitably results from putting an administrative machine devised by foreigners into a society where solidarity of kin still provides the only effective basis of social ethics.

In a country like Somalia, where urbanisation and commercialisation remain embryonic and consequently have made little impact on the traditional tribal structure, graft retains mostly (if not entirely) a solidaristic character; which means that its proceeds are widely distributed. The situation is different in the big cities of West Africa which represent the opposite pole of African social structures, where detribalisation and the spread of European education and values have produced a sizeable mass of rootless or almost uprooted individuals. As it is easier to undermine existing ethical standards than to implant new ones, such people tend to have few scruples of any kind, and eagerly and ruthlessly seize every opportunity to make illegal gains while shirking their duties towards their kin. In Liberia and Sierra Leone most of the venality probably is of the egoistic kind because their elites consist of descendants of slaves sent back to Africa who had been torn away from their blood affiliations.

Under the circumstances of far-reaching disregard for fitness for the job in selecting personnel, while many of the most crucial decisions are determined by bribery, the administration cannot fail to be utterly inefficient. Equally deleterious, however, is the sheer weight of parasitism.

On the whole the British colonial administrators did not indulge in graft but they have manifestly failed to inculcate probity into their successors. Perhaps it was impossible; perhaps it could have been done only if the process of Africanisation had been spread over thirty or forty years or even a century. As it happened, their precipitated departure opened the gates to the flood. Perhaps the only method of decolonialisation which could have left a sounder basis for the future would have been to Africanise gradually the civil and military service—allowing the Africans to compete on merit with European candidates for posts left vacant by normal retirement—and when the process had been completed, leaving the country to be governed by this well-selected and indoctrinated corps. As it happened, power was given to those who clamoured for it most, with the consequence that a few well trained administrators and officers, whose indoctrination with the impersonal bureaucratic virtues had made some progress, were surrounded by half-baked newcomers, and became subordinated to the politicians who had reached the top by demagoguery and huckstering, and who had nothing to lose but everything to gain.

As there is much less wealth in their countries, and as they have been functioning for a much shorter time, the African kleptocrats cannot rival the Latin American top stars like Batista or Peron in the size of the booty. Nonetheless, even a casual inquiry into the ownership of the more conspicuous buildings in any African town reveals that a large part of them are owned by ministers or presidents who a few years ago were simple clerks or teachers. The members of parliament, civil servants and party functionaries possess less sumptuous properties but which nonetheless must have cost many times more than what they had received as salary since they took up their appointments. Such premises are often let to foreign-owned companies for housing their expatriate staff at rents well above the market price. The companies are prepared to co-operate in order to ensure the good will of influential or at least useful persons.

It must not be imagined, however, that foreign corporations do not participate in this game. On the contrary: operating in an environment where such things are regarded as natural, they shed easily the scruples which they might have in their home countries, and do not hesitate to use their financial power to obtain illegal advantages. The only thing that could be said in their defence is that as the indigenous potentates want to have partners, they will favour those who will play and will penalise the spoil-sports. The smaller firms simply allocate to their managers funds for which they do not account in writing but only verbally, and from which they draw bribes for the officials on whom they depend. The big corporations have entire teams whose job it is to operate vast networks of corruption, dabbling in politics, subsidising news-papers, politicians and even judges. The official name for these activities is public relations, and it is the only aspect of business where the Africans can rise to top positions because of their usefulness as go-betweens who know best how to ensure the good will of the politicians by discreetly distributing largesse. These jobs usually go to well-connected people and are very lucrative as no receipts need be presented. More will be said about these activities in the chapter on neo-colonialism.

There was a great deal of corruption in tzarist Russia and pre-war Poland, as there is in present-day Spain or Chile. Nevertheless, as far as I could gather, bribery in these countries was confined to restricted areas connected with the use of official power; and outside this sphere many services were rendered without money changing hands. Furthermore, the rich exploited the poor but within each class there was a strong feeling of solidarity. In Africa, however, genuine solidarity is confined to the clan, and there are no restraints on cupidity beyond its confines.

In urban Africa, venality, far from being a monopoly of the top people pervades all strata and ties up with various old customs and the heritage of slave trade. Many traditional activities and ceremonies involve making payments. A man cannot obtain a wife without paying bride-price to her family (father, uncle or brother). Celebrations of achievements, returns or departures occasion pay-ments to the central person. Even more relevant is the custom of making gifts to a person of higher rank when visiting or receiving him. Clearly, customs of this kind are not equivalent to modern bribery, but it is easy to see how they have provided a propitious ground for it.

In all human societies wealth tends to flow towards power: and until the rise of highly efficient administrative and military machines, only kinship bonds could temper the proclivity to use the power of office for the purpose of acquisition of wealth. So even in the urban environment in Africa, within the bounds of the clan wealth usually flows both towards and from the wielders of authority, even though the former current is normally stronger. In relations between non-kinsmen power normally occasions uninhibited spoliation. Moreover, as it is always easier to release anti-social proclivities than to contain them, the process of detribalisation liberates the people from the sense of duty towards their kinsmen before they have begun to feel under obligation to adhere to more universal norms. In consequence in the urban society almost everybody is trying to squeeze something out of almost everybody else over whom he has power or to whom he is rendering an indispensable service. Thus for instance, if one worker introduces another to his employer, he will claim the first month's wages.

One of the most unsavoury forms of exploitation arises from the handling of applications for jobs. The clerks who have access to them as well as their superiors who have some say in the matter, will reshuffle, remove or destroy the applications so as to favour their kinsmen or those who have paid them a bribe, giving topmost preference to those who satisfy both criteria. Sometimes the competition takes the form of a kind of auction in which the prize goes to the highest bidder while the rest forfeit their bids. Private African firms sometimes openly charge a fee for considering an application, even if it is turned down. Another sinister racket is to demand from the applicants considerable sums as a pledge of honesty sometimes long before they start to work; and when the prospective employer has collected a substantial amount from the applicants he often goes bankrupt or simply vanishes. So many applicants fall prey to such tricks because even respectable big stores and banks demand similar guarantees owing to inveterate stealing by their employees.

Most people who have the power to hire and fire will try to impose upon their subordinates a ransom for being allowed to stay in employment; and if the latter have subordinates of their own, they will try to recover their expenses and make a profit by applying the same technique. So a kind of quasi-feudal network of tribute levying goes right through the public services. Expatriate employees of African public authorities often participate in such rackets. It seems that a kind of negative selection has occurred among the expatriates, so that those who remained or joined since the independence seem to be on the whole less scrupulous than the colonials of the old type. Working under a much stricter control, the expatriate managers of foreign-owned companies do not normally engage in peculation on their own personal account; and the African employees and applicants do not expect them to and do not offer bribes. The common desire of the poorer candidates without kinsmen higher up is to get to the European manager, but African doorkeepers, clerks and foremen usually bar the way.

Being guided in a very much larger measure by the fitness for the job in selecting their employees, foreign companies inevitably surpass in efficiency the African; and this is one of the reasons why the economic power in Africa remains in expatriate hands. The inefficiency of the African publicly owned enterprises, and parasitism and venality of their managers are such that they condemn 'African socialism' to being a pipe dream.

The newly independent African states provide some of the closest approximations to pure kleptocracy that have been recorded. This does not mean that the amount squeezed out of the ordinary people is absolutely or even relatively larger than elsewhere in the world. The slice of the country's wealth appropriated by the pink castes in Rhodesia and South Africa is a great deal larger than what the African elites manage to take. In the former countries, however, exploitation occurs in accordance with the laws debarring the brown subjects from more lucrative occupations, and without recourse to embezzlement or bribery. This contrast does not make the South African method better from the ethical point of view, but it makes it into a distinct phenomenon with different consequences. The same is true about many societies where the lower classes are of the same race as their masters but where exploitation is sanctioned by more or less generally accepted customs and laws, as is the case for instance in Saudi Arabia. The exploitation of the slaves in Rome or the West Indies, of the serfs in old Russia and of the forced labourers in Soviet times or of the nominally free tenants in present day Peru or India, exceeded or exceeds in intensity anything that goes on in tropical Africa, but these forms of exploitation were based on the use of economic or political power within the law (no matter how unjust), and therefore were distinct from exploitation through extortion of bribes. With the exception of Communist Russia, the kleptocratic squeeze was quite widespread in the societies just mentioned but, in contrast to post-colonial Africa, it did not constitute the main fount of inequality and exploitation.

As shown in detail in my *Parasitism and Subversion*, graft is rampant throughout Latin America but it constitutes there a relatively less important channel of the flow of wealth than in Africa; although the sums are absolutely larger. The amount of corruption in administrative machines of Latin America is sufficient to make them utterly inefficient, but the proportion of wealth absorbed by bribes and embezzlement is limited by the political power of the old-established property-owning classes whose chief concern is to preserve their possessions rather than to multiply them quickly. Like their African counterparts, the upstart Latin American politicians usually try to make fortunes rapidly but they cannot squeeze very much out of the powerful hereditary rich. As the latter, moreover, in their capacity of landlords and financiers appropriate the greater part of what can be squeezed out of ordinary people—and as about half of the proceeds from taxes have to be handed over to the army—the proportion of wealth which remains available for embezzlement by the officials and politicians (or extorted as bribes) must be smaller in Latin America than in tropical Africa where (with the exception of Ethiopia) neither latifundia nor the armies constitute equally important agencies of parasitic suction although the importance of the latter in this respect is rapidly increasing.* In Latin America, moreover, the class solidarity among the rich as well as among the poor seems to deter people from applying the squeeze to the members of their own class, whereas in Africa such scruples operate only within the much narrower confines of the clan.

When the new African states came into existence the control over the chief sources of wealth came into the hands of politicians and officials who (with a few exceptions) had no fortunes to defend or lose but only to gain, who did not have to serve as

* Written before the military coups.

watchdogs of an aristocracy or a monarchy and who did not have to reckon with the influence of any non-bureaucratic professions or business circles. Directly or indirectly, therefore, they were free to put a squeeze on all their subjects, with the exception of the powerful foreign companies.

Until the military coup of January 1966, Nigeria was providing the most perfect example of kleptocracy: not only because from the highest to the lowest practically everybody was involved in the kleptocratic circulation of wealth; but also because the positions in the structure of power were bought, and power itself rested upon the ability to bribe. As the apparatus of coercion was relatively rudimentary—and as it was used relatively sparingly—we can say that the regime rested mainly on fraud. The history of military dictatorships in other parts of the world does not encourage one to expect that this form of government will eliminate fraud— but it will certainly add force as the second prop of the regime which will no longer remain a pure kleptocracy.

According to Ronald Wraith, (who was the first to raise this matter in a book):

'What Britain did in 500 years Africans in particular are determined to do in fifty. This is legitimate; what is not legitimate is to be selective—to say that for certain purposes Africa will move at ten times the pace of her former guardians . . . but reserve the right to travel at a more convenient pace in public honesty. . . . The public men on whom wealth has descended in a sudden and unimaginable torrent are not heirs to a tradition of comfortable bank balances and public responsibility; they are nouveaux riches tycoons of public administration. Those who happened to be in the right place at the right time were not all of them cultivated, educated or upright men. . . . Above all, young men from secondary schools and universities who enter the public service do not see a clear road ahead, along which they will travel as far as their abilities will take them in the knowledge that merit will be rewarded and integrity will be their greatest asset. They see a jungle of nepotism and temptation through which they must hack their way unaided.'

The losses caused by corruption exceed by far the sum of individual profits derived from it, because graft distorts the whole economy. Important decisions are determined by ulterior motives regardless of consequences to the wider community. When a useless factory is built in an impossible place simply because the former owner of the site bribed the officials into buying it for an exorbitant price, then the cost to the community must exceed by far the profits of the manipulators. An administrative machine permeated by graft does not respond to direction, so that even a most enlightened and personally honest leader can achieve nothing, his instructions are perverted in execution; and the network of collusion is so thick that he gropes as in a fog. Every bureaucratic machine suffers to some extent from aversion to initiative and originality, from sycophancy and the preferment of intriguers and yes-men. But when graft adjoins these normal diseases the administrative services become a mere machine of extortion, scarcely able to maintain a minimum of public order, let alone to engage in successful economic planning.

The essence of kleptocracy is that the functioning of the organs of authority is determined by the mechanisms of supply and demand rather than the laws and regulations; and a kleptocratic state constitutes a curiously generalised model of laissez-faire economics even if its economy is nominally socialist. However, like pure democracy or pure autocracy, pure kleptocracy is an 'ideal type' which has never materialised because everywhere there are certain bonds of solidarity which interfere with the workings of supply and demand. Until the factor of coercion by the force of arms became decisive, Nigeria presented a very close approximation to this ideal type but only on the level of supra-clan politics, while relations inside the clan and family continued to be regulated by customary rights and duties. Normally kleptocracy is not 'pure' but intertwined with coercion by armed force; so that strategy and tactics as well as price theory are needed to explain the functioning of a system consisting of a mixture of venality and gangsterism, of which the Caribbean republics and the Philippines offer the best examples at the moment.

Chapter 8 FROM COLONIAL TO POST-COLONIAL AUTHORITARIANISM

Until recently one could not express a doubt about the reality of democracy in the new African states without being called a racialist and fascist. In a way this was understandable because as commonly used the word 'democracy' has long ago ceased to have any definite meaning, and has come to indicate a mere approval of the given system whatever it might be. The debates about what democracy 'really' is in fact amount to quarrels about the right to use the approval-eliciting verbal sign in order to influence people's attitudes. If we want to use this term for the purpose of enlightenment rather than propaganda we must specify what we mean, keeping as close as possible to the etymology, but not adhering to it completely because 'government by the people' has never existed and in all likelihood never will: everywhere some people make decisions and others carry them out. In the following discussion, I shall mean by 'democracy' government based on the periodically expressed consent of the majority—in other words, a system of government where there are effective institutional arrangements, sanctioned by laws and customs, which prevent the holders of supreme authority from continuing in office if they are actively disliked by the majority of the citizens. Elections and the plurality of parties constitute important elements of such arrangements, but they can be made ineffective by collusion, fraud, intimidation and bribery. Democracy, defined as government by consent of the majority, prevents only an illtreatment of this majority, and is perfectly compatible with the oppression and exploitation of foreigners or internal minorities, with bellicosity, intolerance, obscurantism and many other evils.

For the benefit of readers interested in methodology I must add that however defined, any political system requires specific conditions for its operation, but we should not include them in the definition of the system. As a general methodological rule, definitions should be as simple (or, to use a more technical term, as unintensive) as possible in order to avoid pre-judging by definition what should be left as an open question to be decided in the light of empirical evidence. Thus, for instance, it is by no means obvious that social mobility always promotes democracy as defined above; although many people are inclined to call democratic any system where the elite are recruited from the lower classes or where some levelling of distribution of wealth or abolition of hereditary privileges has taken place. An authoritarian government may be populist in the sense of genuinely attempting to satisfy the desires of the masses, and it may, (as was the case with Hitler or Peron) enjoy massive popular support, but talking about democratic dictatorships or totalitarian democracy deprives these terms of any recognisable meaning. Totalitarianism can be egalitarian but not democratic.

The process of creating the new African states has provided a vivid illustration of word magic. The usual procedure was as follows: a committee of lawyers would be set up who would draft a constitution containing all the democratic provisions they could think of. Then the rebellious African politicians were told that they could have independence and power if they signed a promise to follow it. Signing a piece of paper was a small price for the bounties of power, while the former overlords could console themselves for the loss of the empire with the idea that they had bequeathed democracy to their former subjects. As with the entire myth of the British Commonwealth, it was a case of a delusion of omnipotence from the grave: though no longer on the spot to order the boys about, the former masters refused to believe that the instruction which they have left behind might be disregarded by the former pupils. The weakness of these farewell exhortations on democracy was that until shortly before their departure the colonial rulers had never tried to exemplify the practice of democracy, and were perfectly content with ruling in a strictly authoritarian manner.

Neither the British nor the French colonial rule was particularly oppressive in areas where there were no substantial settler populations. Especially during the last few decades of its existence, the British colonial administration was the most benevolent government which the African countries have ever had or will have in the foreseecable future: and it had a strong ingredient of paternalism in the correct sense of this unjustly abused word:

that is to say in the sense of a mixture of authoritarianism with genuine concern for the welfare of the subjects. We must not underestimate the selfishness and arrogance of many colonial administrators—and it is not a point which can be proved by statistics—but, at least as far as the British services are concerned, I have no doubt that people with genuine concern for the welfare of their subjects were more common among them than in the midst of the new African elites. Nonetheless, the colonial rule was strictly authoritarian and certainly did not inculcate the ideas and habits needed for a democratic form of government.

Concerning 'paternalism', it may be worth repeating that what we commonly find in politics is a pretended or pseudo paternalism consisting of recourse to images of fatherhood to camouflage an attitude more closely resembling that of a cattle breeder.

The relative virtues of the colonial administration provide no argument in favour of a thesis that it could and should have been prolonged, because, though fairly mild and benevolent in its later days, it could continue only at the price of becoming terroristic once the independence movements had sprung up, which was inevitable. The Africans who had received their education in Britain or France and had heard all about the virtues of democracy, could not fail to see the discrepancy between government by consent and the rule of law in the metropolitan countries and the authoritarian government and racial discrimination in the colonies. In this respect the Portuguese system is less self-defeating and discriminatory because an African who goes to Portugal finds that the people there have to obey and keep their mouths shut just as much as he has in Africa; and for this reason he may feel less humiliated and resentful. It was, moreover, inevitable that Africans who have been educated would no longer stand in awe before the mysterious skills of the Europeans, and would come to feel that they could do the job of governing the country of their birth just as well or even better. This feeling was further stimulated by the circumstance that the Britons and Frenchmen who went to the colonies mostly did not have sufficient qualifications or abilities to obtain equivalent posts at home, and were often less gifted than the educated Africans who were the pick of a large population. Expatriate paternalism holds attractions for peasants, servants and labourers who almost without exception prefer to work for a European or an American than for their compatriot, owing to the better pay and treatment which they normally get from the former. The educated Africans, however, could not fail to be offended by such an attitude, and naturally wanted to put an end to the situation which permitted it. Outside the areas where the European settlers have appropriated the land, the resentment (let alone genuine hatred) against the foreign masters was confined to the educated minority whose aspirations were high enough to expose them to snubbing, and who have materially benefited from independence. Among the ordinary people in the new African states (I am not speaking here, of course, about South Africa) the attitude towards the Europeans is surprisingly friendly and trusting—which does not preclude robbery and murder when the order breaks down . . . but this has nothing to do with colour.

To come back to the problem of democracy: regardless of their merits in comparison with what preceded and what followed them, the colonial administrations have created no foundations for government by consent. The few legislative assemblies functioned only within limited areas, had restricted powers and have made no impact on the prevailing attitudes which were much more influnced by the spectacle of the remote governor who brooked no opposition. However, even if the colonial governments had been making a serious attempt to implant democratic practices before bestowing democratic constitutions, it does not seem that they could have succeeded, for democracy is a tender plant which has thrived only in a few countries for longer than a brief period. In Britain representative institutions have existed for centuries but political rights were confined to a small minority until the Third Reform Bill in 1884 while universal suffrage dates only from 1918. Germany has had a democratic constitution only for fourteen years before the last war and for eighteen years since, although the government of the Kaisers was extremely liberal, law abiding and respectful of the rights of the citizen in comparison with what goes on to-day in 90 per cent of the members of the United Nations. Poland had a democratic government for four years (1922-26), and Russia at most during the six months between the fall of the Tsar and the Bolshevik seizure of power. France was lucky to have enjoyed democracy for over eighty years, but Spain had only five. Most parts of the world, including such parts of Europe as Portugal and the Balkans have never experienced it. So the

Africans need not feel that the absence of democracy in their countries marks them as an inferior race. Democracy, to repeat, is a tender plant which requires very specific conditions.

The inanity of the idea that there is some uniform process of modernisation which (at least normally) comports 'Political development'—by which is meant a trend towards a political system based on free and honest elections—can be seen from the fact that in Africa the only example of peaceful and lawful replacement of the incumbents of the highest offices has occurred in the Somali Republic, which is the poorest and (by any of the usual standards) the most backward state. The explanation lies partly in ethnic homogeneity (unique among the African states) and secondly in the vitality of the old social structure and ethics, which permits the national government to be based on a pact between the three main tribal groupings, which are culturally sufficiently similar to uphold a common code of honour and obligation, and so adhere to the unwritten covenants about the tribal distribution of offices and their rotation. Rather than demagogues seeking the support of a floating and disorganised populace, the parliamentarians and cabinet ministers act as deputies of the tribal chiefs and elders. The wealth, moreover, is so scarce that there is little scope for large scale racketeering. The persistence of the tribal structures rules out efficiency in administration—which is slow and chaotic even by comparison with many other new states—but it permits a consensus about the 'rules of the game' needed for governing by consent. In comparison with the neighbouring lands with their numerous policemen and informers (especially the terroristic imperial rule in Ethiopia and Sudan or the chaotic and bankrupt quasi-totalitarianism in Zanzibar) Somalia is a refreshingly free country where people neither fear to speak about politics nor fawn upon the holders of high office.

In order not to draw false conclusions, we must bear in mind that under a thin varnish of western nomenclature the Somali political system is essentially a tribal league. What is equally important, the class inequalities are absent, as the strength of tribal and clan solidarity ensures widespread dilution of the spoils of office, which consequently cannot be used for building up individual fortunes. In any stratified society no longer constrained by tribal sacred custom, the first necessary though not sufficient condition of democracy is the absence of mass poverty; although representative institutions with restricted franchise can function even if the majority live in painful misery. The conservatives like Macaulay and Burke who opposed the idea of extending the franchise, on the ground that such a step would lead to strife, chaos and eventually tyranny, were perfectly right on the assumption that the masses to be enfranchised would remain as poor as they were when these authors were writing. In all likelihood the democratisation of the British constitution would have had such consequences had it not been followed by a general improvement in the standards of living, due to an acceleration of the growth of productive capacity, accompanied by a decline of the birth rate, while the ample outlets for emigration were also alleviating the pressure of the population upon the resources. The United States, where (apart from the South) democracy began with independence, have always had the highest standard of living in the world. The French were the first nation in the modern world to adopt the practice of restricting their progeny, and in consequence were able to attain the highest standard of living in Europe despite the relatively slow growth of their industry; and although the industrial workers had to suffer misery, the peasants were relatively prosperous and satisfied ever since the Revolution when they became the owners of their plots. Remarks along these lines could also be made about Switzerland and Scandinavia and all the evidence shows that no political system which could be described as democratic has functioned for long in the midst of widespread misery. The explanation of this incompatibility is perfectly simple: democracy requires a consensus on the rules for investiture and exercise of authority, and the expectation that these rules will be observed. These conditions are impossible to maintain when goods are so scarce that people will resort to any means to obtain them unless restrained by force.

Democracy can function only in an atmosphere of compromise, regard for fair play and of agreement on basic values. Once hatreds become violent the verdict of the polls will not be accepted; and indeed it would be foolish for the rulers to hand over the reins to the winners at the polls who intend to slaughter them. As we saw earlier, there are many factors in African cultures which militate against democracy, but they are all of secondary importance in comparison with the curse of mass poverty.

It is really one of the best established principles of political sociology that democracy cannot function in the midst of poverty. Though continuously disregarded, this principle has been formulated by Malthus a hundred and fifty years ago in these words:

'The pressure of distress on the lower classes of people, together with the habit of attributing this distress to their rulers, appears to me to be the rock of defence, the castle, the guardian spirit of despotism. It affords to the tyrant the fatal and unanswerable plea of necessity. It is the reason why every free government tends constantly to destruction; and that its appointed guardians become daily less jealous of the encroachments of power. It is the reason why so many noble efforts in the cause of freedom have failed; and why almost every revolution, after long and painful sacrifices, has terminated in a military despotism. While any dissatisfied man of talents has power to persuade the lower classes of people that all their poverty and distress arise solely from the iniquity of the government, though perhaps, the greatest part of what they suffer is unconnected with this cause, it is evident that the seeds of fresh discontents and fresh revolutions are continually sowing. When an established government has been destroyed, finding that their poverty has not been immolated without producing the desired effect, other sacrifices are called for, and so without end. Are we to be surprised that, under such circumstances, the majority of well-disposed people, finding that a government with proper restrictions is unable to support itself against the revolutionary spirit, and wary and exhausted with perpetual change to which they can see no end, should give up the struggle in despair, and throw themselves into the arms of the first power which can afford them protection against the horrors of anarchy?'

But what about India? The answer is not far to seek: the assertion about the connection between prosperity and democracy applies only to effective democracy where the voters have a real choice and feel free to make it—not to cases where they are prevented from making use of their constitutional rights by terror or fraud or (as in India) by economic constraint combined with the fear of supernatural powers. The recourse to intimidation and fraud has been limited in India (outside Kerala) because the masses have been made so docile by malnutrition and superstitious fears that they do not dare to clamour for a better life; and are content to leave the business of governing to their betters . . . to such extent that even the leaders of the trade unions and of the communist party come from the upper castes. To be sure, the political system is neither dictatorial nor totalitarian and there is a considerable respect for the law, but the poor vote as they are told, and only the wishes of a small majority have to be taken into account. As the traditional restraints, however, are being gradually eroded, naked coercion comes to the fore.

The basic political problem of the underdeveloped countries is usually approached from an unrealistic viewpoint: people argue about whether democracy can ensure economic progress or whether a dictatorship is needed for this purpose, whereas the real question is not so much whether dictatorship is desirable as whether it can be avoided. Such are the allurements of wishful thinking that even serious writers often do not realise that the proposition 'misery necessitates dictatorship' in no way entails the proposition 'dictatorship will cure the misery'. If the choice really lay between democracy and prosperity few reasonable people would advocate the former for countries where millions are starving, but in fact there is a natural affinity rather than incompatibility between democracy and prosperity; and the normal condition of mankind is to have neither.

Naturally, not all forms of authoritarian rule are equally conducive to economic progress; and we must give the communist variant a very high rating in this respect, in view of the appalling record of most other variants commonly addicted to extravagant waste and parasitism. Even the communist variant, however, has not yet proved itself fully, as in none of the communist states does the standard of living approach the level found under capitalist democracies. Moreover, even if the communist system finally does bring prosperity to the masses, there is no reason that democracy would be the next stage; for whereas we can accept as proven that prosperity is a necessary condition of democracy, the evidence for the view that it might be a sufficient condition as well is very scanty indeed.*

The problem of at which point of economic progress does

---

* The factors of liberalisation of the communist regimes, and the problem of convergence of communism and capitalism, are examined in Ch. 23 and 24 of *Elements of Comparative Sociology*.

democracy become viable and perhaps even more conducive to further progress than other political systems is not very relevant to a discussion of contemporary Africa because there is no chance that any of the African states will become democratic within a lifetime, and most of them are moving further and further in the opposite direction. Nowhere in the world has an effective democracy preceded an elimination of generalised misery, and only starry-eyed dreamers can expect the Africans to achieve under particularly difficult conditions a feat which no one else has yet performed.

There can be representative government without democracy if the political rights are restricted to a part of the population, as was the case in Britain when it was laying the foundations of its future opulence. An oligarchic representative government (where only the consent of a privileged minority needs to be obtained) offers certain advantages over a dictatorship by inculcating the respect of law and ensuring a certain continuity and regularity of administration propitious for economic progress. A consensus is easier to achieve as it need not extend beyond the class possessing political rights.*

In comparison with personal dictatorship, a stable oligarchy is less likely to lead to strife and revolution or squander resources on megalomaniac projects and adventures. Provided the bureaucratic machine is not too cumbersome and fiscality not excessive, such an iniquitous system permits fast economic progress even in the presence of corrupt practices. The latter become an almost insuperable obstacle only when the economic functions of the government become extensive—when, that is to say, the slice of aggregate wealth which passes through the hands of the politicians and officials becomes very large.

Even an oligarchic consensus, however, does not exist in African states owing to the ethnic heterogeneity of the new ruling elites. There are, it is true, historical examples of cohesive elites composed of individuals of variegated origins—such as the Catholic hierarchy or the ruling personnel of the Ottoman empire—but

---

* Such was the situation in Britain and France during the first two-thirds of the nineteenth century. Apart from Ivory Coast economic progress is most rapid in South Africa and Rhodesia which have precisely this type of constitution. Unfortunately, however, their racialist basis rules out the possibility of an eventual democratisation in the foreseeable future.

these people were first uprooted, secondly indoctrinated and thirdly inserted into a rigid authoritarian framework. Only the military elites in Africa offer some analogies to this kind of situation, which may be a reason why in so many cases the military rule was the only alternative to disintegration of the post-colonial state. The loose structure of the civilian elites generates no centripetal forces which could counterbalance the centrifugal tendencies stemming from ethnic affiliations. The strong ties of ethnic and kinship solidarity, moreover, transform the fights between the factions of the ruling personnel into struggles between clans, tribes and ethnies.

The fissiparous forces arising out of ethnic heterogeneity are not the only obstacle to an implantation of a representative form of government in Africa. Equally inimical is the set of circumstances which makes political power into the fount of wealth because the acerbity of the struggle for power depends largely on the number of people who will lose their jobs if the supreme authority changes hands. Another aggravating factor is the lack of alternative opportunities of making a fortune or even a bare living, particularly as under an arbitrary and vexatious government success in business also depends on political connections.

As the big business is in foreign hands, while the African capitalists employ only their kinsmen in lucrative positions, loss of office in an elected body or public service condemns the victim to destitution unless he succeeds in safeguarding a substantial part of the loot made while in power. Understandably, the knowledge that these are the only alternatives to continuing in office stimulates venality. There is a vicious circle here because the habit of extorting bribes depresses the earnings of the smaller and more defenceless businessmen while augmenting the profits from access to power, which means that this avenue to prosperity becomes less and less promising in comparison with politics. The consequent further deflection of ambitions into the channel of politics aggravates strife and reinforces the predatory propensities of the rulers and their henchmen.

When I first began writing the present book the British press was still full of praise for the democracy in Nigeria, and for this reason I intended to show in some detail that the Nigerian political system, though not a dictatorship, was not democratic either. Since the military coup of January 1966 there is no need to press the point about the shortcomings of the Nigerian politics because with indecent alacrity the British press began to reveal the sins of its former idols which were never mentioned so long as they had power. The murderers of the pillars of democracy have been described by the professional friends of Africa as 'even greater patriots'. This spineless sycophancy is supposed to serve the purpose of preserving the unity of the Commonwealth. Objectively, Ahmadu Bello (now represented as an archvillain)* merits rehabilitation for, in contrast to the shameless money-grabbers from the more civilised south, he did not keep for himself the funds which he acquired—illegally from the point of the law bequeathed by the British but in keeping with the feudal notion that a master has the right to levy tribute from his vassals. With him the movement of wealth was not only one way: he was notoriously generous to his subordinates, and when he was touring villages he used to have his flowing robes stuffed with banknotes which he then distributed among those whom he judged to be deserving a special reward. Moreover, his actions seem to have been guided to a considerable extent by the ideals of Islam, so that morally he was no doubt better than the completely unprincipled kleptocrats of the south. He was not even particularly conservative: he wanted to make the Northern Region into a fairly modernised Islamic state, as well as to ensure for it a dominant position in the Federation.

When the British government was negotiating with the leaders of the independence movement, the emirs of northern Nigeria had shown little enthusiasm for independence, fearing that it would put them under the domination of the southerners. As a condition of their adhesion to the Federation they have extracted a constitution which not only safeguarded their rights but even gave them a good chance of a dominant position in virtue of the relative size of the Northern Region which inherited the so-called Middle Belt inhabited by a mixed population of Christians, Moslems and Pagans.

In order to be able to govern under a parliamentary constitution and to manipulate the elections the emirs have created a political party called The Northern People's Congress. As the name indicates, its basis was frankly ethnic and its only proclaimed ideology the defence of the Islamic faith and of the interests of

* Written before the second coup.

the Hausas against the southerners—these tenets being interpreted
in accordance with the tacit assumption that what is good for the
Fulani emirs is good for the Hausas and Islam.

In the south, the Western Region came under the rule of the
Action Group and the Eastern Region under that of N.C.N.C.—
which initials meant National Council of Nigeria and the
Camerouns until the secession of the latter, and thereafter stood
for National Council of Nigerian Citizens. Both parties made
attempts to find a following in other regions but finally retreated
to their ethnic bases—the Action Group remaining principally the
party of the Yorubas and N.C.N.C. of the Ibos.

Under the leadership of Awolowo the Action Group made a
bid for supremacy throughout Nigeria, trying to win the support
of the Yorubas and other non-Moslems inhabiting the Northern
Region, and even fomenting the resentment of the poor Hausas
against their emirs. To combat these ambitions the northern emirs
entered into an alliance with the Ibo leaders of the N.C.N.C., in
consequence of which Awolowo has found himself in opposition
in the Federal parliament, although the Action Group continued
to rule the Western Region. However, having control over the
army, the police and the treasury the Northerners and their Ibo
allies have succeeded with the aid of bribery and intimidation in
winning over a section of Yoruba politicians, splitting the Action
Group and finally pushing Awolowo and his stalwarts out of office.
Later Awolowo was accused (with some justification) of trying to
organise a revolution and was sentenced to imprisonment for
ten years.

The political system which arose in the wake of the defeat of
the Action Group—and which was praised throughout the 'free
world' as a model democracy—exhibited the following features.
The dominant element was the Northern People's Congress which
was in fact a league of northern emirs firmly led by Ahmadu Bello,
Prince (Sardauna) of Sokoto, who retained for himself only the
office of the premier of the Northern Region but was acknowledged
as the boss by all northern members of the Federal Cabinet and
Parliament. Every well-informed Nigerian knew that the Federal
Prime Minister, Tafawa Balewa (from whom Mr. Harold Wilson
sought guidance on Rhodesia) was a stooge who could make no
important decision without first phoning Ahmadu Bello at Kaduna.
The Eastern Region remained in the hands of the N.C.N.C. led

by the Federal President Azikiwe and the Eastern Region's premier Okpara. The Western Region was governed by the secessionists from the Action Group under the leadership of premier Akintola, regarded by the great majority of the Yorubas as traitors in the pay of Northern emirs. In the Federal parliament and cabinet the Northerners had a majority but they allowed the Ibo politicians a share in the spoils on which many of them waxed fabulously rich—although the champion in this respect was the Finance Minister, Festus Okotie-Iboh, an Itsekiri from the Mid-West.

In the Hausaland proper the emirs, aided by their relatives and vassals functioning as N.C.P. politicians, had no difficulty in retaining control over the population and fixing the elections. In the Middle Belt, however, where the Christians and the rebellious, largely pagan Tivs constituted a more inflammable material, hundreds or even thousands of agitators were beaten or killed or imprisoned under the pretext of punishment for tax evasion. In the Eastern Region the domination of the N.C.N.C. was equally firm. Every man of ambition knew that the membership of N.C.N.C. was the only road to a good job, while non-opposition was the minimal condition of getting a trading licence or even a fair treatment from the tax collectors. The budding opponents were either intimidated or bought. In contrast, the resentment of the Yorubas against the foreign domination and the rule of the 'quislings' was so strong that neither bribery nor mere intimidation sufficed, and Akintola's government could maintain itself in power only by resorting to outright falsification of electoral counting and an amount of violence which could almost qualify for the name of terror. On the eve of the military coup the condition of this Region was not far removed from a civil war.

Apart from the favourable tracing of the regional frontiers, the Northern People's Congress owed its supremacy to the cohesion of the Fulani semi-feudal aristocracy bound by the links of kinship, which gave it a considerable advantage over the squabbling, corrupt and cowardly southern politicians. As the traditional rulers, moreover, the emirs did (and still do) enjoy at least some measure of loyalty among their subjects, whereas very few people felt any attachment to upstart, money-grabbing and mendacious politicians who could not even behave in a dignified manner. Their disloyalty to one another also contributed to their collective weakness. The Fulani aristocracy, on the other hand, was severely handicapped by their educational backwardness. Even the sole university set up hurriedly in Zaria with the deliberate aim of reducing the Northern Region's dependence on educated southerners, could find only 20 per cent of its students among the Moslems, because so few of the latter had been to a secondary school. Thus the Moslems' aversion to modern education deprived them of the essential levers of power. Notwithstanding the persistent effort on the part of Ahmadu Bello to push the northerners into important positions, the key posts in the federal civil service and (what proved even more crucial) the army, remained in the hands of the southerners—above all the Ibos who, unburdened by a traditional ruling class, have shown most eagerness in availing themselves of the opportunities created by the colonial government and the missionaries.

The Nigerian political system was never what naive friends of Africa imagined, but at least it did not amount to a complete negation of democratic and liberal ideals. It did, however, constitute a blind alley which could not lead to anything better and, as its effortless overthrow by a few officers has demonstrated, it had no power of survival. This, of course, merely seems to confirm the view that nothing even remotely resembling a democracy is viable in Africa. What is more surprising is that even the seemingly semi-totalitarian regime of Nkrumah could be overthrown with equal ease.

The European and the American press have depicted Nkrumah as a bloodthirsty tyrant chiefly because of his many menacing gestures and a few concrete steps against foreign commercial interests. In reality, however, he was megalomaniac but relatively mild. Despite repeated attempts on his life, he had few executions on his conscience, and political prisoners were less numerous under his rule than in many other countries. They were approximately 2,000 early in 1966. Immediately after the coup there were probably more than this number in jail in 'protective custody', but the military government soon began releasing large numbers— and was in fact severely criticised for its rashness in doing this. At one time the remaining total was no more than 250. After the attempted 'mini-coup' in April, 1967, many of those who had been released were put back inside, but the latest estimate in 'West Africa' for September 30th, 1967, is that the number of people in protective custody is now probably between 500 and 800.

Compared with such defenders of democracy as Chiang Kai-shek or Ky or even Mobutu, Nkrumah was an archangel of liberty, fraternity and non-violence. As the struggle for power was limited neither by traditional conventions nor by the prestige of hereditary monarchy, and as all available means (ranging from bribery to armed rebellion) were employed in it, nobody could have governed Ghana through a democratic process. Moreover, like other rulers of the post-colonial states, Nkrumah was facing the difficulty which besets all governments which come to power on the shoulders of a quasi-revolutionary quasi-mass movement, having acquired mass support by making promises which cannot be fulfilled. Wealth cannot be created overnight, and even without the errors of economic policy and the swelling burdens of the bureaucratic machine, the aftermath of independence was bound to be disappointing in comparison with the hopes which had been aroused. And as disenchantment often leads to rebellion, the leader of a victorious movement can normally maintain himself in power only by bludgeoning his supporters into docility. This factor, in combination with other circumstances which exacerbate the struggles for office such as ethnic heterogeneity and the lack of any traditional sanction for the rules of the parliamentary game, have ruled out government by consent in other African states too. There had to be authoritarian rule and the only question was whether it would be relatively beneficent or downright pernicious.

It would, however, be a mistake to suggest that Nkrumah's C.P.P. can really be called 'a revolutionary mass movement' in any adequate sense. Bretton's* opinion on this is very forthright:

'By a curious process of reasoning, many observers of the Ghanaian political scene have concluded that there existed in Ghana, from the beginning (i.e. from 1949 onwards), a mass movement or an organisation that was engaged in some form of mass mobilisation. To this observer, after ten years of inter-mittent study of the Ghanaian political scene, such a conclusion rests on an illusion compounded of wishful thinking, unresearched hypotheses, and purposeful political propaganda. It is a case of mistaking appearance for substance. There is no

* *Rise and Fall of Kwame Nkrumah:* Pall Mall Press, 1967.

reliable evidence at all that the Convention People's Party as a party has ever been capable of, or has engaged in, what might justifiably be termed mass-mobilisation activity or that Nkrumah, its builder, ever actually wanted it to perform that function. He expected the party organisation to help him to power and to keep him there. All that can actually be said of the party is that it succeeded, in 1951, 1954 and 1956, in *contributing* to the capture of majorities in the several legislatures. But that is a far cry from mass mobilisation.

'In Ghana, where the preconditions for mass organisation were difficult to create, it was one thing to coax, cajole, trick and lead 5 to 15 per cent of the total adult population to the polls and persuade them to cast their ballots into the box featuring the red cockerel, the emblem of the C.P.P.; it was quite another to claim that these people, by casting little coloured slips of paper into ballot boxes, had become integral parts of a mass organisation, had been ideologically or otherwise mobilised, shared in any meaningful way the political objectives of the party, and could be relied upon to support other tasks set for them by the party leadership. As a matter of fact, traditional chiefs, who had opted for the C.P.P. in the three elections of 1951, 1954 and 1956, may deserve a far greater share of the credit than the party for the party's impressive victories at the polls. In the urban centres, market women helped mightily, providing the major assistance.'

The first error of Nkrumah (which he shared with Guinea's Sekou Touré and Fidel Castro) was to become enchanted with the so-called socialist economic model. We may sympathise with his wish to curtail the profits and the economic power of foreign capital, but in fact he had less reason to complain than most other rulers of under-developed countries because colonial capitalism had made Ghana one of the most prosperous countries of the so-called 'third world', remarkably free from mass misery. Though not possessing the gadgets of the industrial civilisation, few Ghanaians suffered hunger or even serious malnutrition. A ruler concerned about the welfare of his subjects would have had to do some hard bargaining and occasionally take a tough stand against encroachments by foreign big business, but this could have been done cautiously and without imitating totalitarian models. Instead, he took over a country which at independence had reserves of £200 million and left it with debts of over £250 million—£50 million was spent, over and above direct government income, *for every year of independence*. Most of it went in the last years of the regime. By any standards this is a huge sum for a country of barely 8,000,000 people; it is four times the cost of the Volta Dam and Tema harbour taken together, for example. The manner in which he contracted the final debts, too—i.e., by contractor finance—has saddled the country with a debt which it will take the rest of this century to pay off, even given favourable economic chances.

As with so many other rulers of mankind, Nkrumah's megalomania constituted, no doubt, the chief cause of his misfortunes. He could not wait. The task of building a nation out of an ethnic welter circumscribed by arbitrarily drawn frontiers was sufficiently difficult to daunt the greatest statesman, but for Nkrumah this was not enough. He wanted to be the leader of entire Africa and for this purpose he decided to create a powerful military and industrial base in a few years. Correctly realising that this could not be done under the colonial variant of capitalism, he decided to create African socialism, imagining that what has been achieved in Russia in the way of industrialisation could also be done in Ghana.

The misunderstanding of the Russian achievement has wrought untold harm in underdeveloped countries whose leaders have been persuaded by the Soviet propaganda that the conditions in their land resemble those of the Russia of 1914—which is, of course, an utter distortion of the truth. Tzarist Russia did contain a large mass of poor illiterate peasants but the average standard of nutrition was far above any country in Africa or Asia, and equal to or higher than what it is in Russia now. In any case the mere size and the profusion of natural resources put it into an entirely different category from any of the so-called developing countries. As far as the size is concerned only China belongs to the same category but in comparison with the present or the past standard of living of the Chinese people the Russia of 1914 was a land of milk and honey. Towards the end of the tzarist era the Russian scientists, engineers and economists were as good as the German or British; and, though fewer in relation to the total population, they numbered tens of thousands. In some fields Russian thought was very advanced indeed: the Russian writers like Maxime Kovalevsky or Pavlov-Silvansky were among the pioneers of the sociological interpretation of history, and their works were unmatched by anything that could be found in Britain or the U.S.A. of that time . . . or indeed even much later. Pre-revolutionary Russia had several millions of highly educated people, including a large number of very intellectual Jews who have provided most of the brain power needed for designing and organising the new system. Moreover, during the decade preceding 1914 the Russian industry grew faster than any other in the world, and its output reached one-third of the British. What is equally important from the point of view of being able to organise a centrally controlled economy, the Russians had been running for many centuries a vast administrative machine and the biggest army in the world; in which respect the Chinese communists enjoy a similar advantage. It was an utter delusion that a much poorer country, without any tradition of unity and with only a tiny educated class, could successfully imitate a system which (though cruel and wasteful) has proved to be viable and militarily successful on such foundations.

While aping many of the paraphernalia of recently deceased tyrants, Nkrumah was too mild—or not astute and bold enough —to build a machine of terror which might have ensured the perpetuation of his rule despite his economic follies; although it is unlikely that such a machine would ever have enabled him to curtail graft, and to drill the Ghanaians in hard work and other elementary industrial and bureaucratic virtues needed for operating a collectivist economy. The regime was sufficiently tyrannical to antagonise most people outside the privileged party, but not terroristic enough to frighten and stamp out the opposition which was growing as economic conditions worsened in consequence of extravagant spending on prestige buildings, airliners which had to fly almost empty and grand diplomatic gestures.*

* I hope that no reader will be led to imagine that vaingloriousness is a specifically African ailment, as it hardly needs emphasising that vanity of its rulers has always been the most common cause of mankind's sufferings. The apparently inescapable curse is that those most likely to get power are those who strive for it hardest, and they are precisely the people who ideally ought to be debarred from it, as they are least likely to use it for benevolent ends rather than for assuaging their thirst for more power and glory.

On top of it all, instead of concentrating on the truly herculean task of organising a new state, Nkrumah wanted to become the leader of all Africa and could not refrain from attempting to play a big part on the international arena, not realising the risks he was running. To try to obtain material aid from the communists and the capitalists alike was sensible enough; but to provoke the American secret service by helping the Chinese agents in Africa was an act of folly which, no doubt, brought the final nail for his political coffin.

A new nation needs a unifying symbol, and a dose of the cult of personality may be indispensable, but the crazy doctrinal concoctions of 'consciencism' and the silly extravagancies of Nkrumah worship were undermining the educational standards and preventing the more intelligent people from taking part in administering the state, which task was being gradually taken over by experts in sycophancy.

Both from a general humanitarian and the national Ghanaian point of view Nkrumah deserves credit on a number of scores such as his efforts to promote technical and agricultural education, and to correct the pernicious bias towards training in law or classics, his willingness to stand up to foreign big business, and his perseverance in trying to instil into the Ghanaians a sense of national unity and dignity. Unfortunately, all this was spoilt by megalomania.

Perhaps the most successful political and economic system in tropical Africa is at the moment of writing that of Ivory Coast which shared with Ghana the good fortune of being one of the two richest countries in Africa north of the Limpopo. Houphouet-Boigny's government is, of course, unabashedly authoritarian, though more circumspect and given to consultation than the defunct Ghanaian regime; and, in contrast to Nkrumah, Houphouet-Boigny shows neither the desire to save the entire Africa nor to reveal a new doctrine for the guidance of the entire world. He seems to be content with the job of building a viable state in Ivory Coast and is not too touchy to collaborate closely with the French in capitalist development, in consequence of which the rate of the growth of wealth is estimated to be 10 per cent per annum—faster than anywhere else in Africa. In fact he is doing what the new military regimes in Nigeria and Ghana say they would like to do; but he has the enormous advantage of not having come to power through bloodshed, and of heading a civilian regime which is less likely to waste scarce resources on buying arms and expanding the army for the sake of providing more jobs for the officers. Naturally there is plenty of graft, exploitation, waste and other social evils discussed in the previous chapters; nonetheless, the country has up till now avoided both anarchy and the extremes of repression.

The turn which African politics is taking—and in particular the role of the armed forces—does not appear so surprising if we view it in the light of what I have, in *Elements of Comparative Sociology*, proposed to call the principle of naturalness of despotism. In order to obtain a better insight into the nature of despotism we should invert the problem: instead of attempting to explain the occurrence of despotism we should try in the first place to explain its non-occurrence. This inversion of the problem can be justified on the ground that despotism is the most natural form of government of large social aggregates—natural in the sense of the most probable, that is to say, requiring fewest specific conditions for its emergence and continued existence.

When we look at any example of a non-despotic system of government of a large political unit, we find that it contains an intricate mechanism of balance of power. Montesquieu's principle that despotism can be prevented only by a division of authority remains one of the greatest discoveries of sociology, and has fully withstood the test of time. As is well known, Montesquieu thought that it was the division between executive, legislative and judicial authority that made civil liberties possible in England. The writers on constitutional history usually say that he misunderstood the English system of government, but they are wrong because, although it is perfectly true that the division of authority has never been absolute in England, it was very real in comparison with the situation among Continental monarchies, let alone the despotisms of the East. Like all great discoveries, Montesquieu's idea was very simple: it amounted to the application of the old Roman maxim 'divide and rule' to the rulers themselves, thus converting it into 'divide your rulers in order not to be trod upon'. True, he formulated it in terms which were too legalistic, but as reformulated by Mosca who speaks of the balance of social forces, the principle is unassailable. However, the lack of a predominant centre of power does not need to produce a viable equilibrium:

E

disintegration through strife or paralysis of the body politic are more probable outcomes. A political system based on an equilibrium of forces must generate conflicts, and at the same time contain them within narrow limits compatible with effective collective action. The naturalness of despotism is demonstrated by the fact that all non-despotic regimes were products of slow evolution under circumstances which can without much exaggeration be described as hot-house, and that every severe disturbance of their intricate structures caused a relapse into despotism. The movement away from despotism is long and laborious, whereas the movement towards it is quick and easy.

The recent military coups—in consequence of which the majority of the African states came under military rule—can be explained by the following factors:

(1) The complete lack of consensus on the rights to command and the duties to obey, due to (a) the very newness of the states, (b) their arbitrary frontiers and ethnic heterogeneity, (c) the strangeness of the constitutions which have been foisted upon them by the departing foreign rulers.

(2) The bitterness of the struggle for the spoils due to general poverty in combination with unrealistically high expectations and the fact that political office is the chief and often the only road to wealth.

(3) The weakness of the civilian supra-ethnic organisation.

The first two factors rule out the democratic game and ensure that political authority be based on coercion, but do not predetermine whether the authoritarian rule will be civilian or military—which issue will depend on the relative strength of the two power machines. Where (as in Guinea, Tunisia and Ivory Coast and perhaps Malawi and Tanzania) the ruler has been able to organise an efficient ruling party and secret police, he has been able to keep the soldiers at bay. Where this has proved impossible and the civilian power has been weakened by squabbles among the politicians (as in Nigeria) or the pursuit of ruinously unrealistic policies (as in Ghana), the men with the guns took over. Tanganyika and Kenya have been saved from this fate by the intervention of the British troops but it is by no means certain that they will not follow suit before very long together with other states in East Africa. As the examples of Ethiopia and Morocco show, however, a strong absolute or semi-absolute monarchy, with deep roots in tradition, can constitute an alternative to an efficient mono-party as a bulwark against military take-overs.

Though natural in the sense indicated above, military dictatorship need not constitute any solution, if by a solution we mean a step towards prosperity and peace, let alone democracy. As innumerable examples show, ranging from ancient Rome to contemporary Latin America, pretorianism is one of the least stable forms of government, and not in the least immune to such diseases as corruption, inefficiency and internal strife.* In the Congo there was hardly anything for the soldiers to destroy, but in Nigeria the same centrifugal forces which have ruined the civilian government are at the moment of writing rending asunder the military machine and bringing the country to the verge of chaos.

Militocracy in the contemporary underdeveloped countries is radically different from the militarism which afflicted the European states and Japan. The Prussian militarism—to take the most developed representative of the species—entailed militocracy, that is to say, social and political predominance of the soldiers; but it exhibited few pretorianist proclivities, and its ideology was that of service for the cause of national grandeur. Although the Prussian officers insisted on occupying the places of honour in the society, and expected to live in a manner befitting their exalted position, they were not money grabbers. Even when they became ideologically disoriented after the fall of the monarchy, and began to gravitate towards pretorianist incursions into politics, their chief aim was to prepare a renaissance of German military power. All militarists shared the assumption that what was good for the officer corps was good for the nation, but on the whole European militarism—and the same is true of Japan—was extroverted: it was oriented primarily towards fighting the foreigners, and only secondarily towards the task of protecting the social order from internal subversion. Naturally the relative emphasis varied according to the country and the time, but only in Spain was the protection of the privileged classes against internal dangers the chief function of the army.

Though in varying measure, all the armies of Latin America are debilitated by corruption and indiscipline. If we tried to rank

* For a comparison with other parts of the world on this point see *Parasitism and Subversion* and *Military Organisation and Society*.

them in this respect, we would probably have to put the Chilean army at the top as least addicted to these vices, and the Argentinian at the bottom—at least at the moment. Indeed, as far as Argentina is concerned, it seems that the venality and indiscipline of its soldiers constitute the most important source of the troubles. In most African countries the situation in this respect is even worse, and complete breakdowns of order have been common occurrences. There are some big armies in Latin America: over 150,000 in Argentina and over 10,000 in the tiny and poverty-stricken Dominican Republic. Moreover, in relation to the poverty of their equipment these forces are exceedingly expensive, owing to disproportionately large numbers of high ranking officers, both on active service and retired, and their high emoluments. Argentina, for instance, has as many generals as the United States.

The African armies are exceedingly small in comparison with the Latin American, despite their prominent political role: between the Sahara and the Zambesi there are only 130,000 soldiers, almost entirely infantry or cavalrymen without heavy weapons. None of the tropical African states has an air force or a navy capable of effective action. The armies of the north African states on the other hand add up to over 700,000 men, and possess tanks, jet combat planes, rocket detachments and anti-aircraft units. South Africa's armed forces number over 100,000 men, and Rhodesia has armed 40,000 men (including part-timers). The Portuguese army in Africa amounts to about 100,000. This means that the white southern armies have an almost 2:1 superiority, apart from being better organised and armed.*

Nonetheless, in 1965, the states of tropical Africa spent 2,300 million dollars on arms, which amounts to about 20 per cent of their estimated joint national income and the double of all industrial and agricultural investments. Everywhere the soldiers' pay has been raised since the independence—in some cases drastically. After the murder of the Togolese economy-minded President Olympio by the unemployed former soldiers of the French colonial army, the numbers as well as the pay of the soldiers have been doubled—that is to say, the burden on the tax payer quadrupled. In Uganda, to take an example from the opposite end of Africa, army pay was doubled after the mutiny which took place

* Since this was written the 'civil' war has led to a rapid expansion of the armies in Nigeria and Biafra.

soon after the declaration of independence. Shortly before the army was used to drive out the Kabaka (the King of Buganda) its pay was doubled again; so that now an ordinary rifleman earns ten times as much as a labourer. Furthermore, as the army is now used for collecting taxes the soldiers have ample opportunities for bribery and thinly veiled robbery. Actually in all the countries under a military rule (whether overt or de facto) the soldiers augment their income by exactions; and in the more disordered regions (especially in the Congo) they are hardly distinguishable from gangsters.

Military dictatorships on the whole offer much less hope than the civilian because the army is usually the biggest glutton for wealth, and one tank (let alone a jet plane) costs more than limousines for a dozen parasitic politicians.

Chapter 9 THE EMERGENT CLASS
STRUCTURES

From the point of view of the historical roots of the present forms of stratification, the regions of tropical Africa fall into two broad categories: one comprising societies which were stratified in pre-colonial times; the other being without traditional forms of stratification. As always with social phenomena, of course, there are many intermediate cases with half-formed more or less inarticulate stratification; but let us leave them for the moment and consider some relatively pure examples of either clear presence or clear absence of stratification.

Having been subjugated by Europeans for only a few years, Ethiopia presents the neatest example of an indigenous semi-feudal stratification persisting till today in an almost unadulterated form. Remaining under the despotic rule of an heir of a long lived dynasty, relatively isolated from European influences and economically little developed, Ethiopia has no equivalent of the new ruling elites of Ghana, Nigeria or the Ivory Coast, and the Amharic aristocracy remains at the top of the social pyramid. No other African state is based to the same extent on the old semi-feudal structure. A number of the states, however, comprise areas where such structures remain very much alive and affect decisively the total stratification.

Pre-colonial Africa contained a considerable number of fairly large states which came into existence through conquest. In some of them the conquerors have merged with the conquered; and in consequence the social inequalities have lost their connection with race and language. In other cases (as for example in the kingdoms of Ankole and Ruanda) the lines of stratification continued to coincide with ethnic divisions. In the savannah belt (stretching latitudinally across Africa between the desert to the north and the rain forest to the south) the successive waves of (sometimes partly arabised) Moslems descended from the north upon pagan tribes and kingdoms, subjugated them, and built sizeable emirates, many of which continue to exist and remain under the domination of aristocracies descended from the original conquerors. The aforementioned kingdoms of Ruanda and Ankole are not the only examples of fairly large states created through conquest without a participation of the Moslems: there are other examples in the Lacustrine area, in the coastal belt in West Africa (e.g. the Ashanti kingdom) and in southern Africa (e.g. the powerful kingdom of the Zulus). The West African coastal kingdoms naturally had elaborate systems of ranks but, being situated in the coastal belt where colonial penetration was earliest and most intensive, they were more drastically dislocated by the effect of colonial rule, trade and finally urbanisation. Most of these structures of authority and status have been abolished either during the colonial rule (as in the French colonies) or since the independence (as in Ghana), while some lead a shadowy kind of existence (as in south-western Nigeria). In any case—in contrast to the situation in northern Nigeria—their systems of ranks and privileges have not had a decisive influence on the new forms of stratification which developed in the coastal big towns. Some members of the old royal and chiefly families have succeeded in entering the new elite, but they are heavily outnumbered by the 'mobiles' who set the tone.

As far as the coastal regions are concerned, Senegal constitutes the chief exception to what just has been said: there all the main ethnies (including the Wolof who predominate in Dakar) are divided into rigidly endogamous castes. According to Michael Crowder (*Senegal*, p. 110, Methuen, 1967):

'It is still difficult to get on in politics unless one is noble or freeborn. . . . These castes differ slightly from tribe to tribe, but roughly they are divided thus:

Nobles and Freeborn
Artisans (smiths, including jewellers, weavers, leatherworkers)
Minstrels or *Griots*
Liberated slaves
Slaves

(of course, domestic slaves no longer exist as such in Senegal, but families know who their slaves were). It is certainly easier in Senegal for a Toucouleur noble to marry a Wolof noble than to marry a woman of inferior caste from his own tribe. "A marriage between a freeborn person and a blacksmith" say the Wolof, "is like a horse mating with a donkey". The extent to which caste matters is brought out by the case of a young Catholic girl from a devout family who, rather than marry a fellow Catholic out of caste, in the end became the polygamous wife of a Muslim of the same caste. Within any ethnic group in Senegal marriage out of caste is extremely rare.'

In Zanzibar there was also a gulf between the Arab master-race and the negroid subjects (descendants of slaves) but there independence was followed by a rebellion and a massacre of the Arabs. Perhaps because the former masters were traders the victorious subjects took to marxism and installed a People's Republic whose economy is in shambles despite the subsidy which it receives in virtue of serving as a base for communist subversion.

The strength of the chiefly and royal families varies from region to region in accordance with various local circumstances, but on the whole is adversely affected by the economic and educational development which fosters instability of status, swells the ranks of the educated elites and gives them the powerful apparatus of the state to crush the traditional rulers and the privileged orders. For this reason the chiefs still have a great deal of power in Uganda but not in Ghana. In the former country an acute conflict is developing at the moment of writing between the newly made politicians and bureaucrats (stemming mainly from regions without a traditional indigenous ruling stratum) led by the Prime Minister, Milton Obote, and the old royal clans represented by Sir Frederick Mutesu*.

The first military coup in Nigeria has not only swept away a mass of upstart politicians, but (what in the long run will no doubt prove to have been even more important) it has also undermined the dominant position of the Fulani aristocracy, and has demonstrated that the power of the emirs on the federal scene

* Since this was written, Obote's troops (recruited from the northern part of Uganda) have subdued Buganda and burned its ruler's palace. Mutesu is now living in London as an exile. Obote's victory, however, is not completely secure, and his police are kept busy ferreting out royalist conspiracies.

had much more fragile foundations than was generally believed. The second coup has restored the emirs' position in Hausaland but not in Nigeria as a whole.

In contrast, in Sierra Leone the military coup could be described as reactionary as it appears to have been supported by the hitherto most privileged circles who felt that their position was endangered by 'demagogy'. The Margai regime (especially under Sir Albert) relied to a large extent on the support of the tribes from the interior, and has introduced into high office a number of individuals of that provenience, thus incurring the hostility of the Creole elite. Although of course it is difficult to unravel the details of the conspiratorial manoeuvres which have preceded and accompanied the coup, the very names of the most prominent figures of the present military government suggest a close connection with the old established Creole families.

The turmoil in Uganda stems from the clash between the southern and the northern regions, which, however, is also mixed with a kind of class struggle, or rather a struggle between elites of very different backgrounds. The northern area was populated by unstratified tribes and its elites consist entirely of first generation 'mobiles'; while in the south there existed powerful ancient kingdoms (above all, Buganda), and the modernised elite in that area is predominantly recruited from the royal and chiefly lineages.

An interesting feature of the new elites in most states is that they are recruited predominantly from the areas which before the European conquest were occupied by small independent tribes which had neither privileged classes nor despotic rulers. The disproportionate contribution of ethnies such as the Ibos or the Kikuyus to the formation of the new elites can easily be understood in view of the fact that in contrast to the common people in Hausaland, for instance, their mentality had not been moulded by age-long subjection. Being neither hemmed in nor intimidated by a master-class, they displayed much more initiative in availing themselves of educational and commercial opportunities created by the colonial government and economic penetration. This phenomenon has a number of analogies outside Africa: in Colombia, for instance, most of the native businessmen originate from the Antioquia province which differs from the rest of Colombia in respect of land tenure: instead of the usual big estates cultivated by share croppers and hired labourers whose real position is that of serfs, the rural population of the Antioquia province consists primarily of free and relatively prosperous peasant-proprietors whose initiative and desire for improvement have not been knocked out by oppressive masters.

The indigenous stratification assumes such a variety of forms that even a cursory review of them would require an entire book. As the present work deals with the emerging social structures, the traditional elements will be treated only in so far as they decisively affect them.

The structures of the African societies are so fluid at present that it is debatable whether we can legitimately speak of social classes— although this, naturally, depends on what we mean by a class. If we mean a set of persons distinguished by a similar position on the pecking order of power and prestige, or in respect of income or ownership of wealth, then social classes certainly do exist in Africa, and the inequalities between them are very marked. If we also include endogamy and convivial segregation as our criteria of class, then we shall find no class barriers in African societies. The same is true of the criterion of inheritance of status in those areas (like the Iboland) where stratification is of recent origin. Class consciousness presents an even greater difficulty because of the ethnic heterogeneity of the most privileged people in nearly all the states. If we specify that a social class can be said to exist only if it displays a considerable degree of homogeneity in respect of manners, outlook and the way of life, and has no internal barriers to inter-marriage, then we might (without erring grossly) describe the most privileged people in Sierra Leone as a class, but we cannot speak of a Nigerian upper class because the wealthiest and most powerful people in Nigeria are divided into at least three major ethnies—the most profound gulf being that between the Moslems and the Christians. The Fulani aristocracy and the Ibo self-made big men had in common the possession of power, wealth and high status, and they collaborated for the purpose of running the state; but this ambivalent alliance based on expediency was the only bond, and therefore at no time could we regard these two elements as constituting one upper class. The military coups and the de facto break-up of the Federation have removed the Ibos from important positions in the central government, while the Fulani aristocracy have been relegated to their emirates, their former predominant place in the Federal power structure having been taken by the soldiers.

The most populous state in Africa is also unique in presenting within its borders two extremes of the spectrum of the African variants of stratification: the northern emirates where the pre-colonial aristocracy continues to hold undiminished sway, and Iboland which (as mentioned previously) used to be peopled by unstratified tribes, and where practically the entire elite is of the first generation. The Yoruba elite also consists mainly of mobiles but it also contains the scions of the traditional chiefly clans as well as a larger number of second generation educated men.

The most general feature of the new African elites is their political and bureaucratic character. In other words, outside the less developed areas dominated by traditional chiefly clans, the most privileged Africans are either politicians or high officials or army officers. Landownership—which still determines to a large extent the class structures in Latin America—plays an insignificant role in this respect. The big estates are few, belong mostly to foreign companies, and are run by transient expatriate managers who remain outside the indigenous society. Not even in the regions dominated by indigenous aristocracies is stratification based on the ownership of the land, as the wealth of the emirs, chiefs and their relatives comes as a tribute from their subjects rather than as an income from private estates.

The chief exception to this generalisation is Buganda where the British colonial government has allocated to the chiefs as their private property a large part of the land over which they held a semi-feudal suzerainty. In consequence, Buganda is one of the two areas of Africa which possess an indigenous capitalist land-owning layer—the other being the western part of the Ivory Coast where a somewhat similar class emerged through a process of capitalist accumulation. In contrast to what was happening in the Gold Coast and Nigeria, Ivory Coast had no Marketing Boards to insulate the farmers from the vagaries of the market and to siphon off the profits of the most successful of them into the government coffers. In consequence many Ivorian cocoa farmers went bankrupt and had their lands sold, while others waxed rich and bought up the lands of the bankrupts. In the rest of sub-saharan Africa, however, most of the land is still held by the village communities under forms of tenure which restrict the private rights of sale.

The situation may change if the members of the elite invest a large part of their capital in land, and succeed in acquiring big estates by expropriating the village communities, thus repeating the Latin-American pattern. Up till now, however, landlordship has been more or less restricted to the cities where it does constitute one of the chief mechanisms of exploitation, and an important source of the income of the elite. Big privately owned landed estates play (or played) a preponderant role in the economy only in those parts of Africa which have (like South Africa and Rhodesia) or had (like Kenya and Algeria) numerous European settlers.

On the West Coast there are some very rich merchants among the Africans but they are too few, and the total wealth which they control is too small, to provide a counterweight to the political and bureaucratic element. The really big firms are European, and even the bigger firms based in Africa are owned mostly by Levantines and Indians. In East Africa the Asians (or to be exact people of Indian ancestry born in Africa) used to control the entire trade below the level of British-owned giant companies and still control most of it; and in consequence the African elites are even more purely political and bureaucratic than on the other side of the continent. Actually the East African elites do not even staff completely the apparatus of the state because, owing to the scarcity of educated Africans, expatriate officials still occupy a substantial part of high administrative posts. Apart from the traditional chiefs, these elites are so small and fluid, and so lacking in homogeneity and *esprit de corps*, that the word 'class' seems inappropriate to describe them.

In West Africa in contrast, public administration has been completely Africanised and there are thousands of practitioners of law and medicine. Moreover, owing to the greater development of the towns, trade and education, there are many more Africans in supervisory or even managerial positions in foreign owned companies.

Even in a country as large as Nigeria, the elite comprises only a few thousand politicians, chiefs, high civil servants, lawyers, doctors and university teachers with a sprinkling of a few hundred rich businessmen and managers. More than 90 per cent of the population consists of peasants and labourers; and between the top and bottom elements there is a sizeable mass which could be described as a middle class if we could divest this term of its connotations formed in the light of the European conditions. Acutally the analogies are closer with eastern than with western Europe because of the crucial role of diplomas in determining a person's rank.

Until the recent military coups it used to be fashionable to describe the African elites as consisting of intellectuals; which is completely misleading, if we use the word 'intellectual' in its accepted sense denoting somebody whose primary occupation is elaboration or interpretive dissemination of general ideas. The most striking fact even about the African university teachers is that they are politicians much more than intellectuals. Although many African dons are abler than their British predecessors (who were often people who could never have got equivalent jobs at home), their work is much worse because they devote most of their time to political intrigues, and having arrived, no longer bother about intellectual matters. To a large extent this happens because the prizes of politics are too glittering and seemingly too attainable to be resisted; but, secondly, because once an educational institution becomes riddled with nepotism and cut-throat politics, even people with no taste for this game have to take part in it for the sake of keeping their jobs. The individuals who compose the new African elites are not intellectuals but graduates; and we can say that the new African states are governed either by officers or graduates or both. Probably nowhere else (with the exception of China ruled by the Confucian literati) have diplomas been so decisive in determining a man's social position as in Africa just before and after independence.

If the graduate elites were not so closely tied to their kinsmen in lower positions, we could apply to them the term 'intelligentsia' which in its original eastern European sense denotes not the intellectuals but a much wider class of diploma-holding civil servants and members of what in England are called the professions, to the exclusion of mercantile occupations. The intelligentsia, however, were a fairly endogamous class, consisting of entire families, whereas the African graduates have not only clan-brothers but even siblings right at the bottom of the social ladder.

An extensive discussion on the role of the intellectuals in different societies can be found in *Elements of Comparative*

Sociology, while the nature and the position of the intelligentsia in Poland and Russia is discussed in the chapter on Poland in the collective work on *European Fascism* edited by Stewart J. Woolf and published by Weidenfeld & Nicolson. Here I shall only repeat that utter confusion must result from using a term in a completely different sense according to location. We cannot designate as 'intellectuals' the creative writers in Europe, while affixing this label to all the diploma-holders in Africa, without making comparative analysis (and therefore the progress of sociological understanding) impossible.

Notwithstanding the importance attached to diplomas, the main determinants of status are power and wealth which always go together owing to all-pervading venality. Actually there is no lack of consistency here because the reason for the high value placed upon diplomas is that they are regarded as the chief avenue to influential and remunerative positions—an avenue which seems much smoother and less perilous than business.

There are West African merchants who have made fortunes but they are not many, while not a few have lost everything after initial success. In contrast to the situation in Britain or France the average trader lives miserably in comparison with a civil servant, which is due partly to the subsidised housing provided for the latter, partly to the peculiarities of the salary scales mentioned below and partly to the opportunities for graft open to most civil servants. Politics, of course, provided the quickest road to wealth but it has been open only for a few years, whereas social ascent through gaining diplomas was possible in West Africa during at least two or three decades preceding the independence. Moreover, perhaps precisely because of the latter fact, educational qualifications gave their possessors a great advantage in a political career, as up till now the civil servants, university teachers, doctors and lawyers were the only people who have had comfortable livelihood and high status assured. Furthermore, during the period of Africanisation preceding and following the grants of independence, a man could climb up much faster (and with less risk) by getting a few diplomas than by engaging in independent commercial activities. It is understandable, therefore, why a diploma came to be regarded as the key to the door of success. This does not mean, however, that it must remain so once unemployed and indigent diploma-holders become common.

In contrast to Latin America and the poorer countries of Europe like Italy or Spain, the higher ranks of the public services in the new states of Africa (especially in the formerly British territories) receive very good salaries. The explanation is not far to seek: when in the colonial days the higher administrative and teaching posts were filled by recruits from the ruling country, the remuneration had to be on the same or even higher scale as in Britain or France in order to attract qualified candidates; and by being attuned to the British, French or Belgian scales, the salaries had to be fantastically lavish by African standards. If we take the wage of an average unskilled worker as the unit of comparison, and express the salaries of the top grades of the civil service as the multiples thereof, we find that in Britain the ratio is about 1 : 5, whereas in Nigeria or Sierra Leone it is about 1 : 40. After tax it becomes about 1 : 4 in Britain, whereas in its former colonies the ratio remains unchanged because the equalising effect of the less steeply graduated income tax is offset by taxfree allowances for cars, subsidised housing and free miscellaneous services received by the higher ranks of the public employees. Consequently we can say that in relation to the wages of the unskilled workers the salaries of the higher civil servants, superior army officers and senior university teachers are about ten times higher in English speaking African states than in Britain. I have calculated that if my pay in Britain were to be fixed in the same ratio to the wage of an unskilled labourer as that in which my salary stood in Nigeria at the top of senior lecturer's scale, then I should be getting over £30,000 after tax.

However, in assessing the degree of inequality we must bear in mind the important consideration that in some respect poverty is less painful in a hot climate where shelter is of little importance, and where clothes are not needed for protecting the body (provided it has enough pigmentation) and serve purely as ornaments. The tropical poor may be frustrated in their desire for status which expensive garments might bestow upon them but they are more comfortable in their scanty clothes (particularly if they are full of holes permitting ventilation, or amount to next to nothing) than the rich in their heavy and suffocating attire, whereas in a cold climate wealth and bodily comfort go together in every respect. The increasing consumption of clothes is automatically regarded as evidence that the standard of living is rising, but in reality its contribution to welfare is negative because it adds to bodily discomfort and ill-health while the satisfactions flowing from invidious distinctions can never be multiplied.

In Spain and Italy the higher civil servants earn barely enough to live modestly; in most of the countries of Latin America even less, while the university teachers do not even get enough to feed their families and are obliged to take other jobs at the same time— which largely explains why most of them sympathise with re-volutionary movements, and why their scientific output is so meagre. The impossibility of living decently on their salaries makes graft among the Latin American public employees inevitable, but in Africa this explanation obviously does not hold, and we must take into account the need to provide for the numerous kinsmen, the absence of inhibitions and the other factors discussed in the previous chapters. What concerns us here is not venality but the diploma-holding bureaucrats' supreme position on the social pyramid, and from this point of view we must note that whereas the income of their Latin American equivalents is derisory in comparison with that of the big landowners and capitalists, in Africa the big landowners hardly exist and big business remains in the hands of foreigners. In consequence the diploma-holders' supremacy remains by and large unchallenged, except in the areas where a traditional aristocracy has some power, as even in party machines diplomas are of great advantage. Ghana provided a partial exception to this statement when Nkrumah relied on the support of the less educated party functionaries in his struggle to subjugate the educated elite, and rewarded them with posts which in other countries would normally go to graduates. In this way his regime was based to some extent on a curious form of 'class conflict' (using the word class in a very loose sense) between the more educated and the less educated; although the majority in each group were sons of peasants. Nkrumah himself, however, is a graduate.

Until the series of military coups which have occurred towards the end of 1965 and at the beginning of 1966 the army officers remained at the back of the stage; and, though very well paid, did not constitute a prominent part of the elite, which was in marked contrast to the situation in Latin America.

As in all countries with a large mass of poor peasants and labourers, the division between manual and clerical occupations plays a crucial role in the social structure of modern Africa. The demarcation is slightly blurred by the position of the skilled factory workers and other mechanics who regard themselves (and are regarded) as infinitely superior to domestic servants, labourers and peasants; and who often earn more than most clerks. People like servants or porters regard the chance of getting a job in a factory as a wonderful promotion. The highly skilled and well-paid workers, however, constitute a substantial element of the population only in the few big cities, mining areas and oilfields; and even there they are greatly outnumbered by the servants or the clerks. Consequently, the distinction between those who do and those who do not work with their hands constitutes the lower basic line of stratification. Until recent decades significance of this line was enhanced by its coincidence with the distinction between those who could and those who could not read and write. With the spread of education, literacy ceased to qualify a person for a clerical job, but the fact that it did until recently, endowed even an elementary school certificate with an aura of the means of social ascent. It is one of the chief sources of discontent that people, who have struggled hard to get through the school in the hope of qualifying for a clerical job, find that they cannot advance beyond the station of their illiterate fathers, and either have to stay in the village or work as servants or labourers. Anybody who has partaken of a secondary education (without necessarily finishing it) regards using his hands as utter dishonour, and takes great care to dress in such a way as to indicate clearly that he is exempt from this necessity. For this reason, under no circumstances will he wear shorts which are now regarded as a relic of colonialism, and will have a collar and a tie regardless of the heat. The historic roots and the far-reaching consequences of the disdainful attitude towards manual labour will be examined in a moment, but I must emphasise that such outlook is nothing peculiarly African and can in some measure be observed in all countries of the world, including those professing the communist ideology. Nonetheless, whilst ceasing to play this role in the highly industrialised societies, the distinction between the manual and non-manual occupations divides the lower from what might be called the intermediate layer of African societies.

I have used the term intermediate layer rather than the middle class because the occupational composition of the African intermediate layers differs significantly from the aggregates called middle classes not only in western Europe and north America but even in Latin America. As mentioned above, in the most industrialised countries the distinction between the manual and clerical workers is losing importance, while the division between the routine workers on the one hand and the professional and managerial personnel on the other is emerging as the border between the lower and the middle classes, if we overlook the submerged layer consisting of the old age pensioners, the unemployed and the disabled, the impecunious widows and other unfortunates. In Latin America the distinction between manual and non-manual has retained its traditional importance, and therefore the middle classes there have roughly the same lower boundaries as the intermediate layers in Africa, although they differ in many crucial respects, such as mobility and the pattern of segregation—which is the reason why I am using the word 'class' in one case and 'layer' in another. Equally important are the differences in respect of the upper boundaries.

As everywhere else in the world, there is in each African state a small circle of very powerful individuals; but, if we take the criteria of convivial contacts and similarity of habits, we have to include in the elite persons and families whose occupation and income would put them well outside the charmed circles not only in the highly industrial societies but even in the poorest countries of Latin America. Thus in Britain or France lawyers, university teachers and doctors are regarded as belonging to the middle rather than the upper class, whereas in Africa they belong unquestionably to the top layer of society. The professionals are still so few in relation to the total population that they retain a great scarcity value, whilst the number of people in the power elite in the strict sense is so small that they could not form by themselves a closed convivial circle. The unity of the set, who by the European economic and occupational criteria would be assigned to two different classes (viz. the upper and the middle), is promoted by the gulf in respect of income and the mode of living between the professional (in the English sense) and the ordinary white collar employees, which is much deeper than the divisions between these categories in Europe.

The further circumstance which must be taken into account is the paucity of capitalists and the absence of big landowners in tropical Africa. People who in virtue of their wealth would be assigned to the upper class in non-communist Europe or Latin America—let alone the United States—can be counted on the fingers in the smaller African states, and even in Nigeria hardly exceed a few dozen. Most of them, moreover, are politicians who have amassed fortunes during the few years since they have assumed office—and some of whom have already lost them in consequence of the recent military seizures of power. Apart from the paucity of their numbers, the newly rich have not had enough time to spin a web of relationships of friendship and kinship which would unite them and cut them off from the people lower down the ladder, such as the reasonably successful professionals. Even if we adopted an arbitrary numerical criterion and defined the elite as the top 1 per cent in respect of income and prestige, we would have to include all the doctors, lawyers, university teachers and administrative-grade civil servants—which would certainly not be the case in Europe or America.

The boundaries of the top layer have been fixed by the colonial situation in which there was a very wide gap between the salaries and the prestige attached to the posts normally (and in later times at least largely) filled by the Europeans and the lower posts to which only Africans were recruited. The gulf in income, power and prestige was accompanied by residential segregation involving completely different styles of living: while the clerks dwelt in crowded little houses, tenements or even huts, the higher officials resided in spacious and well-furnished bungalows, built in secluded and wooded areas containing a golf course or a swimming pool. Africanisation has changed the personnel but not the differences in pay or housing. Apart from the governor's palace, the residences of the colonial officials did not differ drastically in quality and the way of life was very much the same for all ranks; and this relative homogeneity of the way of life has been preserved by their African successors. On the whole, then, we can say that the upper layer (or the elite, if you like) consists of all those who have stepped into the positions originally reserved for Europeans.

Summarising the foregoing analysis, we can say that the contours of the former colour bar still determine the lower boundary of the elite while the barrier between the clerical and the manual occupations separates the intermediate layer from the common people who constitute no less than 90 per cent of the population.

The chief differentiation within the lower layer is between the townsmen and the rustics, with the former naturally looking down on the latter. Nevertheless, we cannot regard this division as amounting to a definite gradation because the migration to and from the towns is constant and massive, and in any case most of the townsmen are paupers.

One of the chief peculiarities of the African societies (apart from the areas still dominated by the traditional aristocrats) is the fact that the great majority of the members of the upper and intermediate layers originate from the lowest and have started life as children of peasants. This is especially true of the populations which until recently consisted solely of peasants ruled by European officials, whereas the older towns on the West Coast like Freetown, Dakar, Accra and Lagos have a much longer established professional class, many members of which are second or even third generation. Generally speaking, however, we shall not err seriously if we say that (apart from the semi-feudal areas) very few members of the higher layers owe their status to inheritance. In consequence there is very little connection between the bonds of kinship and the lines of stratification, on which point the Latin American class structures offer an extreme contrast. If we look at the Colombian or Peruvian upper class, we find in its midst a number of newly arrived self-made men, but the core consists of a set of families or rather lineages, linked by common descent or intermarriage and long-standing alliance, which have remained at the top for many generations. The upper classes of Latin America are predominantly endogamous and the ties of kinship seldom cross class boundaries, whereas in Africa the new men of wealth and power are related not to other members of the charmed circle but to people right outside it, often at the very bottom of the social ladder. Two or three generations hence the African elites may envelop themselves in a web of exclusive kinship, but (with the partial exception of Sierra Leone where there is a kind of Creole aristocracy) this has not happened yet; and their cohesion is in consequence far lower than that of the upper classes of longer standing in Latin America and elsewhere. In Africa the majority of top people have fathers and blood brothers (not to speak of more distant relatives and the general body of clansmen) who are illiterate peasants. Many of the potentates have several wives acquired during different stages of their careers, ranging from an ageing peasant woman, who continues to pound yams in the backyard, to a young and sophisticated 'party wife' capable of entertaining important guests.

It is not only in Africa, of course, that we can see elites consisting almost entirely of newly arrived men; all the communist elites are similar in this respect. The Soviet elite, though half a century old could not crystallise into a proper class during Stalin's rule owing to frequent purges which amounted to massive reshufflings up and down the social ladder. The resemblance between the communist and the African elites lies in the absence of kinship bonds linking the members of each, but the difference is that the extended kinship groups do not exist in Russia and have presumably been extirpated in China, whereas in Africa they are very strong, and bind the individuals at the top to their kinsmen placed on all the levels of inequality. The cross-cutting of status and kinship gives rise to a pattern which may be roughly described as inequality without segregation.

From a comparative point of view the cases alluded to in the present chapter fall into three types:

(1) The communist type of stratification where inheritance plays a negligible role in the allocation of status throughout the entire society, and where the elite is recruited from the lower strata.

(2) The traditional aristocracies where bonds of kinship are strong and extended but confined to within the class.

(3) The African pattern characterised by the strength and extension of the kinship bonds and their cutting across the lines of stratification.

Inequality in combination with so little segregation produces within extended families new hierarchies based not on seniority but on the amount of success achieved outside. A successful man, who has acquired an elegant modern house, usually has numerous less fortunate relatives in semi-servant status sleeping on the floors throughout the house—even in the drawing room when there are no guests. The bare-footed boys and girls serving the sumptuously-clad host are more often than not his relatives whom he feeds and houses, and sometimes even educates at considerable expense. Apart from those whom he keeps in his house, a successful man normally maintains partly or wholly a large number of relatives of all ages who have stayed behind in the ancestral village or who live in the humbler areas of the town, lodging in the houses of only moderately successful kinsmen either free of charge or in exchange for doing menial chores. In this way wealth flows through a wide network of kinship solidarity—almost in accordance with the communist ideal of 'from each according to his ability, and to each according to his need'. A much more lavish consumption of goods by the winners in the race is not really regarded as contravening this ideal because most people feel that a person must live in a manner befitting his station in life, so long as he helps his less fortunate kinsmen.

The strength of the kinship ties varies enormously from place to place depending on all kinds of circumstances, but by and large the more Europeanised a person is the more inclined will he be to shirk his duties towards the wider kin. There can be little doubt that under the impact of urbanisation, commercialisation and the cultural influences from outside, the general evolution of the African societies is towards a weakening and eventual withering of kinship solidarity; but this process has not yet gone very far and in consequence the situation is extraordinarily fluid. The consciousness of status, the desire to climb and snobbery are very strong, and there is undoubtedly a great deal of class solidarity—in the sense of a collusion among the privileged to keep their advantages intact and the lower orders down—to which the common people reciprocate with resentment or even hatred. Nevertheless, the poor normally exempt from their wrath those 'big men' who are their kinsmen, in whose reflected glory they bask and from whose good fortune they profit or at least expect to do so. The lines of the incipient class conflict are thus blurred by kinship and ethnic affiliations, which up till now have been more decisive in determining political alignments. In consequence the struggle for power at the top affects directly the material interests of numerous individuals at all rungs of the ladder.

The intersections of the vertical and the horizontal bonds prevent a clear-cut crystallisation of conflicts along either class or ethnic lines, and make African political alignments difficult to unravel; particularly as the relative strength of the vertical and the horizontal bonds and antagonisms varies from place to place and fluctuates in time. In this respect tropical Africa stands in a complete contrast to Latin America where class struggles can be observed in pure form, as shown in detail in *Parasitism and Subversion.*

What has just been said does not apply to Ethiopia, Burundi, Northern Nigeria and other areas where traditional aristocracies have retained their dominant position; and, as mentioned earlier, the situation in Liberia and Sierra Leone is also slightly discrepant. The picture given above fits best the biggest cities in the economically most developed areas—such as Abidjan, Lagos and Accra—which are precisely the centres which are setting the path which the rest of Africa will most likely follow.

In the 'coastal' territories of West Africa, even before the establishment of firm administrative control by the colonial powers, a new elite developed in the coastal towns. In Dakar, Freetown, Monrovia, Sekondi, Accra, Lomé, Cotonou, Porto Novo, Lagos and Calabar a 'Creole' elite was formed by liberated slaves, returned to their native continent but by no means necessarily to their native land. They intermarried with local families but the peculiar nature of their experience led them to adopt a European mode of life and outlook and European education. This Creole elite remained socially dominant until the end of the Second World War, and indeed for some years after it, looking with condescension upon the 'natives' of the 'hinterland' and occupying most of the higher administrative positions accessible to Africans.

The three areas in which the purely indigenous traditional elite retained preponderance are Mauritania, Niger and Northern Nigeria—all predominantly Moslem.

In Guinea on the other hand Sekou Touré and his followers, young men with comparatively little formal education and under the influence of Marxism, appealed to the democratic aspects of Islam and were able to build up a mass following and become the masters of the state. Similar superimposition of a new elite took place in Mali. In Ghana too there occurred the phenomenon of a collective ascent of young, ill-educated men, often ex-servicemen or trade unionists, who took their slogans from Marxist writings, and formed the backbone of the C.P.P., the so-called 'veranda boys' despised by the older elite which they replaced.

In many of the new African states there are neither any traditional elites beyond tribal chiefs nor any modern ones. On the eve of independence, the Congo had only a dozen graduates out of a population of 13½ millions. Until his meteoric rise to fame, Lumumba had never been outside the Congo. In Malawi, the expected yield of graduates from internal sources—from the VIth Form of that country's secondary schools—has been calculated thus:

1966	4	1969	8
1967	5	1970	11
1968	6	1971	12

The number of African VIth Forms in the whole of Nyasaland, Northern and Southern Rhodesia, and the three East African territories put together did not reach ten in 1960.

Although the massiveness of ascent differed considerably from country to country, practically everywhere the dismantling of colonial rule opened fabulous opportunities to educated and semi-educated Africans who stepped into the shoes of the British and French administrators. The former occupations of some current leaders of nationalist movements are instructive: Tom Mboya was an assistant sanitary inspector; Patrice Lumumba a postal clerk; Mobutu a jailer; Kenneth Kaunda a teacher; Joshua Nkomo a social welfare worker. Guinea, for example, has the youngest Council of Ministers in the world: in 1959 the average age of Ministers was thirty-nine years; of Secretaries thirty-six. The Minister of Finance was twenty-nine.

The pro-African liberals had hoped that such a massive renovation and rejuvenation of the administrative personnel would stimulate the initiative and will to work, as has happened after the French, the Russian and the Chinese revolutions, but the absence of a real sense of national identity did not favour collective enthusiasm, and so the ultra-rapid promotions merely stimulated personal appetites and even further undermined the belief in the necessary link between the effort and the reward.

In well-organised societies climbing up the social ladder is a very strenuous and time-consuming exercise, the winners in which commonly reach the higher rungs when their hair is already grey and the stomachs ulcerated. The excessive slowness of this process often produces a government by the senile which leads to stagnation. Provided, however, that it does not prevent people from reaching the top before their energy and the abilities wane, and provided that promotion is based on merit, a moderate gerontocracy has the advantage of making people work hard throughout their most effective years in pursuit of the bait of promotion. In addition by the time the champion climbers reach the top the habit of working hard has become to them second nature, while their desire for fun and their ability to enjoy carnal pleasures will in most cases no longer be strong enough to distract them continuously from their duties. Having worked so hard, they will demand the same from their juniors, and their way of life will help to spread the propitious belief that there is a connection between hard work and success. Almost needless to say, this picture nowhere fully corresponds to reality, as even in the countries most renowned for industriousness, like Germany or Holland, we can find idlers who have found themselves in high office through nepotism. Nevertheless, in the successful industrial countries the picture given above is by and large true, and the number of play-boys in positions of authority too small to set the tone.

In contrast, in the new states of Africa many people were catapulted into high office without having done any work apart from scraping through a B.A. examination or organising a few marches and meetings. It must be added that the unusual distinction of having acquired a diploma was more often than not due not to especially hard work but to the good luck of having been picked for secondary schooling by a missionary or the clan elders; for there were many other young men of equal ability and willingness who never got the chance. Owing to the fantastic speed of ascent, the lucky ones never had the time to learn the habits of hard work and responsibility; and they have reached positions of power and wealth in a flighty frame of mind and still full of desire for amusements and carnal pleasures, which quite a number of them satisfy even during the working hours. Added to the innumerable official receptions, such activities detract of course from the work which the high officials do, but equally serious is the influence of their example on the attitudes to work among their subordinates, as well as among the ordinary people who hear about what goes on in high places. We must, of course, keep a sense of proportion and remember that (as the Profumo affair among many others has shown) Africa is by no means the only part of the world where important people spend time on orgiastic amusements. But a difference of degree can be decisive, and in northern Europe such pastimes find addicts principally among the hereditary rich who are not especially interested in power, rather than among active politicians and businessmen, let alone higher civil servants or managers.

In addition to enabling the lucky ones to by-pass a rigorous and protracted grooming, the massive catapulting into high positions, has undermined the incentives for the later entrants into the administrative machine by ruining their chances of promotion. While the lucky ones at the top do not need to work, those who have graduated a few years too late to catch the crest of the wave find little point in working hard for promotion which must be very distant indeed as their superiors are only a few years older, and therefore will not vacate their posts for a long time to come.

Apart from reducing the incentives to effort, the small difference in age between the ranks aggravates the natural resentment against the authority which is usually less bitter if the boss is considerably older than the subordinates. It is not only that the prospect of seeing the old man off sweetens the pill of submission, but also the envy is diminished when the enjoyment of power and status is counter-balanced by the drawbacks of advancing years, while youthful health and exuberance provide an ample compensation for a humbler position and smaller income. This kind of equalisation permits the relationship of authority to become tinged with paternal and filial feelings, which become much more difficult if the difference in age is very small or inverse.

To the above-mentioned deleterious consequences of the narrow age spread we must add the smallness or even the absence of differences in skill between the ranks. A seniority of a few years is unlikely to create a difference in experience which might justify the gradation; and it is a wasting asset; for whereas a man who has worked for five years may have a substantial edge on a colleague who has worked only one year, this advantage vanishes when they have worked for fifteen and eleven years respectively. Actually the situation is even worse than that because the increase in the supply of qualified candidates in combination with the restriction of demand for their services, has made competition much more severe; and consequently the later entrants have better qualifications than the incumbents of the higher positions. An inverse connection between skill and rank cannot fail to produce widespread discontent and foster the growth of secret subversive organisations in the army and civil service. In the meantime, however, the later entrants into the services of states where the prospects of a revolution are not immediate, employ their talents in devising methods of making illicit gains.

The military seizures of power which have occurred recently can in no way be regarded as a final solution of this problem. On the contrary, they have even further rejuvenated the power elite, thus blocking even more thoroughly the avenues of promotion to those a few years younger. The pressure will, therefore, continue to mount but whether further explosions will take place in any given country will depend on the strength of the explosive forces in relation to that of the containing forces of the ruling politico-military machine, determined by its efficiency, cohesion and resources.

The country which suffers most from the blockage of the channels of promotion is Dahomey, where secondary education has become widespread earlier than in other French colonies, and which consequently used to supply a disproportionately large quantity of the administrative and clerical personnel of French West Africa. When this territory was broken up into independent states the Dahomeyan civil servants and clerks were sent home where there is no room for them. The consequent congestion largely accounts for Dahomey's proneness to coups, of which it has experienced a larger number than any other new state in Africa.

It is very difficult for a ruler or manager to maintain discipline, let alone to get keen and efficient co-operation, if he has no promotions to offer as rewards. For this reason Houphouet and Kenyatta, who have been relatively slow about Africanising the higher posts, have much ampler means of keeping their subordinates in order without resorting to the stick than the rulers who have rashly thrown away the possibility of using this useful carrot in the future by quickly getting rid of all the colonials in the civil service and the army. The continuing possibility of promoting Ivorians without demoting others and thus creating mortal enemies may partly account for the absence of revolts in Ivory Coast.

Whereas Dahomey's troubles stem from the excess of graduates and other diploma holders in relation to the needs of its exceedingly rudimentary economy and exiguous resources, the Congo continues to suffer from a catastrophic shortage, not merely of technical and commercial skills (which is usual in Africa) but even of people with any kind of higher education.

The economy of the Belgian Congo was in many ways the most advanced in tropical Africa: indeed the only one which had a fairly ample supply of native skilled workers and lower grade technicians, while the indigenous traders were distinguished for their efficiency. However, while preparing good foundations for future progress in these respects, the Belgian rulers have done less than nothing to develop an elite capable of taking over the higher administrative functions, taking in fact deliberate measures to arrest its growth such as the ban on visits to Belgium and general restrictions on travel abroad. There were no African officers in the Force Publique, no civil servants above a clerk grade, no managers, doctors or lawyers. At the time of independence the Congo had three graduates. Lumumba was a post office clerk and Mobutu a book-keeper in a jail with a rank of sergeant. The contrast with Senegal or Ghana could not be more striking; and as far as the pattern of everyday contacts was concerned, the Congo resembled Kenya or Rhodesia rather than the West Coast. No wonder, therefore, that when the Belgians suddenly handed over government to the Congolese, a general breakdown ensued, which was particularly disastrous owing to the highly authoritarian and fairly centralised organisation of the economy.

Why the Belgians handed over in such a precipitate manner remains a debatable question. They had the strength to contain the feeble movements of protest for many more years but they might have thought that it would be cheaper to grant an independence which would remain purely on paper, and that the Congolese office-bearers could be manipulated and used as a lightning conductor for popular discontent. Many Belgians, however, claim that despite well-founded misgivings about the consequences they were forced into a rash and disastrous de-colonisation by pressure from the U.S.A. government and the American competitors of the Union Minière who wanted to replace the Belgian monopoly by their own neo-colonialist system.

Concerning the Congolese politicians, it is clear that they were too ignorant to act as sensible but not subservient partners and could only behave as either docile puppets or rebellious vandals. The Belgians, too, were unfitted for a partnership by their excessively authoritarian habits and open contempt for the Africans. Reasonable partners cannot be formed in a day, and it is significant that in the former British Africa, the leader who most obviously puts economic co-operation above racialist or pan-Africanist oratory is Malawi's president Banda, who has lived in Britain for over thirty years practising medicine. On the other side of Africa we have a French language poet, Senghor with his French wife, Houphouet-Boigny who has played a prominent role in the French parliament, and the Ghanaian and Sierra Leonese alumni of Sandhurst.

Chapter 11 ECONOMIC AND POLITICAL
            CONSEQUENCES OF POLYGAMY*

As the tenor of family relations determines to a very large extent people's happiness, an estimation of the value of a social order remains incomplete without an examination of this aspect of life. Nevertheless I shall not venture here into the field of comparative ethics beyond repeating the well-known truth that no specific pattern of social relations can be understood and evaluated without taking into account the context in which it functions, as was shown by implication in the earlier chapters in connection with the problem of disintegration of the traditional structures.† The theme of the present chapter is confined to certain important political and economic consequences of polygamy under the conditions of urbanisation and commercialisation, and in particular its impact upon capital accumulation and social mobility, leaving aside whether it is propitious or inimical to happiness or justice.

Polygamy affects the accumulation of capital in several ways. Firstly, it represents a certain form of investment which means that it diverts the capital from other possible uses: instead of buildings or machines men buy wives. In the traditional agricultural society (but not among cattle herders) this was the only kind of investment available; and although additional wives were also acquired for prestige and pleasure, it was definitely a productive investment from the point of view of the man whose wealth depended on the number of wives tilling his field. From the collective viewpoint, the acquisition of wives by any given individual amounted merely to a redistribution of wealth because the women

* Polygamy includes polyandry as well as polygyny, but as the former does not occur in Africa, no misunderstanding can arise from using the wider and less technical term.

† A detailed treatment of the changes in Nigerian family and sexual patterns is contained in a forthcoming book by Iris Andreski: *Old Wives Tales from Ibibioland.*

would be tilling the land anyway, and the only question was whose, although in tribes engaged in incessant warfare polygamy was the only way of ensuring that every woman had a husband, and that neither her working nor procreative powers were wasted. The latter function was particularly important because the survival of the tribe depended on the speed with which the ranks of its young warriors were replenished.

In steeply stratified societies the wives or concubines of potentates do no work, or at least not much, and are looked after by the servants and eunuchs. Some handicrafts may be produced there but on the whole the harems are places of consumption not production. Under urban conditions polygamy ceases to be economically productive at any level because whatever job a woman is doing (whether it is washing, or market trading or nursing) she could be doing it without a husband, who under agricultural conditions had at least to get a field for her to till and to take part in defending it. Among the urbanised rich polygamy has the character of more or less pure consumption. From the point of view of accumulation of real capital (that is to say objects serving production of goods or services) the crucial question is whether collecting wives merely diverts wealth from other forms of consumption, or whether it raises consumption at the expense of saving and investment. To put it in a simplified way: whether the choice is between wives and limousines, or wives and lorries and tools. It is difficult to be absolutely sure about the answer but on the whole it does seem that polygamy diminishes the propensity to save because more rather than fewer limousines will be needed if the wives increase in number. What is even more important in the long run, wives beget children, and therefore polygamy increases the number of dependents. As the number of wives in polygamous societies depends primarily on a man's wealth, this means that the wealthier the man the more children he will have.

The steep positive correlation between the number of children and wealth not only impedes accumulation of capital during the life of the progenitor owing to the cost of maintaining a large household, but it also accelerates the process of dispersion of fortunes in consequence of the large number of heirs. Under the communal property in land, which remains the rule in the traditional African village communities, the property was inherited by the clan and distributed in accordance with the rules which varied from one clan to another, but under the Islamic law or in towns where laws imported from Europe are in force, the property is divided among the sons which means that the more numerous they are the more likely is the capital to be dispersed. Under these circumstances the slow building up of family firms—which was precisely the process through which industry and trade have developed in Europe and America—becomes much more difficult.

Perhaps even more important is the effect of polygamy on vertical social mobility. In a situation where the richer the man the more numerous are his progeny, the unavoidable consequence is that some of them must be eliminated from the charmed circle, unless external conquests are taking place. Constant strife is the natural outcome of such circumstances. Sometimes the extermination of candidates to high office may be institutionalised: in the Ottoman Empire, for instance, a sultan was obliged by law to kill off all his brothers upon his ascension to the throne. In the Central African kingdoms of Ankole and Kitara the sons of the kings had to fight for the succession until only one of them was left alive. Sometimes, however, this process of elimination is peacefully regulated. In Siam the rank of the descendants of the kings (his successors excepted) was lowered after every generation; after the fifth they became commoners.

Extensive polygamy intensifies external and internal conflicts in other ways too. Firstly it accelerates the replacement of the killed, owing to the fact that under this pattern the birth-rate depends only on the number of women available. The result is that killings, i.e., wars and revolutions, must be more frequent. Secondly, polygamy which is always practised more extensively by the upper classes than by the lower, and which therefore produces an upward movement of women, accelerates the numerical increase of the upper classes in relation to the lower because the rank is inherited through the father. If the privileged classes are growing faster than the lower, then, in order to maintain their customary standard of living they must be continually raising their share of commodities produced by the latter, thus exacerbating the antagonism between classes, or they must subjugate outside populations. The same situation may arise, though in a rather milder form, in a monogamous society in consequence of the lower

F

morality among the upper classes, due to their better conditions of living.

Christianity enforced monogamy as the best way of limiting sexual pleasures (of men, of course; women did not count), which were thought intrinsically evil. Its effects on politics were not envisaged. Nevertheless monogamy was one of the chief factors which made European political structures remarkably stable in comparison with Asia, and which made the internal politics of European states relatively free from violence. This was undoubtedly one of the chief causes of the distinctiveness of the Occidental civilisation.

The theory connecting the differences in the rate of numerical growth between upper and lower strata with the variations in the intensity of their conflicts, helps to explain a number of phenomena including certain political events in Latin America, and Asia. The excess of the reproduction rate of the upper classes over the increase in their wealth severely restricts the opportunities for social ascent, which has several far-reaching consequences. In the first place, it ominously lowers the level of ability of the administrative managerial and personnel by excluding many gifted potential recruits and including many medicore but well-connected individuals. Secondly, this limitation of social mobility leads to an accumulation of frustrated ability in the lower classes, thus accentuating their rebelliousness: as on the whole people obey more willingly those leaders who surpass them in relevant skills and ability than those who do not—especially in an epoch when belief in the hereditary transmission of magical powers no longer holds sway. As a further consequence, the present ruling elite could easily be replaced by a new one recruited from below, which improves the prospects of creating a new social order through revolution.

Students of the fascist movements in Europe have noticed the connection between their spread and the distress of the middle class. The same connection existed in Colombia with this difference: there the natural growth of the middle class was even more important than inflation. Indeed, we have here a confirmation of what Francis Bacon said nearly four hundred years ago in his essay 'Of Seditions and Troubles':

'Generally, it is to be foreseen that the population of a

kingdom (especially if it be not mown down by wars) do not exceed the stock of the kingdom which should maintain them: neither is the population to be reckoned only by number; for a smaller number that spend more and earn less, do wear out an estate sooner than a great number that live lower and gather more: therefore the multiplying of nobility, and other degrees of quality, in an over proportion to the common people, doth speedily bring a state to necessity.'

In the essay 'Of True Greatness of Kingdoms' he adds: 'Let states that aim at greatness take heed how their nobility and gentlemen do multiply too fast. . . .'

In Colombia for instance the birth rate is extremely high in all classes, but, owing to their lower death rate, the higher classes reproduce themselves faster than the lower. That this must be so is evident from the survival tables; but the 'whitening' of the population, despite the absence of immigration from Europe, provided additional evidence that this deduction is not mistaken, although here there is the doubt as to the constancy of the criteria on the basis of which people are classified into racial categories. As industrialisation is insufficiently rapid to create a very large number of managerial and highly technical jobs, the young men of the middle classes compete desperately for posts in the civil service or as retainers of politicians. In this respect Colombia is not unique, but the situation there is graver than in Chile or Argentina because the reproduction rate of the higher classes is higher whilst the chasm between the classes is even greater and more closely related to racial differences, which make a downward crossing of class frontiers more repugnant.

In Africa polygamy is universal among the rich Moslems, and common among the rich but not highly educated merchants in non-Moslem areas, but it is less frequent among Christian diploma-holders. Wherever it is prevalent it cannot fail to generate a strong downward current of men. Numerically this may be partly compensated by an upward current of women but it is the men who are likely to fight when forced to go down the social ladder.

The proliferation of the privileged strata stimulates nepotism, as the powerful will do their utmost to find sinecures for their less able descendants. This has three main effects: firstly, it lowers the level of ability of holders of offices; secondly, it blocks the ascending movements and thus aggravates strife; thirdly, it fosters parasitism.

⌈In non-Arabised Africa, especially on the West Coast, polygamy places few restrictions on women's freedom to move about, engage in economic activities and even own wealth. As is well known, market trading on the West Coast is predominantly in the hands of women. With the exception of rich chiefs, the men are glad to see their wives ply trade and bring money home. Men's inclinations run towards parasitism rather than tyrannous jealousy; and in consequence women have developed a spirit of initiative and make better and far more reliable workers than men. However, as we move northwards towards the centres of Islam, the position of women approaches more closely chattel slavery.

It might be worth mentioning in this connection that, contrary to the commonly held view, I do not believe that fatalism—which is often singled out as the most important obstacle to economic progress of the oriental lands—can be regarded as a direct product of religious teaching because there is as much fatalism in the tenets of Christianity (including its Calvinistic variant generally regarded as especially propitious to business enterprise) as in Islam. I am convinced that the most important explanatory factor is the subjection of women. A woman brought up for a life of inescapable slavery—in whom every impulse towards initiative and freedom or even rudimentary self-respect has been stamped out—cannot fail to transmit to her sons a fatalist outlook which, imbibed during the most impressionable years, cannot be erased by later education.

To come back to the position of women in West Africa: the undermining (in many cases a complete destruction) of the traditional pattern of family and marriage—a confusion about the rights and duties, accompanied by a striving towards emancipation on the part of the women and an inclination towards shirking of fatherly duties among the men—has given rise to a furious sex war which provides an inexhaustible topic for chatty newspaper columnists and forms an essential part of the Hobbesian situation.

Chapter 12 THE HIDDEN ASPECTS OF FOREIGN AID*

Only people with little knowledge of the indigent societies can imagine that simply by pumping funds or goods into them we can ensure economic progress. The most obvious obstacle is graft, and the clamour for aid without strings often amounts to little more than demanding freedom to embezzle. Simple misappropriation, however, could be (and to some extent has been) reduced to modest proportions by channelling the aid into concrete projects, such as dams or factories and making it available in the form of goods and services required for construction of these objects. Even in such cases there are considerable opportunities for graft in connection with awarding sub-contracts, but at least the subsidy cannot be entirely wasted, and something concrete will remain.

It is more difficult to avoid the waste occasioned by inefficiency and bureaucratic parasitism. In societies severely afflicted by parasitism the number of parasites seems to be governed by the amount of surplus (surplus being defined as the stock of goods in excess of the minimum subsistence requirements of the producers). An augmentation of the surplus tends to increase the number of parasites and, therefore, their force in relation to the productive elements of society. We have here another vicious circle: the more rampant the parasitism, the stronger are its powers of perpetuation and growth; and the more difficult it is to eradicate it.

An influx of funds from abroad usually stimulates the proliferation of superfluous administrative posts remunerated on a scale incongruous with the economic possibilities of the receiving country, which whets the appetites and fans the scramble for the spoils. This type of waste is seldom criticised because it brings commercial advantages to various interest groups in the donating

* Most of the statements made in this chapter apply equally to the problem of aid to poor countries outside Africa. Hence some repetition of what has been said in Parasitism and Subversion.

countries and direct benefits to the parasitic elements in the international bureaucracies.

Not everybody who advocates aid to the poorer countries is prompted by altruism: when speaking about starving children, he may be envisaging a new post with a large salary and an expense account, free trips, conferences in pleasant places, a pretty secretary and what not. Even in the best administered unilateral schemes of technical assistance a very substantial part of the funds is wasted on needless trips and conferences. In international organisations the waste assumes gigantic proportions.

One could fill a whole book with examples of wanton squandering but I shall mention one incident from my personal observation. When I was living in Port Harcourt, one day the local newspaper carried a notice of the arrival in the town of a photographer travelling on behalf of an international agency which is supposed to be helping the starving children. This institution saw fit to spend a sum which would suffice to feed hundreds of children for years on sending a good-looking woman photographer of twenty-two on a trip of thousands of miles, as if no local residents could be found who would supply photographs of starving children free of charge. In comparison with the international organisations the work of the British Council is wonderfully economic and productive.

Somebody has described the British diplomatic service as a system of outdoor relief for the aristocracy—a diagnosis which fits most diplomatic services of the world. In no other region except Latin America, however, do diplomats weigh so heavily on the economy of their countries as in Africa where the multiplicity and smallness of the states make their cost exorbitant. As on the whole African states trade little with each other and cannot fight, the two chief normal concerns of diplomacy occupy little attention of their diplomats who are free to devote themselves to their purely decorative functions at exorbitant cost to their poor countries. Their proclivities to ostentation and to living beyond their means are further stimulated by the presence of numerous officials of various international agencies, many of whom do little useful work of any kind and devote much time to intrigues. In view of the growing interdependence of the nations, U.N.O. provides a needed forum for discussions but it can neither prevent wars nor rescue the poor nations from their plight. The sorry state of the Congo in the aftermath of the United Nations intervention should dispel any illusions about the capacity of that body to save the poor countries which cannot save themselves.

An additional folly must be mentioned: for the sake of national status and private gain, countries which do not have enough qualified personnel to staff the most essential services delegate to various international bodies an absurdly high proportion of their educated men, who learn there the leisurely habits of a diplomatic existence, and get inveigled into high level intrigues. There is a story—no doubt allegorical—that when Khrushchev met Kennedy he jocularly proposed to draw a joint list of agents so as to avoid paying the same people from both ends.

Both the Americans and the Russian conveyors of diplomatic pressure seem to have found that 'buying' African politicians is very tiresome because (in contrast to similar people in Europe) they cannot be bought but only temporarily hired. Whereas a Dutchman or a Norwegian who has accepted money from a foreign diplomat or secret agent is very much concerned about concealing the fact, and therefore can be compelled to render further services by blackmail and without much further payment, an African politician (provided he shares the money with his kinsmen and friends) will be acclaimed by them as a hero, and may even boast about his cleverness in getting it out of the mean foreigners. Consequently, he cannot be blackmailed, will constantly ask for more, and may even repeatedly and almost openly hold a kind of auction.

To be effective, technical aid must comprise an element of moral education. This does not mean that the members of the less fortunate nations are less moral in private matters or in any absolute sense; but, the absence of customs conducive to efficient work and wise management constitutes at least as serious an impediment to economic progress as the lack of capital. For this reason, the aid can have good effects only if it is administered by people who can give a good example to the citizens of the receiving countries, and this condition rules out most of the agencies active at present in this field. People learn each other's vices much more readily than virtues and pressure groups operating under a cloak of spurious impartiality, and the divergence of values and ethical standards, leave their personnel with no common interest other than the vested interest in their positions and salaries.

The American Peace Corps, the British Voluntary Service Overseas and the equivalent bodies in other countries, provide a valuable education for the youthful volunteers; although even in this respect the outcome is by no means assured because a prolonged stay among people with different customs often stimulates antipathy and contempt instead of liking and understanding. As far as the countries in which these organisations operate are concerned, it is clear that the benefits are not very great and may well be outweighed by undesirable effects. This has little to do with the lack of good intentions on the part of the volunteers—although we must not imagine that they are all prompted by pure altruism rather than by a self-regarding though innocent desire to see the world—and seems to be an inevitable consequence of casting youngsters into the role of mentors of communities with strong traditions of gerontocracy; especially as they know little or nothing about the local conditions, mentality and manners. One does not need an excessive power of empathy to understand why an arrival of juvenile apostles is often felt as an insult which stimulates an ill-feeling towards their country of origin. The resentment is further stimulated by the apostles' adherence to the bland ethnocentric assumption that 'resistance to change'—that is to say the reluctance to adopt the American (or at least the European) Way of Life—can only stem from ignorance. Here we have another example of ideology masquerading as science, for if we study resistance closely enough, we can see that given the circumstances and the scale of preferences, most people do in fact behave more or less rationally so as to maximise their satisfaction. Adam Smith's conception of what makes a society tick was right up to a point: where he has erred was in postulating the ubiquity of the tendency towards a harmony conducive to progress, whereas in reality a trend towards stagnation, decadence or destruction is just as (if not more) likely to result from the interplay of individual interests.

To get back to the Peace Corps and similar bodies: the main point is that although their principal official task is to teach useful skills and organise self-help, the most conspicuous effect of their stay is the undermining of the traditional beliefs without replacing them by anything adapted to the local circumstances. Transmitting the values of an affluent and highly mechanised society to people living under very different customs and in the midst of poverty can only sow confusion. Even if they live frugally by their own standards, the volunteers' habits of consumption appear as princely to the young native men and women and cannot fail to stimulate the latters' dissatisfaction with their lot.

True, there must be some dissatisfaction with one's present lot if any progress is to be made, but it is an error to imagine that this stimulant is wanting in contemporary Africa—apart perhaps from some very inaccessible and conservative (usually Moslem) areas. The stories about the Africans not desiring many material goods are thoroughly out-of-date; on the contrary, the present problem is how to canalise the pursuit of wealth into constructive rather than destructive channels.

Friction and hostility can arise out of all kinds of discrepancies and incompatibilities, and the following example provides an illustration of how good intentions unguided by the knowledge of local circumstances can lead to an unpleasant situation. In a certain town in West Africa an international student association organised a camp for volunteers from Europe and America who had offered to work without pay during their vacations to help to build a school. There were among the volunteers some troublesome individuals who misbehaved or found the work too hard or who simply wanted a trip and had no intention of requiting it, but most of those whom I met seemed quite genuine or even high-minded. Nonetheless, their presence caused a riot, and the police had to be called out to protect them from an angry crowd of local unemployed who felt that they were being robbed of an opportunity to earn something. The organisers conceived the idea—very good in principle—not only to foster international and inter-racial goodwill, but also to do something to enhance the regard for the dignity of labour and to counteract the pernicious association between high status (as indicated in the past by a pink skin) and the contempt for manual work. On the other hand, it is difficult to deny that the local unemployed had some justification when clamouring to do the work themselves when we see that the mere food for an overseas volunteer costs many times more than the normal wage of a native labourer, and that the money spent on transporting one volunteer to Africa and back would suffice to pay a local worker for several years.

The moral which emerges from this example is not that voluntary services can do no good, but only that they are not doing much good as run at present. Let the donating countries not delude themselves: as things stand at present the cost of sending youthful volunteers overseas should be regarded as part of the expenditure on the education of their own people rather than as a cross-continental almonry. Moreover, no matter how operated, the voluntary services of foreigners must have important drawbacks which can be compensated only if their activities form a part of a well conceived and efficacious action aimed at removing the crucial factors of the present predicament. Vague good works benefit chiefly the souls of the benefactors but cannot make much difference to the fate of the sufferers.

On the whole, the aid administered directly by the more prosperous countries remains fruitless chiefly for two reasons. The first is sociological ignorance. Owing to the parlous state of the social sciences, the policy makers receive little guidance from them, and act (or at least have acted until quite recently) upon uncritically accepted and unwarranted assumptions such as the view that industrialisation must bright propserity and social harmony, or that the rate of growth of an industry is governed solely by the supply of capital. These errors, however, appear trifling in comparison with the perversely obtuse determination to ignore the effects of the demographic explosion.

The faultiness of the aid is not surprising in view of the fact that the nations blessed with a relatively decent social order acquired it not through deliberate planning but in virtue of a fortunate and fortuitous confluence of circumstances. Naturally, many beneficial piecemeal reforms have been planned and carried out more or less systematically but the basic underlying conditions (such as, for instance, the decline in the birth rate or the spread of religious tolerance) did not come into existence as products of deliberate policies. The knowledge of how to engineer a good society does not exist and may very well be unattainable because of an ineradicable basic antinomy: social engineering requires power over human beings, which because of its dimensions is inevitably turned to evil ends.

The second reason for the scant fruitfulness of the external aid is that, in spite of the noble phrases it remains subordinated to the goals of buying allies and cajoling customers. The subsidies given to the international organisations, with the aid of which numerous sinecures are created for well-connected persons from countries with exiguous resources, serve the same purpose. It seldom matters to the donors whether their gifts do any good so long as they secure compliance in diplomatic or commercial matters. On the negative side of the balance of aid as operating at present must also be put its tendency to undermine the self-confidence and the spirit of self-reliance, and in the extreme cases to foster a beggar mentality anxious to evade difficult tasks. For this reason, measures designed to help the needy countries to sell their products would have a healthier psychological effect than outright gifts. In any case, what determines the wealth of nations is efficient organisation and hard work, whereas aid from outside can play only a very subsidiary role.*

As misery and strife cannot be eliminated without a slowing down of the growth of the population enlightened aid would necessarily comprise a contribution to the spread of birth control. Nevertheless, although the donors are ready to spend vast sums on measures conducive to multiplication of the sufferers, they refuse to do anything about the factor which makes widespread misery inevitable. One reason for this inaction is that aid in the form of free supply of contraceptive appliances, though more effective in reducing misery than steel mills and highways, could not be

* The fourfold increase in foreign students' fees, recently decreed by the British cabinet in spite of protests from the universities, casts a serious doubt upon the sincerity of their professions of good will towards the poorer countries of the Commonwealth. When the Labour Party came to power it set up with great fanfare the Ministry of Overseas Development which has been endowed with a budget of about 200 million and, it must be added, has created a considerable number of rather pleasant jobs. Now the prophets of aid to the developing countries have decided to try to save a couple of million pounds by shutting the door on the poorer students who lack the connections and money which are becoming increasingly necessary for securing a place at an African or South-Asian university, and who are already handicapped by immigration regulations which make it difficult for them to pay for their studies by part-time work. It is precisely the type of student who gets his education the hard way that is likely to do most for his country, but our socialists obviously prefer the idle sons of sheiks and kleptocrats.

Since it requires no great perspicacity to see that no other form of aid can be more beneficial than helping people to learn useful skills, and that to debar potential future leaders from getting education in this country is the best way of ruining what remains of British cultural, political and even commercial influence, what can we surmise about the background of this decision?

equally spectacular. Moreover, as it concerns topics under a taboo, a discussion of this deadly serious matter often provokes levity which reflects on any reformer active in this field, who runs the danger of being cast into a comic role. And many people would rather risk death than ridicule. In addition to other deterrents, the very finality of this form of aid diminishes its attraction: for if children destined to starvation ceased to come into the world, the fortunate would lose the opportunity of making themselves feel virtuous by giving alms.

On the receiving side the preoccupation with economic development and the desire for foreign aid stems not so much from the concern for the fate of the poor as from the lust for the paraphernalia of power and glory. With a few honourable exceptions, what the rulers want are cars and aeroplanes, wide roads, elegant airports, big buildings and arms. Apart from the lack of altruism, sheer ignorance plays an important role. The connection between overpopulation and poverty cannot be seen in the literal sense, but only understood through moderately abstract reasoning which requires a certain amount of intelligence and the ability to free oneself from mental blinkers; and which is, therefore, beyond the capacity of many politicians and their followers. When the majority is plunged in deep ignorance, only an authoritarian government (provided that it is sufficiently enlightened) can push through a sensible demographic policy, because the voters lack the foresight to support it.

If aid were really designed to alleviate suffering and injustice, the rational policy would be for the donors not only to include an abundant supply of goods and services needed for birth control, but also to make the rest of the aid conditional upon the adoption on the part of the receiving governments of adequate measures of encouragement and propaganda. The concern for the susceptibilities of the receiving nations is overridden easily enough when commercial, military or diplomatic concessions are at stake, and therefore should not be used as an excuse for inaction in this grave matter.

A common excuse for inaction is the claim that the traditional social structures present insurmountable obstacles to the spread of birth control. But if this is the case then we might as well stop pouring money down the drain, suspend all aid and prepare ourselves for the inevitable racial war of extermination. Above all, let us refrain from any attempts at peace-keeping and allow the unfortunates to dispatch one another to the grave—for surely it is preferable to fall in battle than slowly starve to death.

Some benighted demographers have been issuing warnings that we must not foist birth control upon traditional societies before studying its possible deleterious social and psychological effects. That such effects are possible or even probable I would not deny. I would go even further and say that a suspension of natural selection—that is to say, of elimination of the unfit—must bring about a biological degeneration unless it is replaced by some artificial technique performing the same function. The eugenic problems are very important in the long run but the most urgent task is to avoid a global starvation and holocaust. To delay pressing for birth control because of its possible dislocating effects upon the structure of agrarian societies (which in any case are being shattered by the population pressure, apart from other cultural forces) is like dilly-dallying about calling the fire brigade when the house is on fire because squirting water might ruin the furniture.

Actually, if only the leaders of the few richest countries—perhaps even of the United States alone—were enlightened and courageous enough it would be quite feasible to stabilise the world's population by applying the following policy. Firstly, the amount of aid offered should be substantially increased but the actual granting thereof should be made conditional upon the willingness of the receiving governments to allow the donors to organise extensive family planning networks in the receiving countries, just as the oil companies are allowed to set up their distribution services. Such birth control stations would not only dispense the requisite devices and services free of charge, but would also make a payment to every woman who had undergone the treatment as well as to her husband. Subsequently a small yearly or even monthly payment would be made to them for retaining the device, or simply for not being pregnant, and medical assistance would be offered to their living children. Some arrangements could also be made to induce people who have not yet had any children to space them out. Naturally, the details would have to be adapted to local circumstances.

Of course such a scheme would require a tremendous effort and expense if it were to be applied on an adequate scale. Apart from providing the money, it would be necessary to train more than a million medical assistants, to build thousands of clinics, to set up an administrative machine capable of keeping check on millions of women, taking their fingerprints and ensuring that the funds and the equipment are not misappropriated. Nonetheless, all this would in all likelihood cost less than what is spent on the useless or even harmful gadgets like supersonic airliners and telstars, not to speak of the crazy race to the moon. It would certainly cost less than the weapons and soldiers employed, or about to be employed, in keeping at bay the proliferating and increasingly desperate multitudes.

Concentrating the aid on those who are willing to help themselves (and whose rulers will allow them to do so) may seem a cruel policy, but it is the only one which holds out a hope of a real and permanent improvement. Indiscriminate charity may help the lucky few—although even that is not certain because one extra meal per year may not make much difference—but it is mainly good for the soul of the donors, and is like trying to stop a flood with a bucket.

Forcing birth control upon starving peoples, however, will be regarded as proof of hostility so long as the donating governments do not adopt a more enlightened outlook at home; because encouraging one's compatriots to multiply, while telling another race not to, can easily be interpreted as (or even really amount to) a form of aggression which calls for a retaliation.

So long as the birth rate remains at the level prevalent in Africa at present the choice is not between democracy and social justice on one side and despotism and exploitation on the other, but between hostile and friendly tyrannies; and the only attainable goal of foreign aid can be the purchase of allies and customers. Hospitals and schools cannot do much good if people have to starve as soon as they leave these laudable institutions. And simple arithmetic suffices to show that they must starve so long as they multiply so fast.

Chapter 13   NEO-COLONIALISM

In contrast to imperialism pure and simple—that is to say, the tendency to expand the area of political control by force of arms, neo-colonialism (or economic imperialism as it is called in Latin America) is an elusive phenomenon. A conquest is normally a deliberate act, but control over a country's economic life may pass into the hands of foreigners without any concerted endeavour on the part of the latter, and simply because the foreigners are more willing to engage in commercial and industrial pursuits or possess greater skill. In such a case the outcome may be economic domination but we can hardly describe the spontaneous process which led to it as imperialism. We must remember, however, that a process of economic penetration which began as an unintended product of uncoordinated activities of many traders becomes deliberate and concerted when control over economic activities comes to be concentrated in a few hands.

Strictly speaking we could apply the term economic imperialism (of which neo-colonialism is a variant) to all cases of concerted striving on the part of the nationals of one country to extend their control over the economic life of another country, without attempting to become its official rulers. If fully successful, however, economic imperialism ceases to be merely economic because if all the wealth is in the hands of foreigners the national government can hardly avoid being a puppet. And as the history of the British East India and Dutch East Indies Companies shows, commercial penetration may lead to an outright conquest. Conversely, every conquest or extension of a sphere of influence, even if it is motivated by purely strategic or diplomatic considerations, affects the distribution of wealth, and therefore there can be no purely political imperialism, although the importance of the economic aspect varies greatly. For these reasons, the concept of economic imperialism is not easy to employ, particularly as it carries pejorative undertones which imply that extension of economic control across political frontiers is always evil.

To the 'liberal' economists all commercial transactions appear beneficial to all concerned, and they see no reason why the benefits bestowed upon a country should diminish when these activities are carried out by foreigners. The Marxist propagandists in contrast, depict the activities of foreign businessmen as *a priori* detrimental to a country, making the assumption that all private commerce is harmful, which is clearly absurd in view of the fact that capitalism is so far the only system which at least in some countries has succeeded in eliminating mass poverty. Both the 'liberal' economists and the Marxists are wrong: activities of foreign businessmen may either benefit or impoverish a country, depending on the circumstances under which they take place. It remains true, however, that from a nationalistic standpoint it is possible to regard dependence on foreigners as evil even if it brings economic benefits.

In his book on neo-colonialism Nkrumah takes it as too obvious to require examination that the amount of foreign investments constitutes an indubitable proof that the African countries are badly exploited. On the other side, the economists of the creditor countries speak as if every loan had to benefit the receiving country. In reality, a loan may be harmful or helpful according to the conditions on which it is given and the use to which it is put.

Lending at interest for unproductive purposes really amounts to preying on weakness, and the medieval schoolmen were right in condemning it. Indeed, it is only when the capital is used for increasing production that lending at interest can be socially useful; and unfortunately many international investments do not differ greatly from the harmful usury of a village money-lender who exploits the improvidence of his clients. To this category belong the loans given to the rulers of African states for the purpose of buying arms or erecting ostentatious buildings or monuments, or distributing gifts to their friends and supporters. It is impossible to know exactly how large has been the proportion of investments of this kind but it seems that it has been very substantial in the worst governed countries. It may, of course, be said that the use to which a loan is put is the responsibility of the borrower, but it is difficult to absolve the creditors from guilt when they know that the funds will be squandered by the kleptocrats, whereas the money for repayment will be extorted from their unfortunate subjects. Such investments amount to collusion in oppression and exploitation.

Like so many other political expressions, neo-colonialism is a pejorative term applied indiscriminately or shunned absolutely according to ideological preferences. There is little agreement about its meaning even among those who habitually use it, and it covers almost any kind of contact between the highly industrialised and the economically backward countries, ranging from politically uncontaminated trade to outright military intervention. As far as the latter is concerned, there is not much point in calling it neo-colonialism, as it constitutes the oldest and the most common instrument of subjugation. So it seems advisable to restrict the meaning of 'neo-colonialism' to the exercise of power based on economic and technical superiority without assuming formal sovereignty and without a recourse to arms. As the possession of power, however, seldom fails to bring some profit, we could emphasise the economic end-result and define 'neo-colonialism' as 'the exercise of political influence in a legally foreign territory on the basis of economic power and with the aim of enhancing or maintaining profits'. There can be little doubt that in both senses 'neo-colonialism' is a very real phenomenon, although it is something new only in those parts of the world where political suzerainty as well as the economic power was until recently in the hands of foreigners. In China a very similar situation used to be called semi-colonialism. In Latin America this form of domination has operated ever since the collapse of the Spanish empire, and there it is labelled imperialism. The practice of influencing foreign politics through bribery naturally goes much further back, but the tremendous disparity in economic power between industrialised and non-industrialised countries, coupled with their mutual dependence, has created new incentives and new possibilities for applying economic pressure which have no parallels in the earlier epochs. In the pre-industrial world a powerful monarch had a very much larger amount of wealth at his disposal than a tribal chieftain, but an ordinary inhabitant of a big kingdom was no richer (and was often much poorer) than a tribesman whose resources might have been slightly more exiguous but who did not have to support a parasitic aristocracy or officialdom. Nor did the empires and the surrounding tribes have much need for each other's products. We can fairly safely surmise that Roman vases did not appeal to the Teutonic chieftains so irresistibly as do Cadillacs to the sheiks of Arabia today.

The first step towards understanding the phenomenon of neo-colonialism in the sense indicated above must be an examination of the main ways in which it operates, the most obvious interpretation being in terms of sheer commercial bargaining power. There are grounds for claiming that the poor agricultural countries do not get fair prices for their products, while having to pay too much for manufactured imports, because the latter are produced and marketed principally by giant companies able to manipulate the prices as well as the quantities offered, while the agricultural produce comes from smallholders selling in perfect competition and often even operating under the conditions of negative elasticity of supply—which means that when the price drops the quantity put on sale increases rather than decreases. This can happen because such small farmers do not aim at maximising the difference between the costs and the proceeds—which they could hardly do without accountancy—but try to earn a given sum which would enable them to buy whatever they need most. Moreover, as the factors of production—their labour and the land—often have no alternative uses (and therefore no exact price), a reaction to a drop in the price of the produce leads to an increased production thereof. As everybody knows on the other hand, a giant monopoly tends to restrict the supply so as to keep the price up and to secure the largest possible net profit. Nonetheless, it is not easy to judge a claim that a sovereign country (one, that is to say, which cannot be taxed from outside) is being exploited in consequence of the unfavourable terms of trade . . . for how can we tell which terms of trade are fair? We could surmise there must be exploitation where a monopsonist (i.e. sole buyer) deals with a large number of unorganised sellers, but as far as the dealings between the Africans and the foreign businessmen are concerned, this is most obviously the case on the labour market and it is common knowledge that the expatriate firms treat their workers a great deal better than the indigenous firms or the state-owned industries like the railways or the post office.

To remedy the weakness of the peasant producers various marketing schemes have been devised in African countries—mostly still under the colonial rule. To prevent foreign big buyers from bargaining directly with illiterate peasants and beating the price down, state corporations were set up to buy produce from the peasants and sell it abroad more advantageously in virtue of a massive bargaining power. After independence, however, these schemes ceased to help the peasants because the state (most notably in Ghana) insisted on a big margin between what it paid to the peasants and what it got from foreign buyers while dishonest administrators proceeded to exact big rake-offs on their own account, as shown in the chapter on kleptocracy. To the peasant it does not make much difference whether the monopolistic power which reduces what he gets for his produce is in the hands of the foreigners or the indigenous rulers, except that if the latter is the case, then he might expect theoretically to get some of it back in the form of roads, medical care, education and similar dispensations. In fact, however, this happens to a very small extent, as most of the wealth appropriated by the government is consumed by their top personnel. An enquiry conducted in 1967 in Ghana by a special commission into the activities of the agencies responsible for cocoa-buying and marketing under Nkrumah found farmers so distrustful of their compatriots on these bodies that they expressed a wish for the return of the former European buyers.

Though it is very difficult to assess its dimensions and consequences, the use of superior bargaining power undoubtedly constitutes an important element in the cluster of phenomena which can be called 'neo-colonialism'. Equally important, however, (and more pregnant with deleterious consequences) is the method of securing high profits by bribing the indigenous politicians and officials. On a small scale this can be done on an entirely private level without meddling in high politics, but big affairs of this kind cannot fail to impinge on international relations, particularly as the foreign firms may induce their governments to foster their interests by applying diplomatic pressure or even by instructing their secret services to lend a helping hand. This is most likely to happen where strategically essential supplies are concerned or where resistance to commercial penetration is mixed up with communist infiltration. Trade may no longer follow the flag but it still follows political influence which it fortifies in return. Foreign businessmen may get help from their governments for three distinct (though not mutually exclusive) reasons; (1) in virtue of their efficacity as a pressure group at home;

(2) because of the benefits which they bring to the economy of their country as a whole; (3) owing to their contribution towards extending or maintaining the political influence of their government in the countries in which they operate. In these days of far-reaching governmental control of trade, commercial and financial dependence inevitably entails some degree of political subordination. Whether this leads to something which might be legitimately called exploitation depends on how great is the disparity of strength between the trading partners and how upright and principled are the rulers and administrators on both sides—for the more self-seeking and money-grabbing they are, the more willing they will be to serve as tools of exploitation of the weaker by the stronger.

Acquisition of wealth by force is common at all stages of civilisation and the examples thereof range from a tribute exacted by one small band from another to the massive confiscations which took place during the Second World War and its aftermath. A somewhat subtler procedure of this kind is an alteration of the terms of trade by open or veiled threats of which we have examples in the commercial treaties concluded with various eastern European states by the Germans before and during the last war, and by the Russians afterwards. To this very day Poland, Czechoslovakia, Bulgaria, Hungary and Eastern Germany are obliged to buy from the U.S.S.R. many kinds of goods at prices well above what they would have to pay elsewhere, and to sell to it other goods below the prices on the world market. However, as the internal prices as well as the rates of exchange are arbitrarily fixed, it is difficult to calculate the resulting gains and losses.

Unlike the expeditions at the beginning of the century, the recent interventions by the U.S.A. in Guatemala and Santo Domingo had the aim of preserving the social and economic systems in these countries, and of keeping them within the American political orbit, rather than of protecting specific commercial interests of its citizens; although it must be admitted that the two aims were intertwined. Similar interwovenness of trade and politics can be observed in Africa today where, for instance, the French troops help indirectly the commerce of their compatriots by making themselves useful as an internal police to the African rulers who are willing to maintain the diplomatic, commercial and cultural links with France. In other words, in exchange for propping them up, the French are able to obtain from the francophile African rulers considerable commercial preference. The British are much less adept at this, as can be seen from the situation in Tanzania where Nyerere (who would have been overthrown by a military mutiny had the British troops not come to his rescue) continues to twist the ex-lion's tail economically as well as politically. Whether the commercial advantages obtained by the French method amount to exploitation depends in the first place on comparative prices: for if by political or military moves the French induce the Africans to buy from them, then the magnitude of the latter's loss will depend on the difference between the French prices and those of other possible suppliers. Even if the Africans were losing considerable amounts in this way, we would have to set them against the sums received as aid in order to find out whether in fact they are being exploited; although we would also have to consider how the aid is being spent and whether it does not in reality amount to something more than mere bribes given to the rulers to satisfy their thirst for palaces and other prestige buildings. Judicious estimates of exploitation would be of great value but despite all the talk about neo-colonialism nobody has up till now attempted to provide them.

There are no grounds for doubting whether the Romans did exploit their empire when we know that they imposed heavy tributes, carried into slavery large number of the inhabitants, expropriated most of the landowners and robbed all the treasures. It is equally obvious that there is exploitation in South Africa where most of the land has been appropriated by the descendants of the conquerors, and where people of conspicuously non-European descent are prevented by law from engaging in more profitable occupations, setting up businesses, buying land and so on. It is also reasonably clear that there was exploitation in the Congo (particularly in the early days) when the natives were forced by a capitation tax or straight conscription to work in the mines while receiving very little benefit from the exportation of what they have dug out, and when large tracts of land had been seized and appropriated by the European colonists: although an apologist of the Belgian rule could claim that most of the gains from mining returned to the Congo in the form of new investments which went into buildings, cities, roads, harbours and so on. Most of the colonies, however, were less profitable than the Belgian Congo and in many cases it is debatable whether more wealth was taken away than put into them or the other way round. Some of the colonies with scant natural resources (like the Somaliland or Haute-Volta) had to be subsidised, and they were acquired for strategic or prestige reasons, or under the promptings of the expansionist tendencies of the colonial bureaucracy. Vilfredo Pareto has argued that the Italian colonies in particular were completely unprofitable, and that their chief effect upon the Italian economy was to effect a transfer of wealth from the totality of the taxpayers (who were bearing the cost of colonisation) to the restricted groups who were making big profits in the business with the colonies or occupying remunerative posts in the colonial administration.

Nefarious activities of private firms and individuals bolstering up their profits by bribing the African politicians and officials into committing their state to unprofitable deals, may add up to something which could be called neo-colonialist exploitation, but on the level of government policy there is no evidence of any general conspiracy among the industrial nations to keep the prices of their exports up and of the imports from the under-developed countries down: there seems to be no world-wide cartel-like squeezes and the competition among the exporters of industrial goods and competition among the importers of raw materials appears to be quite brisk.

From the point of view of strictly economic calculation, the terms of trade with the underdeveloped regions are of secondary importance to the industrialised nations. The real danger to Britain, for instance, is that it might be driven out of the markets by German or Japanese competition—not that it might have to pay Nigeria more for wood. It would matter a great deal to any of the chief industrial exporters if it could buy raw materials from Africa or anywhere else more cheaply than its competitors, but if they all have to pay the same price, it does not matter all that much what that price is . . . within certain limits, naturally, because a hundredfold increase would certainly make a difference. The reason for the relative unimportance of the price of raw materials is that they represent a very small fraction of the total costs of manufacturing. On the other hand, what matters most from the strategic point of view is whether certain key materials can be got at all. When it is the question of who will get the uranium from the Congo or molybdenum from Vietnam the most drastic means will be employed—ranging from propaganda and bribery to guerilla warfare and massive armed intervention. It seems less credible, however, that strong diplomatic pressure would be exerted or the secret services called into action for the sake of preventing the price of a bar of chocolate from rising from sixpence to ninepence. Such matters may be of considerable importance to individual importers who have to compete with other firms, but for the governments of the European states (let alone the U.S.A.) these are trifles. Seeing the big blotches on the maps and hearing romantic talk about the developing countries too few people realise how small is the wealth of Africa. The aggregate purchasing power of Nigeria—the most populous country in Africa—is less than that of a city like Manchester or Düsseldorf. In view of this disparity, no industrial country could base its welfare on exploit-ation of Africa because even if they reduced the income of the Africans to nothing they could increase their own only by a small percentage. On the other hand, exports make such a small contribution to the income of the average African that even if their prices were doubled he would hardly feel the difference. Furthermore, the considerations of strategy and international politics are often given precedence over the questions of commercial advantage.

Ours is a strategically-minded age, overshadowed by the struggle for world domination between super powers, in which economic power is used to secure political advantage rather than the other way round: and in consequence even the questions of the markets often assume an 'all-or-none' character. The overriding concern of the U.S.A. government is not that they may have to pay more for tin or rubber but that important sources of such materials may be denied to them altogether if they fall into the hands of the communists whose power will be thereby enhanced relatively as well as absolutely. Manipulation of the African governments by the bigger powers is something very real—and we can call it neo-colonialism if we wish—but it is something practised by the communists at least as assiduously as by the capitalist powers—and, to repeat, the chief motivations stem from power politics rather than the desire for profit, although it would be going too far to say that the latter plays no part at all.*

* The 'dollar imperialism' in Latin America is examined in *Parasitism and Subversion*.

This is how Carey Jones describes what was happening when Kenya was acceding to formal independence:

'As the transition period progressed foreign interference began to play a larger part. Foreign funds flowed in to K.A.N.U., the party likely to win. Some of this, no doubt, was a matter of keeping in with the future government and more on a par with those in business, particularly Asians, who were persuaded to make subscriptions for fear of victimisation later on. The foreign funds, however, did not go into party coffers, but into the hands of individuals, and different individuals became the disposers of funds from different countries. This, of course, made personal divisions within K.A.N.U. acute and the buying of support and votes became common. A leading politician, three months before the elections for internal self-government, who had been watching this, said: "If I had enough money and wanted to do so, I could start a new party today and win the election in three months time."

'The effect of this foreign money was wholly evil and disruptive. It set up powerful foci of differences within the governing party, each focus being in some degree a vassal of the foreign country supplying the funds. The seeds of division within the post-independence African leadership were securely planted and well watered with golden showers. The different vassals were given the power to buy support and divide counsel. The natural forces making for division were sufficient, without this reinforcement, to make unity difficult. The effect was likely to paralyse a sane appreciation of problems. All the nutshells and shibboleths of the outside world—free enterprise, non-alignment, socialism, pan-Africanism, anti-mercenaries, anti-South-Africanism—became firmly embedded in the Kenya scene. Kenya in becoming independent was already becoming dependent, but to several masters.' (*The Anatomy of Uhuru*; (pp. 142-3) N. S. Carey Jones, Manchester University Press, 1966.)

One of the more effective methods of neo-colonialism consists of supplying weapons free of charge in exchange for diplomatic compliance or commercial concessions: and it may be coupled with a military protection against the neighbours or against internal uprisings as is the case with the relationships between

Britain and Kuwait. We should not imagine, however, that the gifts of weapons give the supplier an infallible control over the recipient: in Indonesia, for instance, the army has employed the Soviet weapons in the greatest massacre of communists ever carried out. Nasser, too, keeps a large number of communists in jail in spite of gifts of arms and money from Russia. The power which the supplier can exercise depends on the availability of alternative sources of supply and on the urgency of the need. At the moment supply is easy because of the abundance of obsolescent weapons which can be given away at very little cost to the donor. On the other hand, the demand for weapons has so far not been very great in Africa except in Ethiopia and Somalia which have a bitter frontier dispute.* Moreover (in contrast to Latin America) no large forces are needed for an internal use because the common people are so fragmented ethnically and so lacking in class consciousness that the danger of concerted mass uprisings seems remote. Nevertheless, the armed forces may be expanded either to satisfy the vaingloriousness of the rulers or in response to the expansionist tendencies of the officer corps.

On the whole it seems that the influence of the former rulers or the new American, Soviet or Chinese mentors can be preponderant only where the government is so weak that it cannot maintain order without foreign help, as is the case in the Congo. Similarly, the influence of expatriate officials and experts is strongest where they are most indispensable—that is to say, in the countries where even the minimally qualified men are too few to staff the administration, which is the case in East but not West Africa. Normally an expatriate official will favour his country of origin in some ways, but we must not under-rate the strength of the emotional bond with the country in which they work, which in some cases is very great.

The predatory aspects of neo-colonialism constitute a special case of the more general phenomenon of parasitic involution of capitalism. In Latin America the indigenous as well as expatriate capitalism has been affected by this tendency. In Africa, however, the indigenous capital is still very exiguous and in consequence it is mainly the foreign capital which is drawn towards a parasitic involution. The chief cause, however, is essentially the same; namely, the absence of social forces which

* Written before the Biafran war.

might canalise the capital into uses beneficial to the general population.

The chief concern of businessmen is to make money, and their choice of the means to that end depends on the relative difficulty of various types of activity. So there is no reason to assume that they will choose to behave in ways that are socially useful if socially harmful methods of conducting business bring larger rewards. Investments of capital in bribery (for the purpose of driving a competitor out of business, for example) may be very profitable but socially they are not merely unproductive: their indirect consequences cause a diminution of aggregate wealth.

A thorough involvement of businessmen in political strife and graft not only gives them harmful means to keep the wages down and the prices up but also affects adversely the possibilities of small businessmen who cannot use political influence so effectively as the big capitalists. Particularly important in this context is the stranglehold which small cliques or big capitalists have on credit facilities, which enables them to make enormous profits on usury, but this applies much more to the native capitalists with political connections than to foreigners.

Capitalism tends towards a productive orientation when the capitalist entrepreneurs can neither use coercion for the purpose of parasitic exploitation, nor are so devoid of strength as to be exposed to exploitation themselves—in other words, when businessmen are too weak to prey upon the other classes, but too strong to be preyed upon. Such a situation—which in my previous books I have proposed to call the situation of equipendency—requires a certain degree of balance of power between the business elite and the political elite. An important implication of the principle of equipendency is that capitalism can function beneficently only in a society where money cannot buy everything, because if it can, then the power of wealth can have no counterweight and a parasitic involution ensues.

Prevalence of graft increases the power of money because it nullifies the force of legal constraints and reduces to impotence even those rulers who might be personally incorruptible; and for this reason the African governments can seldom oppose socially harmful uses of wealth. This is a common failing elsewhere too but in Africa it assumes more extreme forms than in the more prosperous countries. Under these circumstances politics becomes a strictly money-making activity, and capitalist groups invest in it large sums—an expenditure equally wasteful and even more pernicious than advertising from a social point of view, but which brings rewards in the shape of concessions, permits, contracts and the leniency of tax-collectors. The nature of such transactions prevents us from discovering the magnitude of the sums involved but we can be fairly certain that they are substantial.

As they have few incentives to behave responsibly or even to obey the laws, it is not surprising that businessmen, foreign as well as indigenous, augment their profits by dishonest means and resort to massive tax evasion, although the expatriates undoubtedly pay more taxes out of a given income than the local potentates. In addition to the obvious method of outright buying fiscal leniency with bribes, there are many other tricks such as purchasing goods or services at exorbitant prices from another firm owned by the same shareholder in order to deflate the profits of the first. This dodge is also used for circumventing the restrictions on repatriating capital; and it is difficult to see how it could be forestalled even by an incorruptible civil service because who is to say whether the price paid for some imported goods is too high or not? In supplying public bodies, shoddy goods or phoney medical supplies may be delivered and the key officials bribed into accepting them. Obversely, public property may be sold at absurdly low prices in exchange for bribes. As in the days of Cecil Rhodes (though not on an equally grand scale) the acquisition of lands (be it merely as temporary concessions) often entails recourse to sharp practice or even clear fraud, the most common being a legalistic distortion of the land tenure. For example, a headman or chief, who in customary law is merely a guardian of the communal property, will be construed by legal subterfuges into an owner in the sense of the English or French law and then induced to sell the land. This will usually cause a commotion but bribed officials will arrange for the transfer of ownership to be enforced by the police or even the army.

It must be remembered, however, that bribing officials, politicians and officers may not only be the easiest way of smoothing one's path, but it may even be a condition of remaining in business, as any firm which refused to play the game would be handicapped in competing with less scrupulous rivals. So the big firms employ public relations managers (usually Africans well connected with the top people) whose task is to pass the bribes. The expense thus incurred is more than recovered through evasion of taxes or import duties or passed on to the consumer in higher prices. The only thing that could be said in justification of these practices is that the administrative machine is so cumbersome, disorderly and slow that it would bring the business to a complete standstill if its cogs could not be moved by bribes.

If we want to apportion the shares of guilt for the sorry state, we must blame in the first place the richer and more powerful: although we must take into account that exploitation and graft are just as common in Ethiopia as in the former colonies. It is more useful, however, to concentrate on the factors which have brought about this state of affairs and contribute to its perpetuation. Earlier I have indicated the circumstances which stimulate the predatory and venal proclivities in African societies, as well as the difference in attitude to the country of residence between the old style colonials and the commercial employees who now predominate among the expatriates. The most general factor underlying the deleterious aspects of foreign commercial penetration of Africa today, however, is the disparity of size between powerful big business from the northern hemisphere and the invertebrate African states. Given the extent of social dislocation, venality and cut-throat struggle for money would be rampant in Africa in any case, but the presence of commercial giants able to offer bribes which are irresistible in the midst of general misery, creates another unmanageable impediment to improvement of political morality.

The colonial administration systematically favoured the trade of its compatriots. Nonetheless, during the last decades it acquired a genuine concern for the welfare of its subjects, and did in fact try to do something for their welfare. With the exception of Kenya, Rhodesia and Algeria where the settlers were so numerous that they were appropriating a very large share of wealth, and of the Congo (and to a lesser extent Northern Rhodesia) where the returns on the capital were quite extraordinary, the colonial rule was comparatively beneficial by the standards of the utilitarian ethics, even though it remained very far from the liberal ideals. For the ordinary Africans the last decades of the British and French colonial rule were a golden age of prosperity and peace when they were treated better than ever before or since. Owing to the paucity of its personnel, the colonial administration had the additional advantage of being relatively cheap. The officers lived very comfortably but without extravagance—indeed much more modestly than their African successors—and what is more important, they were far fewer. With the exception of the Congo, the colonial governors, though co-operative, were not mere stooges of businessmen and did occasionally defend the interest of their wards as they understood them.

While leaving or even enlarging the mercenary element of the population, decolonisation has removed the relatively responsible element and replaced it by predatory elites severely addicted to proliferation. Consequently, parasitic suction increased drastically—tripling perhaps—less wealth remained for productive investment, and the new rulers became more dependent, collectively as well as personally, on money supplied by foreign big business than the colonial civil servants ever were.

The purchasing power of the population cannot be suddenly increased because it is limited by the amount of goods produced, which is limited by the existing skills, equipment and resources; whose growth depends (among other things) on the demand for their products. As is well known, economic expansion consists of a beneficent circle of increasing production creating demand for the goods, which in turn stimulates the growth of production and so on; whereas constriction or stagnation creates the opposite vicious circle. Parasitic suction is not only unjust, but it also prevents the expansion of the economy by restricting the market. Transfers of the purchasing power from the masses to the privileged few act as a brake upon the growth of production because they reduce the market for goods which can be produced cheaply in large quantities, and swell the demand for luxury goods and personal services. Furthermore, they lower the efficiency of labour by debilitating the workers and depriving them of incentives. There would be some advantage in an extremely unequal distribution of income if the rich invested most of their wealth in expanding production but this is not at all the case in the African states. The booty of the potentates is mostly spent either on lavish ostentation or on dispensing largesse to innumerable relatives—which in either case means consumption which does not depend on making a contribution to the production of wealth. The part which is saved is either tucked away in Swiss banks or invested in real estate in the cities. As the accumulation of capital takes place mainly through manipulation of political power the big African capitalists have neither the time nor the skill to manage industrial establishments and prefer the simpler task of collecting rent. The export of capital to foreign hiding places cannot, of course, be measured but it certainly involves sums which (though moderate by the standards of big Latin American kleptocrats) are very substantial in relation to the poverty of the African countries. The export of parasitically acquired capital aggravates the economic difficulties which fan strife and thereby endanger the prospects of the rulers continuing in their present position. This danger makes them even more eager to provide for a comfortable life in exile, thus further aggravating the capital drain . . . a perfect vicious circle which can be found in most poor countries of today, with the exception of those which have fallen into the strait-jacket of totalitarianism.

The permanent economic crisis, engendered by parasitism and the export of illegally acquired funds, has several unfortunate effects upon the behaviour of foreign business. Firstly, as the market contracts or at least fails to grow as fast as the population, investment in manufacturing or distribution for the local population becomes or remains less attractive than extraction of minerals and oil, or plantations producing exclusively for overseas markets. As the profits from exports thus generated are either repatriated by the foreign firms, or appropriated by the parasitic elite and then also invested abroad, the population benefits very little from these activities, particularly as wages remain low owing to widespread unemployment. The vicious circle is completed by the factor of uncertainty (itself largely due, as just said, to the permanent economic crisis) which makes foreign businessmen eager to repatriate their capital as quickly as possible, unless the profits are high enough to compensate the risk of destruction or confiscation.

It must also be mentioned that in East Africa the anti-Indian currents have had an extremely deleterious effect on business. Like the Jews in pre-war Poland and Rumania, the more the Asians are persecuted, the less willing are they to behave in ways beneficial to the country, and the more eager to make profits quickly (and if need be dishonestly) and to locate their capital abroad. Being much less numerous in proportion to the population, and far from having a monopoly on trade, the Lebanese and Indians in West

Africa, although often targets of ill-feeling in times of crisis, have never aroused the animosity shown towards the Indians in East Africa. Stemming primarily from the struggle for scarce opportunities for making a living, the persecution of the commercial ethnic minority further aggravates the general poverty which has sparked it initially.*

Fearing for their possessions, the big foreign firms are inclined to try to make sure that their men get to the top or remain there, and thus get drawn right into the political arena. The political influence of big business is, of course, nothing new and it can be seen in all the capitalist countries. However, in the relatively law-abiding polities such an influence is exercised through the means of donations to a sympathetic political party and newspapers or other controllers of mass media, whereas in dictatorial but corrupt one-party states only the more pernicious weapon of bribery can be used for this purpose. The constant recourse to this weapon makes the attainment of orderly and law-abiding government ever more difficult, and thus perpetuates the conditions which have made its use advantageous or even necessary in the first place.

In its strictly political aspects neo-colonialism is a method of influencing weak and corrupt governments by bribery, cajolery and intimidation, as well as through infiltration by secret and not-so-secret agents into key positions. As it is the governments of the United States and of the Soviet Union that are most successful in using these weapons, we could say that the advent of neo-colonialism in this sense amounts to a replacement of the overt rule by Britain, Belgium and France by the thinly camouflaged hegemony of the super powers; although France has been exceptionally successful in conserving a large part of its sphere of influence with the aid of the new techniques. As covert power is even more likely to be irresponsibly used than overt authority, it is not surprising that the change has been on the whole to the detriment of the dominated populations.

The relationship between the African rulers and foreign business is of such a nature that each is encouraging the vices of the other—preying upon the predatory proclivities of the other—as has been happening for a long time in Latin America and in

* The vicious circle of antisemitism and economic distress in eastern Europe is analysed in Ch. 21 of *Elements of Comparative Sociology*.

Liberia which is the worst governed country in Africa. In its economic aspects the essence of neo-colonialism is the combination of a rapacious, dictatorial and proliferating ruling clique enmeshed in a vicious circle of exploitation and strife, with a laissez-faire capitalism, tamed neither by any democratic forces nor even by a bureaucracy guided by *raison d'état*, and operating under the conditions of insecurity which make a socially beneficent conduct of business unprofitable or perhaps even impossible.

The foreign businessmen cannot be blamed for making Africa poor for without them the aggregate wealth would have been even smaller than it is. The problem of neo-colonialism is not that of a giant conspiracy to rob Africa: for the reasons already indicated such an attempt would be much less profitable than a participation in a more rapidly growing market. Metaphorically speaking, it is a problem of elephants in rickety china shops. The big foreign firms can upset the traditional way of life and aggravate the vices of the indigenous elite, but they have no power to create a well-ordered and prosperous state. Anyway, they feel that their business is making money, not state-building or social reform.

Chapter 14 AFRICAN SOCIALISM

It may not be entirely accidental that the two frankest books on the obstacles to progress in Africa have been written by Frenchmen: René Dumont and Albert Meister.* Having been less addicted to racial contempt in the past, the French seem now to be less prone than the English to fall over backwards into an inverted racialism according to which nothing African must ever be criticised. Despite their realism in analysing the present situation, the two authors recommend 'African socialism' (administered by the 'pure and hard' according to Dumont's specification) as a cure for Africa's ills.

When following in the footsteps of Fourier and Proudhon, Marx and Engels were preaching the coming of the workers' paradise, they could only imagine what might be the effect of abolishing private property. In fact they did not even bother to draw any plans for the future socialist social order, and concentrated on analysing the workings of capitalism and castigating its iniquities. It is precisely because (in contrast to other prophets of socialism) they have left a blank cheque that they can be used as patron saints of a social order which negates their ideals, as can be seen by anybody who looks at what they have written about such things as censorship or bureaucracy. A hundred years ago, however, even a great mind could underestimate the dangers of bureaucracy and fail to realise that in large human aggregates communal property must remain a legal fiction covering the reality of the control by the officials. In the second half of the twentieth century, and with the sad experiences of eastern Europe staring us in the face, the belief that the so-called 'national planning and control over wealth' *must* bring about a just and

* *L'Afrique Noire est Mal Partie:* René Dumont, Collections Esprit, Editions du Seuil, Paris, 1962. Published in London by André Deutsch Ltd, under the title *False Start in Africa.*

L'Afrique peut-elle Partir?: Albert Meister, Collections Esprit, Editions du Seuil, Paris, 1966.

G

prosperous society amounts to a doctrinaire blindness camouflaging the desire to boss people around.

As P. T. Bauer puts it:*

'The possible, and indeed likely, increase in the inequality of power seems an important and little explored aspect of an increase in the role of government in economic life. For various institutional reasons, such as the absence of a well-informed and effective public opinion and the differences in effectiveness between the urban and the rural population in many under-developed countries, this range of problems is of special importance in the underdeveloped world. But its relevance is wider. For instance, measures designed to promote greater equality in conventionally measured income and wealth may result in greater inequality of power among members of a society, notably in greatly increased power of some individuals or groups over others. This is obscured by the habit of regarding inequality of wealth as commensurate with inequality of power, notably as indicating the ability of some individuals to control others. In fact, freedom from control or dictation is a function of access to independent alternatives, and not of equality of wealth or incomes conventionally measured.'

A collectivist economic system would work in Africa even worse than it does in Europe. Actually, as things stand at present, it could not work at all; and even the diluted versions which have been tried in Ghana, Guinea, Mali, Tanzania and Congo-Brazzaville have remained legal fictions adorning a kleptocratic reality. Kleptocracy as a system of government consists precisely of the practice of selling what the law forbids to sell: appointments, diplomas, government contracts, public employees' time and so on; and so long as venality persists money reigns supreme. Nor is there any evidence that totalitarianism constitutes an infallible cure for venality and that there can be no such thing as totalitarian kleptocracy. After all, with the waning of the remainders of revolutionary fanaticism and the elimination of terror, venality is reviving in Russia; and the unleashing of the Red Guards is probably Mao's desperate attempt to prevent a revival of corruption in China. In Poland practically everybody takes part in illicit trade

* *Economic Analysis and Policy in Underdeveloped Countries:* pp. 124–5, P. T. Bauer, Routledge & Kegan Paul, London, 1965.

in objects secretly produced or removed from state-owned establishments.

In the revised 1966 edition of his path-breaking book (*L'Afrique Noire est Mal Partie*) pp. 205–14, René Dumont more or less recants his advocacy of socialist system for Africa in the chapter called 'Premature Socialism', in which he assesses the situation in Guinea and Mali as follows (the rather free translation and arrangement is mine):

'In Mali the plan was too ambitious, for the government had neither the finances and material means, nor the organisation, nor the personnel required for its realisation. . . . the administrative personnel for which they budgeted was excessive . . . and the people were reluctant to make the necessary effort.

'The Mali leaders, and above all the officials, in dealing with the peasants, simply give orders just as did the colonial administrators. . . . Therefore no extensive change has been achieved in the attitude of the peasants, whose interest in innovation and technical progress remains largely dormant. The bureaucracy in Bamako is too remote from the realities and the daily life of the bush. . . . Resources allocated on a national level are, all too often, considerably diminished as they pass down through the different administrative levels. . . .

'In 1965, the 35 nationalised concerns showed a deficit of more than 5 million C.F.A. francs. Le Somieux, a national import and export firm, showed losses comparable to the aggregate of the profits of the private companies which it had replaced. . . .

'Samir Amin was right in emphasising that there was less corruption in Mali than in Guinea and Ghana. Nonetheless, the quarter which the Bamako people call "Ministerial" is ornamented with villas built with public loans. Shops gradually become emptier, millet fetches a high price on the black market. . . .

'The Guinean failure is a more severe blow for the future of Africa than the Mali difficulties. For this time it is a question of a rich coastal country, with supplies of bauxite and hydro-electricity. Its agricultural exports, especially bananas and coffee, have rapidly declined, while the food shortages are becoming increasingly widespread. Only the Fria aluminium factory, which is controlled by foreign trusts, makes a profit. It is American aid which is now preventing Guinean bankruptcy; but America is merely holding the country's head just above water, without really contributing towards its development. . . .

'To nationalise foreign commerce presupposes the existence of officials capable of efficiently and honestly organising the nationalised concerns. Ameillon (an African writer killed in Cameroun) regards Guinean administrators as "very mediocre" with only "very rare exceptions", and describes "the golden rain", that is to say, big salaries with exceedingly large allowances and free accommodation, for the new princes of the regime. Why does his analysis suddenly come to an end when the question of the complete failure of the nationalised firms arises? . . . For the answer would permit us to define more precisely the practical and economic limits of nationalisation at the present moment. These limits are defined above all by the ability and more especially by the honesty of the staff. . . .

'The Guineans (the products of the French system of higher education) thought that it would be possible with the aid of modern equipment to surpass the rate of Chinese growth, while working much less. . . . Such a tempo of development would require, in Africa, a constraint superior to that of the Stalin era, or of the Chinese "great leap forward": which can hardly be recommended for Africa, in view of its dubious success in China. For the human environment presents problems far more difficult than does the natural environment.

'The only guests in Israel, all expenses paid for two months, who refused to work for a week on a kibbutz, were the young Africans. . . .

'In Tanzania, the students went on strike when they were required to sleep two to a room. In Hungary, students sleep in eights; there, the Africans protested as well.'

Venerable experts keep telling us that private enterprise has brought damage rather than benefits to the poor countries, and that what they need is socialist planning, although it should be obvious that under kleptocracy planning is impossible. To be exact, planning as a paper exercise is not only perfectly feasible but also great fun—what is impossible is to carry out such plans when the officials disregard the instructions and sell their decisions to the highest bidder. A striking case of the unreality of planning as everything but a façade was the much-trumpeted Seven-Year Development Plan in Ghana, which bore no factual relation to anything actually done by the government and was regarded with utter cynicism by officials working for the Planning Commission itself. The choice open to the African countries is not between central planning and free enterprise, but between an open and a clandestine pursuit of gain.

Even without venality the sheer inefficiency would be enough to rule out effective planning.* Speaking of Kenya, N. S. Carey Jones says:

'The trends tending to weaken the economy far outweigh those likely to strengthen it, and are likely to be accelerated as all the divisive and disruptive forces from outside are given full play. The possibility of the country attaining sustained economic growth seems remote and the probability is that the economy will gradually decline. It is a matter for speculation how far the decline in medical services and health services will offset this by keeping population growth within bounds. If it does not then there is a future for most people of increasing impoverishment, although, of course, many Africans will be richer. As statistics (and colonial statistics were notably poor) get poorer some of the problems of government . . . will disappear. If you do not have information you do not know what problems you have to tackle or how to do it. Who now knows or, indeed, cares, whether the population of the Congo is increasing or decreasing, the people getting poorer or richer, as the Kasavubu–Tshombe triangle is formed and re-formed, and foreign interference ensures that no stable policy can be worked out? . . . As impoverishment increases, so the material available for both foreign subversion and for dissident or power-seeking individuals is increased and made more inflammable . . . with the potential for growth which existed under colonial rule turned into a decline; nature taking its toll of human life as it did in the past until a new equilibrium is reached at a lower level. This would be masked by foreign aid, foreign technical assistance and slowed down by them. . . .

* The same problem in the Latin American (especially Cuban) context is examined in *Parasitism and Subversion*.

Independence came at a greater speed than that generated by internal causes, because of outside influences and Britain's world policies; i.e., Britain's attempts to meet outside influences in its much weaker post-war condition. The same outside influences will not leave Africa alone. . . . The one-party state, like foreign aid, is a check to the unstable influences, but they can still work within it, while foreign aid from too many sources will give outside influences a chance to cause disruption and confusion under official protection. It seems probable that the newly independent countries will fall under Communist control, particularly Chinese.' (*The Anatomy of Uhuru*: p. 207.)

The more enlightened and less hypocritical advocates of socialism for Africa would agree that the existing administrative machines could not direct a centrally controlled economy. What they hope for is a revolution like the Chinese which would bring to power dedicated and incorruptible puritans. Such views raise two questions: the first being whether such a solution is feasible, and the second whether it would be desirable. To begin with the second, I can simply state my opinion that it would amount to jumping from the frying pan into the fire. Viewed against the background of the terrible age-long oppression and misery of the Chinese masses, the present regime may be regarded as an improvement or at least as no worse than the preceding. In contrast the substantial majority of the inhabitants of Africa south of the Sahara are still quite far from having reached equal depths of degradation. Though poor, very few of them are actually starving, and most remain gayer and more vivacious than the denizens of northern welfare states. It may be said that this is a matter of temperament; nonetheless, nobody can be vivacious who is badly undernourished and lives in the fear of the lash—and it is important to remember in this context that the majority of the African peasants still live in free village or pastoral communities without landlords or usurers or policemen. One could well claim that the life of a Somali camelherd is freer, more interesting and satisfying than that of a clerk in London, but nobody can doubt that it is better to be a bored clerk than a drudge labouring to point of exhaustion under the fear of starvation or a lash. If we take laughter and merriment as indications of happiness, we must conclude that in most of tropical Africa things are not yet too bad, and that its inhabitants are a great deal happier than ordinary Indians, Ibero Americans, Arabs or Europeans—although the unhappiness of many of the latter must be attributed to isolation, insecurity and nervousness engendered by the rat-race rather than to material privations.

No totalitarianism could make the fate of the Indian or Peruvian peasant worse than it is; and bullied, poor and exhausted as he is the Chinese peasant probably fares better under the Communists than before. In Africa, however, the acute sufferers from tyranny and rapacity still constitute a minority; and therefore a replacement of the present venal and ineffectual rulers by totalitarian fanatics would substantially augment the sum of human suffering. Unfortunately, if the present combination of ultra-rapid population growth with economic stagnation persists, it will impoverish and degrade the African poor to such an extent that like their Indian or Arab equivalents they will have nothing to lose.

At the present juncture in Africa, the undesirability of a totalitarian solution coincides with the difficulty of applying it. Detribalisation has not yet gone far enough to produce a large mass of rootless individuals who might yearn for integration into a para-military party of ideologues. The persisting solidarity of the clan, which makes it impossible to get the administration to function in accordance with the laws and the ideals of impersonal efficiency, also prevents the development of efficient and fanaticised party machines, capable of imposing totalitarianism. Owing to the invertebrate character of the states, a communist system could be set up through infiltration with secret agents, and with the aid of bribery, intimidation or armed force, if the big communist powers had a free hand in Africa. But this would amount to communist crypto or not-so-crypto colonialism—government by puppets put into power and maintained there by external force.

The ruling graduates have acquired the taste for the socialist phraseology during their studies in Paris or London because the socialists, and above all the communists, were the only Europeans who favoured the cause of African independence before granting it became imminent and took trouble to befriend lonely African students. The ideology itself has never acquired the power to move the masses; and even the founder of Africa's first socialist dictatorship—Sekou Touré—derives more sustenance for his power from the reverence felt by the masses for his royal blood than from the appeal of his Marxist slogans. In so far as such slogans have any appeal, it stems from the tradition of passivity towards the government and the habit of expecting it to do everything. Hopeful expectations of true paternalism bear a good testimony to the character of the British and French colonial rule but they constitute another impediment to the development of voluntary associations in addition to ethnic divisions.

As mentioned earlier, for Nkrumah the chief attraction of the socialist model was the illusion that it offered a short cut to industrial and military power. The disastrous failure of his attempt can partly be attributed to his personal shortcomings: firstly, his megalomania which prompted him to discard honest and competent advisers, and to listen only to sycophantic quacks and secret agents; secondly, his lack of administrative skill; and thirdly, his insincerity and failure to give a good example—for while preaching socialism and dedication, he was a highly successful practitioner of capitalism who had accumulated a substantial fortune.

His whimsical decisions made a consistent economic policy, let alone detailed planning, quite out of the question while the cult of personality and the crazy ideological hodgepodge aggravated the loss of the sense of reality. Consequently even the few real and important additions to Ghana's productive equipment made under his rule cannot bear much fruit for want of integration with the rest of the economy. True, the catastrophic fall in the price of cocoa to less than half of its 1953 level has seriously undermined Ghana's economy, and can be blamed for the ensuing bankruptcy, but a policy must be judged by its adaptation to the actual situation—not to what might have been—and the fact remains that Ivory Coast which has suffered just as much from this price drop, has weathered the shock much better because of realistic economic policy which ensured a continuation of French help. One of the main reasons why the Soviet economic model cannot succeed in small countries is precisely their dependence on foreign trade.

In their recent book in Polish on *Socialism and the Modernisation of Africa*, S. Chodak and J. Kleer come to the conclusion—a remarkable one for members of the communist party—that tropical Africa is not ripe for socialism. Even more remarkable is their claim that neither is China, also based on a reference to Marx's view that a full development of the capitalist form of production must precede the advent of socialism—which is exactly how Karl Kautsky tried to explain why the revolution in Russia has produced terror instead of socialism. Despite their Marxist inurement to woolliness, our authors rightly find Senghor's sermons on African Socialism completely vacuous.

In comparison with the other African governments aspiring to socialism, however, Nkrumah enjoyed the great advantage of being able to start with much greater assets, and of having at his disposal a much larger and better educated administrative personnel. Even if Nyerere is free from megalomania, hypocrisy and the lack of the sense of reality, which bedevilled Nkrumah's rule, and is more willing to learn from experience, his personal virtues cannot compensate for the complete absence in Tanzania of skills and habits required for operating a centrally planned economy.

⸱Where the government is in the hands of natives but the capital belongs to foreigners, an ideology advocating the state ownership of the means of production naturally appeals to nationalist sentiments. This partly explains why state-capitalism has been set up in Burma and Egypt, and why communism and nationalism reinforce each other in Latin America, and why anti-big-capitalist semi-fascism was much in vogue in Poland before the war.* The low motivating power of socialist and communist ideologies in Africa is largely due to weakness of nationalism because a stronger feeling of national solidarity would enhance the appeal of the idea of confiscating the foreigners' possessions. Though weak, this factor is by no means entirely absent, but in any case the sheer and short-sighted cupidity of the rulers provides a sufficient motive for expropriations. No matter how ruinous in the long run— no matter how incapable is the government of managing the establishments which it acquires—a forced purchase normally brings profit to somebody.

On the East Coast, especially in Tanzania, African socialism furnishes the justification for the attempts to despoil and drive out the Indian traders, and to replace them with a bureaucratically controlled distribution under the guise of co-operatives; just as national socialism provided a perfect formula for anti-semitism

* See on this point, *National Characteristics of Fascism:* ed. Stewart Woolf, Weidenfeld & Nicolson.

in central Europe, because the Jews (like the Indians in East Africa) could be condemned from a nationalistic point of view as aliens, and from a socialist standpoint as capitalists. In Zanzibar racialist socialism provided the slogans for exterminating the Arab mercantile master-race which has been oppressing their African slaves for centuries. The Indian traders on the mainland have never been the ruling caste, but their wealth and notions of superiority, coupled with numerical and political weakness make them into an ideal scapegoat for collective frustrations, apart from being the object of envy. The policy of replacing Indian traders by African public employees finds much favour with the candidates for office, but whether it will benefit the peasants is more than doubtful, because having a machine of coercion at their disposal, the kleptocrats can fleece their victims much better than politically powerless alien usurers.

During the final correction of the present chapter the news has come that the Tanzanian government has decided to expropriate the banks and the bigger trading companies—although unspecified compensation has been promised to their foreign or Asian-descended owners. If the Asians are excluded Tanzania has no personnel capable of managing banks or other kinds of big business. Furthermore, as the Africans will not entrust their money to their compatriots unless they are their kinsmen—least of all to people connected with the government against whom they can get no redress in a court of law—this measure cannot fail to bring about a complete disappearance of private deposits, a reversion to hoarding of gold and foreign currency, and consequently a drastic reduction of the already miserable private saving and investment. For a few months, however, this step will enhance Nyerere's prestige in the eyes of the populace who imagine that the premises of the banks contain inexhaustible wealth which will make them all rich. Perhaps Nyerere is resorting to such short-sighted demagogy in order to stave off a military revolt, but this will not help him much in the long run unless (like, for instance, Duvalier in Haiti or Somoza in Nicaragua) he builds a dependable terror machine which will be all the more necessary when the aroused hopes of material improvement are irretrievably disappointed. The recent purges indicate that he is sliding rapidly towards terror.

Nyerere has many merits. In contrast to other rulers of Africa (or for that matter of other continents too) he is not addicted to ostentation and dresses simply and (what is important) in a sensible fashion appropriate to the climate. He has had the courage to admonish repeatedly his paladins for their parasitic proclivities, and even to reduce their salaries. What is more, he has even dared to criticise the African men in general for their inclination to leave all the work to women. It is all the more pity, therefore, that he has not been able to free himself from the socialist superstitions learned in Britain. He should know that, in spite of the fact that there is less corruption in Tanzania than on the West Coast (owing to the greater prevalence of village self-sufficiency) the newly established co-operatives are as riddled with bribery and embezzlement as any public institution in Africa.

Africa is not the only part of the world where a lot of people are attracted by socialism or communism mainly because they promise a massive multiplication of public posts. In Africa, however, apart from the desire for the foreigners' possessions, this motive is almost the only one because of the absence of the components of proletarian protest, due to the ethnic divisions and inarticulateness among the poor. At least in the former British colonies, moreover, one gets the impression that the ordinary Africans like the expatriate capitalists better than the bureaucrats of their own race, although this preference does not seem to extend to the Asians. This feeling stems not from any kind of masochism but from simple knowledge that the colonial officers were juster and more benevolent than their indigenous heirs, and that with very few exceptions the expatriate businessmen treat their employees very much better than do the native employers or officials.

The reasonable belief in the value of education has been pushed
to such doctrinaire extremes that the idea that there might be
too much education has the flavour of a forbidden thought
banished on pain of ostracism. Yet it would be strange if education
were the only human activity exempt from the usual rule of the
golden mean. One of the reasons why so few people dare to
question the desirability of expanding educational services
regardless of the circumstances is that nowadays most writers
derive their sustenance from educational institutions, and therefore
do not like to uphold views which run counter to the vested
interests of their profession. But the argument *ad hominem*—so
often hurled against capitalists, militarists, bureaucrats and trade
unionists—can also be applied to those occupied in education;
and there are no grounds for believing that this profession is
exempt from the sway of Parkinson's laws of bureaucratic
expansion. In wider social circles education is often valued less
for the sake of the knowledge it imparts than as a status symbol.
In Africa such extraneous considerations interfere with the rational
choice of how much and what kind of education is needed.

The missionaries were primarily concerned with teaching
people to read so that they could absorb the lessons of the Bible,
while the colonial governments needed only clerks. No large
demand for technical skills was envisaged, owing to the conception
of the colonies as purveyors of raw materials and foodstuffs
produced by uneducated peasants. Adapted to the purpose of
forming clerks, ministers of religion and later lawyers and officials,
the educational institutions in colonial Africa laid stress on literary
and legal studies, and neglected industrial and commercial
training, not to speak of the agricultural, shunned by everybody
and stigmatised by the notion that anything to do with the
cultivation of the soil is fit only for a poor and illiterate rustic.
Almost everywhere the lawyers outnumber scientists by at least

20:1. The abundance of lawyers is a general feature of under-developed countries; and one could advance an hypothesis that law-abidingness is inversely correlated with the proportion of the law graduates in the population. The disadvantages of this imbalance have been recognised by many African governments who have taken steps to foster technical education and to curtail the production of lawyers. On the other hand, however, even greater distortions have taken place since the independence in other respects.

Almost needless to say, Africa is not the only part of the world where education is valued primarily as a means of getting a paper which opens the road to social ascent. Nevertheless, it does seem that in the post-colonial states this common human tendency has become particularly pronounced under the influence of several factors, the most obvious of which is irrelevance of what is taught to everyday life. A student of engineering may be concerned above all with getting a diploma, but he knows that even with a diploma he will need what he is learning for making a living, and that in the world of engineering even the highest degree would not help if his knowledge were blatantly inadequate. But when an African boy is studying British or French constitution or history in the hope of getting a job in the post office he does not expect ever to be able to use the knowledge which he is acquiring with great effort and expense; and is inclined to view education as a kind of endurance test (resembling somewhat the torments inflicted at the tribal initiation ceremonies) eventually rewarded with a magic paper which can open the gate to white-collar employment. The following incident shows the magical aura surrounding the diploma: a man who had lost his Cambridge School Certificate (obtained with the aid of a correspondence course), when his house burned down took the course and examination all over again instead of applying for another copy. It may be said that (apart from this incident which must be rather unusual) this kind of approach to education is common enough even in the most highly industrialised countries. True, it is all a matter of degree: in the African states it is simply much more prevalent . . . in fact completely dominant.

As so many people were clamouring for education—that is to say, access to diplomas—the governments responded by expanding schools and universities with scant regard for economic limitations. However, as with the issue of banknotes, what is good for an individual may not be good for the country: if everybody gets more money while the amount of real wealth does not increase nobody is better off than he was. Having witnessed how some people have made fabulous careers in consequence of getting a degree or a school certificate, the ordinary African somehow came to imagine that through education everybody could be quickly lifted up to the level of affluence enjoyed by the successful graduates. Unfortunately, things are not quite so simple, particularly when the education is unrelated to production of wealth.

In addition to this inflationary illusion, the international keeping up with the Joneses accounts for the unrealistic approach to education. In the first place quantitatively: the rate of illiteracy has become a symbol of international low status of which the rulers are ashamed and therefore try to eliminate, even if it leads them to devote 25 per cent of the budget to education, as in the case of Haute-Volta. Unfortunately, however, these attempts often amount to little more than sweeping the thing under the carpet; packing the classrooms with more than a hundred pupils in order to make the statistics of school attendance look good even if nobody learns very much. Owing above all to the population explosion, even such sacrifices are mostly futile, and in many countries the percentage of children attending schools is falling even though the absolute numbers are rising. In the poorest countries the percentage is still very low: 9 per cent in Niger and Haute-Volta. At the other extreme are Gabon with 90 per cent and Congo-Brazzaville with 80 per cent. In any case, even where schooling is widespread the results are meagre because of overcrowding, bad organisation and incompetence and corruption of the teachers and educational administrators. The commonest method is learning by rote in the manner of Koran or Bible classes.

This, however, does not prevent the imitation of the external paraphernalia of the educational institutions of the opulent countries; and here the intrusion of the American influence has even aggravated matters because on the whole, the greater the disparity of wealth, the more inane and pernicious is the imitation. The wealthy United States can afford to maintain its youth for years in idleness—learning nothing and just expressing their personalities until the time when they have to learn strictly vocational skills—but in a poverty-stricken country such models are disastrous and the education must be shorter and begin at once with bread-earning skills, except for the very small elite.

Illiteracy constitutes a serious handicap for someone who has to work in a factory and read the notices and instructions, but not for a peasant engaged in stone-age agriculture. The kind of improvements in agricultural methods, which could bring the African peasantry to the level reached in Europe by the medieval serfs, could be learned without the knowledge of the alphabet. Even birth control could be introduced before literacy, as it indeed must be, because without it there will always be too many children to be taught. Rather than multiplying semi-literates for the sake of cutting a good figure in U.N.O. statistics and providing U.N.E.S.C.O. officials with excuses for trips, what is needed is a small body of proper literates with elementary technical training in agriculture and birth control—instructors on the level of village school teachers but whose job would be to help the villagers to live on the spot rather than prepare their young for great careers in the town. Literacy campaigns are a relatively easy way of keeping up with the Joneses, whereas it is much harder to alter the habits of the villagers than to get the children into the class-rooms with the bait of false hopes of social ascent. The extent of mental improvement through literacy is usually overestimated because people from countries where illiteracy is rare, and therefore mostly confined to morons, imagine that it automatically entails abysmal ignorance and stupidity, whereas in fact one can find in primitive societies illiterate philosophers.

Education which neither helps in the work nor opens the gate to promotion, nor gives access to genuine intellectual or artistic satisfactions, can only generate discontent with the work which a person finds himself compelled to do, and which in consequence he will be doing worse than if he had never received this kind of education. This is true even of elementary schooling, if regarded as a vehicle of social mobility, but applies particularly to the higher grades. Over-production of graduates is the surest means so far discovered for conjuring up subversive movements. The turmoil in Latin America and Asia is closely connected with this factor and the same was the case in Eastern Europe until the communists put an iron lid on this cauldron. Particularly dangerous is over-production of lawyers, as they naturally take to politics.

The mushrooming of schools and universities in Africa, and the production of diploma holders at the rate much faster than that of economic growth, accounts to a very large extent for the flare-up in Nigeria which occurred as soon as Nigerianisation of the civil administration and the army had been completed and the government services had to suspend recruiting. In East Africa the number of Africans even with only secondary education was so small when independence was granted, that for the next few years, room can still be made for new graduates by pushing out the British laggards and the Asians but the limit of absorptive capacity is not far off, and we can expect some explosions when it is reached. All this does not mean that there is too much education in any absolute sense but only that given the rate of economic expansion, the type of education and the associated expectation backed by a disdain for labour, issuing large numbers of diplomas and certificates means creating a mass of unemployables.

Travelling around Africa one is struck by the visual manifestations of the discrepancy between education and economy. In Europe or America the premises of educational institutions (even in the university towns) seldom surpass all other buildings in respect of size or munificence, whereas in Africa they usually stand out unique. A town consisting mostly of shanties and containing only a small number of sizeable buildings may have a university campus surpassing in beauty anything that can be found in Europe. A village consisting of little huts with mud walls will often have only one solid building: the school. In a way we might rejoice that the things of the spirit are valued so highly; nonetheless such contrasts do depict the dilemma: where can the products of these schools go when they leave? Into the surrounding hovels? Or the shanty towns?

To be useful education must be adapted in quantity and kind to the society which it is supposed to serve and not be simply transplanted from another country where the circumstances are entirely different. What the African countries need most is firstly relatively good education for a very small elite but also adapted to the local needs by its practical orientation rather than an imitation of Oxford or the Sorbonne. It is unlikely that within the next two or three generations Africa could produce large numbers of scholars or scientists capable of making important contributions to knowledge, while a few exceptional individuals of this kind could extend their education abroad. A certain intellectual minimum must be reached at least by a sizeable elite before the advancement of learning can become a legitimate concern. The most important point, however, is that the spread of education will aggravate parasitism, exploitation and strife unless its recipients live frugally and do not imbibe the habits of consumption of students in wealthy countries. This means that training should be done on the spot by either modestly-paid indigenous instructors or expatriates who are prepared to live frugally for a while: at least without a car and without whisky, let alone the diplomatic privilege of free importation.

A very substantial progress in agricultural and technical skills could be made without all the peasants (or even the majority) becoming literate. Putting literacy in the first place stems not from any rational ground but from status seeking, fed by the inferiority complex and encouraged by international organisations which have a vested interest in pretending that the differences between 'the nations' are smaller than they really are. Even the strictly technical training received in Europe or by instructors from Europe and America is often inappropriate because it teaches the pupils to rely on equipment which in Africa will not be available.

Up till now education has contributed very little to the welfare of African peasants, and is creating or has already created a distorted society with a largish number of graduates and secondary school leavers whose knowledge is of a very unproductive kind, while elementary technical and agricultural education is utterly neglected. Even apprenticeship does not function as it ought because, owing to the lack of customs regulating this relationship, it usually is a means of extortion: the apprentice not only has to do all kinds of jobs which in no way help his learning (which is common enough in other parts of the world) but he also has to pay to the master very substantial sums which rules out most of the potential candidates. The whole business is permeated with the ideas surrounding apprenticeship in sorcery, with the craftsmen trying to conceal their knowledge. Even in fairly big establishments where all the employees receive regular wages it often happens that the more skilled extort payment from the new recruits for showing them how to do the work, and the craftsmen take care that none of the latter is spying on them to find out how to do the job. Such attitudes have a similar effect as the equally anti-social restrictive practices of the British Medical Association: namely the shortage of people with the needed skills. It must be said, however, that not even the sorcerers could surpass the American Medical Association in the ruthlessness of monopolistic exploitation.

While lawyers and graduates in Latin abound, it is extremely difficult to find a competent African middle-grade technician or even an ordinary really skilled craftsman. A possible exception to this is Ghana, in at least certain types of craft, such as carpentry. The Belgians also concentrated on technical training in the Congo, and the results are usually said to have been good as long as they remained there to keep order and direct the work. In consequence even the countries where the civil service and magistracy have been completely Africanised have to import expatriate foremen and pay them three times as much as they would get in their country of origin, which is quite fantastic in relation to the average wage of the Africans. In addition to constituting a fatal burden on the budding industry and stimulating the cupidity of their African colleagues, such people have the worst possible influence on race relations, as they are mostly too uneducated and unintelligent not to regard alien ways as evidence of stupidity, and too coarse not to voice loudly their contempt.

It requires a good deal of imagination to be able to teach industrial skills or guide the work of somebody who has never handled even such a simple mechanical object as a lock and key; and in consequence of entrusting such tasks to people of very moderate intelligence, contempt is engendered on one side and bewilderment and resentment on the other. This problem, however, is diminishing in importance as tribesmen untouched by modern civilisation are becoming rare. As a matter of fact, many African villages nowadays contain self-taught mechanics able to get a car on the move after a breakdown. Linguistic misunderstandings, on the other hand, continue to give rise to ill-feelings, particularly because of the habit, common among unintelligent and uneducated people who only know their own language, of assuming that anybody who does not understand them must be either dim or deaf, and that shouting might help him to grasp the meaning.

An adequate supply of appropriate skills is a necessary condition of economic progress but it is not a sufficient condition. Parasitism, corruption or an overcentralised bureaucracy stultifying initiative can maintain a country in utter poverty regardless of how much skill is available. As for politics, it suffices to remember that the most educated nation in Europe succumbed to the crude and vicious preachings of Hitler to realise that schooling alone cannot ensure a decent social order.

The vicious circles of stagnation and strife do not exist simply in consequence of ignorance. People pursue the satisfaction of their desires within a determined field of opportunities. Whether the resultant behaviour, as well as its cumulative effects, will conduce to relative harmony and welfare or their opposites depends on the total structure of the society as well as on the character of its constituent units.

Chapter 16 IS THERE A WAY OUT?

As rapid economic progress requires not merely capital but also appropriate skills and customs which cannot be evolved in a year or two, there is no quick way of making the African states into replicas of the wealthy countries of the northern hemisphere, particularly as their natural resources are by no means over-abundant. Industrialisation can help only up to a point. Many of the imports can eventually be replaced by locally manufactured goods, but the possibility of living by exporting manufactures and importing food and raw materials is not open to the African countries because this would involve not only overtaking but actually displacing the established exporters of manufactured goods, as obviously only a small proportion of the countries of the world can gain livelihood in this way. In any case, so long as the birth rate remains at the present level, war, famine and disease will continue to play the role of checks to population growth with increasing efficacity. Which of these checks will be more important will depend on the circumstances; and we might see either endemic warfare (internal or external) or harsh despotisms holding down their subjects in such misery and degradation that the victims of disease, hunger, terror and crime will be sufficiently numerous to compensate the high birth-rate.

There are many customs which make the introduction of birth control difficult: the beliefs that posthumous peace depends on having male descendants, pride in the number of offspring as a proof of virility or femininity, dependence of the status of a wife on the number of sons which she has produced (which in poly-gamous households can lead to a procreation race), the philo-progenitive admonitions of the religions—to mention the most obvious factors. All these customs correspond to the necessary conditions of survival of a tribe engaged in incessant warfare. When war is endemic a tribe which fails to keep up with the numerical strength of its foes will be destroyed. Furthermore, with very high mortality anybody who wants to have some children surviving into adulthood must beget a large number—and we must remember that in the absence of any public assistance or pensions, having adult children constitutes the only safeguard against starving in old age for people who own no income-producing capital. These philoprogenitive customs are adaptations to a high death rate but the effects of their persistence after this rate has fallen are of such a nature that they tend to bring the death rate back to its former level. If the birth rate remains at its present level, the effects of the medical improvements which have reduced the mortality from various diseases will be to increase the number of those who die from hunger or violence.

Despite the obstacles indicated above, the most populous parts of Africa (all situated on the West Coast) offer a more propitious ground for introducing birth control than many other parts of the globe owing to a relatively high status and remarkable independence of women who are neither so intimidated nor so debilitated by undernourishment as their Indian or Arab sisters. The prospects in the Moslem interior of Africa are much worse because there the women are much more timorous and ignorant, and the men much less educated and more traditional, and polygamy would be much more difficult to abolish.

Under the present African conditions, an elective government (even if it were feasible in other ways) would speedily bring its demise by its inability to cope with the growth of the population. True, in north western Europe the habit of regulating the number of children has spread not only spontaneously but in most cases against the opposition of the government; but, where the cultural and economic circumstances do not favour such a spontaneous change in the prevalent pattern, only an authoritarian government can foist upon the population a practice which contravenes their old and cherished customs, and appeals to no powerful vested interest. Even worse: where political allegiances stem from ethnic divisions, a party can gain voters (and therefore seats in the parliament) only if its supporters multiply faster than the other ethnies. In consequence, electoral competition incites the politicians to encourage a procreation race as well as to tamper with the results of censuses. The last census in Nigeria—which took place when the parliament still reigned—almost led to a civil war, and constituted an important precipitant of the chain of events which has led to the military coup. The party spokesmen were accusing the other sides of fraudulent counting, and at one point the premier of the Eastern Region offered to accept the results if the figure for his region were raised by a million. Under such circumstances there can be no question of a policy of slowing down the population growth.

As things stand at present, the problem of Africa is not how to ensure quick progress but how to prevent, or at least to slow down, the spread of misery and violence under the impact of the population explosion and of the rapid growth of parasitic power groups. If nothing is done about birth control, the march towards starvation and increasingly brutal oppression cannot be arrested; and under such circumstances the only feasible policy for the outsiders is to ensure that their friends obtain or retain power, regardless by what means. Only on the assumption that birth control will spread is it worth discussing the question of other measures necessary for alleviating the fate of the African masses.

As shown in one of the preceding chapters, the favourite remedy of socialist planning can only make things worse. Given the ethnic frictions and the all-pervading venality, every extension of governmental control raises the stakes and, therefore, intensifies the struggle for power, in addition to stultifying private initiative and enlarging the burden of bureaucratic parasitism.

Reliance on foreign aid amounts to wishful thinking or an ostrich-like attitude firstly because this aid is unlikely ever to become commensurate with the need. As it is motivated mainly by the desire to maintain political influence, it tends at the moment to diminish in amount in consequence of the rapprochement between the Russians and the Americans, while the Chinese are much too poor to be able to resort effectively to this method of winning friends. Moreover, even if the amount of the aid were to be increased, its wise administration presents insuperable difficulties because in addition to the factors of corruption and inefficiency (which impede the application of the remedy of collectivist planning) inter-racial and international misunderstandings and animosities, as well as the real clashes of interest, constitute serious obstacles to effective co-ordination. In any case the flow of funds from abroad can provide no substitute for internal reforms, without which it may even aggravate the situation by whetting cupidity, and teaching people to rely on alms rather than their own effort.

Nor can salvation come from the influx of private capital. Without a sense of security, and having to deal with a fickle and corrupt bureaucracy, foreign capital can create highly profitable enclaves principally concerned with extraction or production of exportable bulk materials, but it cannot create the network of medium and small firms needed for internal progress. This can only be done by native enterprise. A gradual growth and multiplication of indigenous firms is also necessary from the point of view of the human basis of an industrial civilisation. The habits conducive to efficient organisation and high productivity have nowhere struck root in a few years. In northern Europe and America they have been cultivated for centuries in small workshops and businesses before they were applied on a large scale.* Recurrent wars have also occasioned frequent high pressure training in efficient co-operation of large numbers. The Africans, whose deeply introjected norms concern only co-operation within a narrow circle of kinsmen, have not yet developed attitudes necessary for the efficient operation of small shops let alone large organisations. And it must be emphasised that this is a matter of values, principles and feelings which must be imbibed from the environment at the most impressionable age and cannot be learned from a book.

What Africa needs most is the human capital of millions of knowledgeable, hard-working and enterprising small businessmen; and this capital cannot be imported from abroad. The Europeans cannot play this part because their standard of living spreads among the Africans entirely inappropriate expectations of gain, and incites spendthriftness which must be either ruinous or based on cheating or extortion. Despite their thrifty habits, the Asians cannot perform this role well either because (as was the case with the Jews in pre-war eastern Europe) their monopolisation of commercial activities (always more lucrative than agriculture) stirs envy and wrath in the hearts of the impecunious majority, and thus leads to a sidetracking of all political issues into the blind alley of ethnic strife, which conjures up a vicious circle of its own. Alienated, afraid of confiscation or massacre, the commercial minority export the capital, organise rings to keep the members of the majority from encroaching upon their preserves, often

* Further information about this point can be found in Chs. 13 and 14 of *Elements of Comparative Sociology*.

conduct business on the double-morality principle and buy security or even privileges with bribes. Their behaviour feeds the enmity of the surrounding population, and constitutes one of the factors which aggravate the economic difficulties, which, in turn, fan the inter-ethnic strife. Monopolisation of commerce by an alien minority may cause little friction in a static agricultural society where the ethnico-occupational boundaries remain steady and sanctified by tradition; but under conditions of rapid change, a co-incidence of occupational and ethnic divisions constitutes a source of grave conflicts which may easily give rise to catastrophic conflagrations. By any humane standards the people of Asian origin have a right to live in their African birthplace—and a humanitarian sociologist should think about the ways of harmonising their interests with those of the African majority, and avoiding persecution and bloodshed—but nobody in his senses can regard immigration of foreign traders as a solution to African poverty.

Owing to a much older tradition of trading than on the East Coast, the West African business class was developing well until independence. Afterwards, unfortunately, illegal or semi-legal squeeze has caused the ruin of many small businessmen without political connections and too poor to afford adequate bribes; and a concentration of ownership of capital in the hands of the ruling cliques. Arbitrary fiscality and corrupt licensing have been used to despoil budding small manufacturers, traders or owners of repair shops for the benefit of parasitic officials and politicians. The uncertainty has led the big foreign firms to repatriate much of their capital which was previously used to give credit to small traders, while the state banks have restricted their lending to the charmed circle.* While the big foreign firms are treated with subservience which they did not get from the colonial administrators, the small native enterprisers have in most countries fallen victim to bureaucrats' and politicians' or soldiers' predacity. The best advice which can be offered to the African governments is 'do not strangle small business'.

The African governments ought to restrict their regulation of economic life to the minimum not only because they cannot do it

---

* The African situation is better understood in the light of partly analogous developments in Latin America, analysed in Chs. 3 and 4 of *Parasitism and Subversion*.

effectively but also because without such a restriction the process of a gradual curtailment of graft cannot even start. The soldiers who have taken over under the pretext of fighting corruption have become just as venal as soon as they began to make decisions on which profits depend. The administrative systems relatively free from corruption have developed in Europe during the era of liberalism when the officials had little power, could be checked by other groups and had few bounties to offer. Even the Prussian administrative machine was more corrupt in the eighteenth century when its supremacy had not yet been challenged by countervailing social forces, than during the era of relative liberalism in the nineteenth. When the bureaucratic machine is riddled with venality any further extension of its power makes the eradication thereof more difficult. As far as possible cures for corruption are concerned the alternative seems to be: either a fair approximation to laissez-faire or a terroristic totalitarianism of Stalin's kind. Even the latter system, however, might fail to eradicate venality and nepotism in a society where the bonds of kinship remain very strong; and anyway, under the present circumstances such a system probably could not be erected in Africa.

Within the limits of what is possible under the present circumstances, the government of the Ivory Coast comes more closely than any other to what is desirable. It is not, of course, free from bureaucratic parasitism, corruption, ostentatious waste, and other evils analysed on the preceding pages but at least it has been able to achieve a very fast economic growth at the rate of 10 per cent per year which has outstripped the population increase. A substantial measure of economic progress, as distinct from mere growth, is an achievement unique in tropical Africa; and in the entire continent the only other country where wealth grows faster than population is South Africa. As in the latter country the wealth is more unevenly distributed and the racial conflict shows no signs of abating, while in Egypt the population has more than caught up with the increased production, Ivory Coast is the only country in the entire continent which can be said to be progressing. What is the secret of this remarkable achievement?

Ivory Coast shares with Ghana the privilege of having started its existence as an independent state with a more favourable relation of population to resources than any other part of the continent with the exception of South Africa. Unlike Gabon or

Malawi (not to speak of Rwanda or Gambia) it is not too small for economic growth; yet (unlike Nigeria, Sudan or Congo) it is not too big and heterogeneous to be governed effectively. Moreover, unlike for instance Senegal, Sudan or Niger, Ivory Coast does not have to bear an overwhelming burden of Islamic conservatism and obscurantism. And in contrast to Ghana which shares the same advantages, it had the good fortune to get a ruler who is free from megalomania.

Houphouet-Boigny stands out among the African leaders by his readiness to admit that his country is backward and not merely poor. When asked why he governs as dictator, he did not claim to have invented a superior brand of democracy or socialism, but simply said that if it took France several centuries to reach democracy, how could a new undeveloped state do the same in a few years? Nor has he ever tried to emulate Nkrumah in claiming the leadership of the whole of Africa, or in attempting to turn his state into an industrial and military power in a few years. He does not bother much about Rhodesia or South Africa, does not try to cut a great figure at U.N.O. or at the gatherings of the so-called Third World, realising that the task of building up one nation is big enough for any man. Unlike Nkrumah or Sekou Touré, he offers no ideology to save Africa: and so far as possible keeps out of big power politics. To Nkrumah's principle of 'politics first' he replied with a policy 'economics first' with the result that he is the one who has retained 'the political Kingdom', to use Nkrumah's expression. He is even prepared to rely on the French troops to guard against the possibility of a military coup, which also enables him to save on military expenditure.

In a new book, *Le Développement du Capitalisme en Côte d'Ivoire*, Samir Amin, an Egyptian economist, analyses what he regards as the unfavourable aspects of the Ivory Coast experience; although he maintains that the economy has since 1950 grown at an average annual rate of 9 per cent or even 11–12 per cent since independence in 1960, which is almost double what the Ivorian government claims. According to Amin, the amount invested in the economy, compared to gross domestic product, rose from 15 per cent in 1950 to 19 per cent in 1965, private sector investments rising from 30 per cent of the whole to 67 per cent. The recurrent budget has increasingly provided surpluses for development spending and there were no balance of payment crises at any

time during the fifteen years. Nonetheless, claims Amin, there are
many examples in colonial history, 'analogous almost to the last
detail' of countries which experienced boom conditions for
lengthy periods—e.g. Senegal, Ghana, Western Nigeria and
Congo—but in them the boom took place over a much longer
period while in 1950 the Ivory Coast was still undeveloped; which
means that Ivory Coast has been doing no more than catching
up with the more advanced African countries after a late start.
The three main trends on which growth has been based have
probably now reached the point where further rapid growth is
unlikely unless policies are radically changed: the boom in
agriculture has been almost entirely in export crops and due to
unoccupied land being brought under cultivation, while non-
industrial investment has been primarily in transport infrastructure
rather than in agriculture itself, least of all in food production. On
the other hand, limits to the creation of light industry capable of
replacing imports are likely to be reached very quickly. Furthermore, the growth has been entirely dependent on outside capital,
'whose domination over the whole of the country's economy is
exercised in the most absolute way'; with the consequence that
the salaries of the European staff 'still account for about 40 per
cent of all salaries in the productive sectors of the economy
(against 60 per cent in 1950), because non-Africans still occupy
all the key posts. In agriculture the situation is different, and
whereas there were only a few hundred African planters in 1950,
there are now about 20,000 rich African planters 'exploiting
almost a quarter of cultivated land, employing two-thirds of total
paid labour and enjoying an annual income of some 400,000
francs, which leaves them an important surplus for prestige
consumption', but up to now circumstances have not induced them
to invest productively.

As in Uganda, the planters are mostly chiefs who have fore-
closed as their private property big chunks of land under their
jurisdiction, turning them into plantations worked by hired
labourers—in the Ivorian case mostly immigrants from the countries further north, especially socialist Mali. Thus a kind of rural
capitalism has developed—with an embryonic landed aristocracy
on the one side and a mass of landless labourers on the other,
occupying one third of the cultivated areas, and resembling
faintly the Latin American pattern.

The industry and large scale commerce, on the other hand, remain in the hands of the Europeans and the Lebanese. Apart from a few hundred bigger traders (among whom Ghanaian women occupy a prominent place) only market traders and hawkers are African. Indigenous non-rural capitalism is confined to letting tenement houses and financing taxis, but the investors here are not full time businessmen but higher officials who usually succeed in doubling their salaries by these means, despite spending very little time on managing the business. So the Ivorian elite consists overwhelmingly of civil servants, with no more businessmen than elsewhere in tropical Africa. Hence, if one can speak of the development of capitalism in the Ivory Coast one can hardly speak of the development of an Ivorian capitalism.

Now let us suppose that Amin's analysis is entirely correct and that Ivory Coast is doing no more than replicating the spurt of development which Ghana, Nigeria, Senegal and Congo experienced during the later years of colonial rule. Even then we would still have to give Houphouet's government credit for the unique achievement of being no less efficient than the colonial rulers in promoting material welfare; while the fact that this is achieved by an indigenous rather than a foreign administration holds out much better hopes for the future.

The advantage of having a lot of unused land, and therefore unusually wide opportunities for relatively effortless development, has undoubtedly made the task of government easier than in countries where economic progress required technical advances as well as structural changes. Nonetheless, a mere availability of easily accessible resources in no way provides a guarantee of progress: as is proven by the case of neighbouring Liberia, where the relation between population and resources is not much less favourable but where the ruling class (consisting mainly of the descendants of liberated slaves from America) is much more segregated from the common people and much more rapacious than is the case in Ivory Coast, while the external influences are guided more by the quest for immediate profit, and less by long term political considerations or a sense of a cultural mission.

As many key administrative posts continue to be occupied by Frenchmen, and the French troops remain in the country, Ivory Coast is often accused of being a colony in all but name. The facts of a close collaboration with France cannot, of course, be disputed, but is it evident that a gradual and slow transition from the colonial situation to independence is a bad thing? On the contrary, we can see what has happened to those countries, like Guinea and the Congo which had quickly severed the links with their former masters.

For readers more theoretically minded (the others can skip this) I must add that a comparison of Ivory Coast with Nigeria— which was equally willing to collaborate with 'capitalists and imperialists' but had fewer unused resources and more political dynamite—illustrates the general principle of unlevelling politico-economic feedbacks (as I propose to call it) which, much more than strictly economic factors, accounts for the widening gap between the fortunate and the handicapped countries. Both these feedbacks are positive up to a certain limit, but from an ethical standpoint we can label one of them as a vicious circle and the other as a beneficent circle. The principle in question obviously calls for a further elaboration, but for our present purpose the following brief and informal description will suffice.

Impoverishment fosters strife and predation, which further impoverish the country, which leads to even more strife and predation, which bring about still further impoverishment . . . and so on, until a certain nadir is reached. On the other hand, economic improvement fosters peace and order, which permit further economic improvement, which further strengthens peace and order, which then permit even further economic improvement and so on . . . until some events break or reverse this circular causality.

To come back to Ivory Coast: we cannot deny that bureaucratic parasitism and corruption, ostentatious expenditure, especially on prestige buildings, inequality of wealth, and a harsh suppression of opposition are all there, but at least are not getting worse and they occur in combination with economic progress from which nearly every inhabitant benefits, instead of a widespread deterioration as is the case in the rest of Africa north of the Zambesi. In any case, on the score of bureaucratic exploitation, Ivory Coast compares well with other countries in Africa, Asia and eastern and southern Europe. Before 1958 the situation in Ivory Coast did not differ from that in other French colonies, and despite a very fast economic growth the administrative expenditure grew faster than the aggregate product. Even the critic of the present regime,

Samir Amin, admits (op. cit. p. 242, my translation) that 'between 1958 and 1961 the evolution is very similar to that of all the other African countries which have acceded to independence, and is marked by a radical rise in the level of administrative expenditure. After 1961, however, the Ivorian trend veers in a very different direction and, while the economic growth attains 11 or 12 per cent per year, the administrative expenditure rises by no more than 5 or 5½ per cent per year, whereas almost everywhere else in Africa we witness after independence . . . a slowing down of economic growth, accompanied by an acceleration of the rise in administrative expenditure.* . . . In the few African countries where economic growth has accelerated after independence, as in Gabon . . . administrative expenditure seems to have been rising very rapidly . . . '

The weak point is that when Houphouet-Boigny goes, a struggle for power may flare up and destroy what has been achieved, or that a less masterful successor may not be able to hold in check the bureaucracy's appetite for expansion and increased emoluments. The other cloud on the horizon is the ubiquitous menace of the population catching up with the growth of wealth; which must happen unless a vigorous policy of spreading birth control is put into practice. In this respect Ivory Coast is in a worse position than Ghana because of the greater power of the Catholic clergy, although this is at least partly counter-ballasted by strong currents of anti-clericalism.

As the economic progress enables Houphouet-Boigny to offer the population more tangible benefits than political circuses, he does not have to distract his subjects' attention with neo-colonialist or southern racialist spectres and can even let Africanisation take its natural course rather than force its pace. What is perhaps most important, the awareness of how much better off they are than their neighbours has given the Ivorians a vested interest in the integrity of their state, which has stimulated the development of a really felt nationalism more effectively than all Nkrumah's oratory.

Ivory Coast offers the best example of the relatively beneficent variant of neo-colonialism but, to repeat once again, this does not mean that it is free from the evils prevalent in other countries. Nonetheless, it is no mean achievement to have escaped so far

* As in that rapidly under-developing country—Britain—since 1964.

from the general decline of living standards and the deterioration of public order which are evident throughout Africa north of the Zambesi.

Having within their borders great sources of wealth in the shape of copper mines, Zambia and Katanga could have perhaps emulated the Ivorian success. Katanga, however, has been forcibly incorporated into a chaotic aggregate torn by strife, which can hardly be called a state let alone a nation, while Zambia is suffering from the friction between its native inhabitants and the still indispensable pink miners, traders and specialists, which has been aggravated by the conflict over Rhodesia and which stands in strong contrast to the relatively harmonious race-relations in the Ivory Coast. Furthermore, Zambia has suffered much more than Rhodesia from the economic sanctions aimed at the latter, losing its most convenient access to the sea as well as its usual sources of supply. Instead of by rail through Rhodesia, oil for Zambia has to be carried at a much greater cost over bad roads from Tanganyika with losses en route estimated at 40 per cent. To punish the pink Rhodesians, goods are bought directly from South Africa and transported by the Portuguese who have to be paid much more than what the Rhodesians would get for the transit of copper through Angola.

It must be added that the evidence from other parts of the world suggests that a flow of wealth from extractive industries (normally employing only a small fraction of the labour force) often constitutes a dubious benefit because mines and oil-fields may remain 'foreign bodies' within economy and society which do little to spread the attitudes conducive to economic progress, and may even foster parasitic and predatory tendencies. This has been the case in a number of Latin American countries, as I have tried to show in *Parasitism and Subversion*.

The spectacle of the Ivory Coast should gladden the hearts of conservatives throughout the world, as it underlines the merits of gradualness and of building on the traditional foundations. To a greater extent than any other political system in Africa, the Ivorian regime rests upon an alliance between the new bureaucratic elite the traditional chiefs and the French government and big business. There is, however, a crucial difference between the Ivorian chiefs and the emirs of Northern Nigeria or the kings of Buganda or Ashanti: namely, they are many and none of them has enough power to present a threat to the government. They are, moreover, much more westernised and less traditionalistic than the potentates of Moslem regions. Houphouet-Boigny himself is a son of a wealthy chief, and the undoubted (though, of course, relative) success of his regime suggests that a mixture of the traditional chiefs with businessmen and the inevitable bureaucrats makes a sounder ruling class than the latter ingredient alone— not to speak of upstart demagogues or military mutineers.

Another important factor of success is the equanimity with which the dependence on France is accepted. Houphouet has often stated his conviction that Africa is the prolongation of Europe, not of Asia, and that the unity of Africans on a continental scale is a dream. His pro-western outlook derives from his attachment to France; but also from his distrust of Asians and Arab leaders. His general scepticism about the efficacy of those international bodies is shown by this statement to an interviewer 'I cannot see how the United Nations, composed of countries with different and divergent interests and objectives, could aid a country without there appearing the elements that divide that organisation'.

Houphouet's attitude may be due to his personality but it also seems to present an extreme exemplification of the general tendency of the relations between the rulers of the French speaking states and their former masters to be franker and less guarded than is the case in the former British colonies. The explanation of this contrast seems to lie at least partly in the differences between the French and the British manners. Of all the colonial master races the British have probably committed the fewest atrocities in recent times, and have been the most correct in personal relations. The English writing African novelists, for instance, endow the characters of their masters with much less brutality and greed than do their francophone counterparts. Despite the relative infrequency of criminal propensities, however, the British have been less able to make initimate friends among their subjects than any other colonisers owing to their customary stand-offishness. The practice of snubbing—which is a peculiarly English art, the name of which cannot be translated in its full meaning—seems to have created a more unbridgeable abyss than the grosser abuses of other colonisers, with the exception, perhaps, of the Belgians. True, this has affected solely the educated or rich Africans (because one does not snub one's servants) but they are

the people who decide foreign policy. The vaingloriousness of
Nkrumah was partly a matter of temperament but partly an
assertion of racial self-respect: and the talk about economic
exploitation is more often than not an expression (or 'rationalis-
ation' in freudian terminology) of injured pride.

Snubbing generates if not hatred then at least a permanent
touchiness because it is so difficult to parry and to reply to in
kind: anybody who is not powerless can shout back if openly
insulted, but one has to be trained in the art to repay a snubbing;
and in any case an opportunity may never arise.

True, in British Africa too there have been indigenous
dignitaries with whom the colonial administrators were quite
friendly. Nonetheless, the conviviality was rather strained and
formal, and based on peaceful co-existence or alliance rather than
integration. Significantly, the relations were most cordial with the
Moslem notables who could not be excluded from clubs or cocktail
parties, because they did not wish to go there, and anyway had
no desire to mix too much with the infidels whom they regarded
as an inferior breed despite their power and technical proficiency.
The French colonial system has produced a sizeable number of
black Frenchmen, whereas black Englishmen have always been
a rarity and the most obtrusive symptom of this difference is the
more common occurrence of faultless French than of faultless
English among educated African officials.

The French rulers had fewer scruples about harsh means of
coercion but, on the other hand, British visitors to Dakar at the
beginning of the century were amazed to find French and Senegalese
children in the same school. In the colonial troops African officers
sometimes commanded French juniors—which was absolutely
unacceptable to the British. Even more: the Senegalese and
Moroccan soldiers stationed in France had free access to fully
integrated brothels. These examples show that segregation and
ill-treatment (however defined) are not the same thing. In the
Portuguese colonies (to mention another case in point) the use of
power and the methods of economic exploitation have been (and
remain) harsher than anywhere in British Africa but no strict
colour bar has ever existed. Arriving in Mozambique, I was
struck by the sight of workers being prodded with whips by
foremen (the like of which I have not seen in Rhodesia) and, on
the other hand, by the abundance of African customers in good

H

hotels and restaurants where some of the cooks and waiters were Portuguese. This was in 1950 when even in Nigeria the clubs were for Europeans only.

Nkrumah and Houphouet epitomise divergent paths to power; on the one hand we have a man who was in jail when elected to supreme office, on the other, a former minister of the French cabinet and a former speaker of the metropolitan parliament who had to keep the quarrelling French deputies in order, and who would have become the temporary head of the republic had the then president died in office. Small wonder, therefore, that the first has a chip on his shoulder while the second is sufficiently self-assured to accept dependence on France.*

If we compare Ivory Coast with Liberia—which has been the worst governed country in Africa ever since it was created—we can see the advantages of coupling effective power with overt assumption of some responsibility by the stronger government— or, if you like, the superiority of deliberate governmental neo-colonialism over the policy of leaving power in the hands of a commercial company (in this case Firestone). A country with such substantial resources in rubber and iron could be developed very fast given a modicum of honest and conscientious government. Liberia has never had a census, but it appears to be the view of qualified observers that the official estimates of population are grossly inflated. The official total is some 2½ million, but there are probably less than a million Liberians.

If Houphouet can achieve some improvement in the standard of living of the common people, however slight in comparison with the luxurious living of the elite—no mean feat in the context of continent wide retrogression—by collaborating closely with the former colonisers, why cannot Kenyatta do the same despite his willingness to follow a similar course? There are several reasons in addition to the psychological factor mentioned earlier: the first is that Kenya's economy depended on large estates owned by European settlers which have been the bone of contention in the struggle for independence and the Mau Mau uprising, and had to be largely dismantled to assuage the land hunger of the Kikuyu—

* Houphouet is said to have practised as a medicine-man, which function demands a good dose of realism and a great skill in manipulating people; it is certainly a better preparation for ruling than learning slogans at a European or American university.

with deleterious consequences for productivity. Secondly, the general level of education and political experience of Kenyan Africans cannot rival that of the Ivorians. In Kenya politics, big business and large scale agriculture were reserved for the Europeans while the middle sized commerce and the middle and lower grades in the administration were in the hands of the Asians—that is to say immigrants from India or their descendants. The Africans were rustic tribesmen or labourers with the exception of a few Kikuyus who had obtained some education but never got anywhere near the positions equivalent to those which the Ivorian elite occupied in the colony and in France. Consequently there could be no continuity of development, and independence had to entail a severe dislocation and deterioration of the economy as well as of the machinery of the Government.

We must also take into account the damage wrought by the fighting against Somali rebels in the northern provinces; and, above all, the effects of the friction between the autochthonous majority and the minority of Asian provenience. As with anti-semitism in eastern Europe before Hitler and the hostility towards the Chinese merchants in Burma and Indonesia, ethnic antagonism distracts people's attention from more promising issues and engenders a self-aggravating vicious circle of strife and economic deterioration. Kenya's situation, moreover, is especially precarious because, owing to the paucity of skilled Africans, the Indian traders, clerks, artisans and other specialists are really indispensable, and a policy of heedless Africanisation must produce a disastrous retrogression in efficiency in every walk of life. Underlying this short-sighted racialism is the usual African attitude towards jobs falling outside the tribal traditions, which treats them solely as sources of revenue and completely overlooks the contribution which they ought to make to general welfare.

'In looking at the transitional period', says Carey Jones,* 'we have seen how rapidly the balance of political strength changed and how quickly the economy deteriorated. An African government would start the battle for development from a point well behind that at which the economy had reached under colonial rule. . . . The invisible umbilical cord connecting Kenya with Britain, and through which it was fed with capital and skills and entrepreneurial ability, which flowed easily in both directions, was being broken,

* *The Anatomy of Uhuru* pp. 179–180.

and the system was showing itself unable to digest the skills left and was ejecting them. . . . In encouraging Africans to dispose of British skills, other countries were offering different skills, but skills that had no long-term interest in the future of the economy. Their main interest was in perpetuating ideologies from private enterprise to socialism and establishing or maintaining foreign spheres of influence which were bound to compete. . . . Those who knew the country and its problems would be replaced by those who did not and who were interested in other things. The African leaders were persuaded to think that they would be able to play off the West against the East, and reap the maximum benefit for their country. What, of course, they were doing was surrendering their country to the play of forces that they could not control.'

Even in its fully developed forms, the industrial civilisation presents many defects and grave dangers; its achievements, far from being consolidated for ever, remain in a precarious balance; and it is by no means easy merely to keep the system going. But it is even more difficult to make a sudden jump from primitive agriculture to a complex industrial economy; and, as we have seen, the obstacles stemming from social structure and culture are even more formidable than merely technical shortcomings. To become no less conducive to human happiness than the old tribal way of life, the new order must be given time to evolve; which means, among other things, that the growth of the population must be slowed down to a manageable rate. Authoritarian governments will remain inevitable in Africa for a long time yet, and no one can say whether they will eventually give way to more democratic political systems. But if we have to decide which of them to applaud or help, or at least not to condemn, we should choose those which are preparing the ground for progress by maintaining order without recourse to draconian methods, curtailing corruption, limiting the expansionist and parasitic tendencies of the bureaucracy and the army, fostering indigenous small businessmen, spreading birth control, practical education and respect for work.

INDEX

INDEX